Mike Nappa is my competition. We both ⬛⬛⬛⬛⬛⬛⬛⬛⬛⬛⬛⬛⬛ ut the Bible. So, I'd like to say *Bible-Smart: Matthew* stinks. And that Mike uses big words when he should use small words. And that he skips the hard questions in this book. And the writing makes us all fall asleep. But all of that would be a lie. So, doggone, I'll confess. Truth: Mike is an excellent and engaging writer who knows the Bible and knows how to tell its story. The guy is gifted, and *Bible-Smart: Matthew* is a shred of the evidence.

STEPHEN M. MILLER, Mike's competitor and bestselling and award-winning author of *The Complete Guide to the Bible* and *Casual English Bible*

Finally! A book that helps the non-academic dig deep, wrestle with questions, and grow closer to God when reading the Bible. I will be recommending *Bible-Smart: Matthew* to my family and friends—this is the series we've all been waiting for.

MARLO SCHALESKY, Executive Director of Wonder Wood Ranch and award-winning author of *Beyond the Night* and *Women of the Bible Speak Out*

Do you want to talk? If so, *Bible-Smart: Matthew* is for you. Some Bible commentaries are meant to be read. This one invites you into a conversation. It is built around honest questions every reader of Matthew faces. Mike Nappa offers bite-sized answers that are clear, thoughtful, and engaging—yet, they are not the final word. They are the first words designed to stimulate a conversation with Matthew that will linger long after you set this commentary aside.

DR. JOHN A. BECK, faculty at Jerusalem University College in Israel and bestselling author of *The Holy Land for Christian Travelers* and *The Baker Illustrated Guide to Everyday Life in Bible Times*

Bible-Smart: Matthew is both wonderfully accessible and beautifully deep. Mike Nappa offers his readers surprising insights into well-known texts through historical explanation and contemporary application. It is a wonderful resource for preachers, Bible teachers, and anyone who wants to learn more about the story of Jesus as recorded in Matthew.

DR. MARY L. VANDEN BERG, Professor of Systematic Theology at Calvin Theological Seminary

Author Mike Nappa's idea of "just hanging out, looking at Scripture together" is a worthy one, and well accomplished. *Bible-Smart: Matthew* addresses the kind of questions we all have about God's Word with interesting and easy-to-understand answers. Mike has done a great service to those of us who want to better know the Bible and the loving God behind it.

PAUL KENT, bestselling author of *Know Your Bible* (over 3 million copies sold)

BIBLE-SMART™

Matthew

Q&A for the Curious Soul

MIKE NAPPA

ROSE
PUBLISHING

Bible-Smart™: Matthew: Q&A for the Curious Soul
© 2023 Nappaland Communications Inc.
Published by Rose Publishing
An imprint of Tyndale House Ministries
Carol Stream, Illinois
www.hendricksonrose.com

ISBN: 978-1-64938-033-3

Bible-Smart™ is a trademark of Nappaland Communications Inc. All rights reserved. Find Bible-Smart online at: www.Bible-Smart.com

This book is published in association with Nappaland Literary Agency, an independent agency dedicated to publishing works that are: Authentic. Relevant. Eternal. Visit us on the web at NappalandLiterary.com.

The views and opinions expressed in this book are those of the author and do not necessarily express the views of the publisher. The publisher is in no way liable for any context, change of content, or activity for the works listed. Citation of a work does not mean endorsement of all its contents or of other works by the same author.

Book design by Cristalle Kishi; edited by Jessica Curiel.
Cover images by AWelshLad/iStock.com and Mrs. Opossum/Shutterstock.com.

Library of Congress Control Number: 2022035675

Printed in the United States of America
011022VP

For Dr. Zahea H. Nappa
who gave to me my very first Bible

Contents

Miracles, Parables, and Teachings

The Resurrection!

Preface
Shout-Out to Pastor Chuck

The first time I met Pastor Chuck—excuse me, "Reverend Charles R. Swindoll"—I was making copies in the break room at First Evangelical Free Church of Fullerton, California.

I'd been hired while he was on vacation, joining the church as one of several youth pastors working in his ministry. It was my second week on the job and I was very aware that I was, well, dressed like a youth pastor and the absolute lowest-ranked person on the entire church staff. He walked into the room to get a cup of coffee and I suddenly felt very much out of place.

There's Chuck Swindoll, I thought. *World-famous radio personality, author of a zillion bestselling books, pastor of one of the largest megachurches in the nation.*

I swallowed hard and tried not to be noticed. Out of the corner of my eye, I saw him glance toward me. *Don't make eye contact, Mikey,* I told myself. *Important people hate it when the little people do that.*

I hit the button to make more copies, even though I was already done. Next thing I knew, the man was standing next to me, his hand outstretched.

"You must be the new youth guy," he said, smiling. "I'm so glad you're here. My name is Chuck."

Inside I was screaming, *Of course your name is Chuck! Everybody knows who you are!* Outside I said, "Um, thank you. Yes. Uh. My name is Mike."

My starstruck brain didn't capture everything that happened next, but I do remember that he stood and chatted with me for a few minutes, told me his office door was always open, and to stop in and say hi sometimes if I felt like it.

Then it was just me and that copier making flyers no one needed. I told my boss about it later and he just laughed. "Yeah," he said. "Chuck isn't too impressed with himself. Get used to it."

Over the next few years, I found out that Pastor Chuck really was the same humble, friendly guy I'd met in the break room. In the pulpit, out of the pulpit, down the long hallway at the church, he was always just "Chuck."

To be honest, I didn't work with him directly very much (did I mention I was w-a-a-y down the org chart?), but I learned to trust him. In fact, I learned a lot from that man, including things like …

> The Bible isn't just a record of God's inspiration; it's an invitation to know and love Jesus more intimately.

> Studying the Bible doesn't have to be a chore, or something you do because a theology professor made an assignment, or because you're obligated to teach from it next Sunday. There is honest joy in discovering "insight for living" from God's Word.

> Curiosity is the first step toward understanding. When we pursue that which makes us curious about Christ, we naturally draw closer to Jesus—and his truth.

> It's OK to ask questions about the Bible, about truth. In fact, if you're not asking questions, you're missing out on one of God's great gifts to his children.

> Knowledge of Scripture isn't simply a matter of education or academia; it comes from the activity of Christ's Holy Spirit within and around you. Learning to listen to his Spirit is essential for growth and understanding.

I think it's no exaggeration to say that watching Pastor Chuck every day, listening to his teaching, witnessing his passion for God's Word, discovering a kindred spirit, and experiencing his encouragement—all of that shaped the Christian man I am. Chuck Swindoll inspired in me a lifetime of biblical curiosity that continues even more strongly today.

It's been a few decades since that random meeting in the church break room. I don't wear surf pants and mismatched Converse All-Stars anymore. In time, I've managed to publish a few Christian books of my own, sell a few copies here and there, speak to audiences far and wide—and never forget the pastor who modeled authentic Christianity to me. So now I figure it's time to say publicly what's been in my heart for years:

Pastor Chuck, thank you.

Your shadow looms large over my life, and I am forever grateful.

Mike Nappa, 2023

Introduction
Welcome to Bible-Smart™

There was a time when only clergy and the educated elite were able to read and understand the Bible. Today, however, we have dozens of English Bible translations and an astonishing *wealth* of biblical knowledge—available to anyone!

We truly do live in an unprecedented time in history, when it's easier than ever before to read and understand God's Word.

So why do so many of us struggle?

And why is it so hard for us to talk about the Bible without "making it weird"?

Well, despite its modern accessibility, the vast majority of biblical knowledge is still held in the ivory towers of educational institutions and pastoral study rooms. It's obscured by Greek-English Lexicons, awkwardly unfamiliar theological terms, absurd, hair-splitting arguments ("seminal transmission of sin" anyone?), overly intellectual writing styles, and academically imposed restrictions in communication.

There's truth to be found, yes. But few of us have the time or desire to wade through all that "extra stuff" just to glean the straightforward answers we're looking for when we read God's Word.

Now, don't get me wrong. I'm all for teaching the Bible, and preaching and scholarship and theological commentaries, and research, and doctrinal accuracy, and being a person "who correctly handles the word of truth" (2 Timothy 2:15 NIV). In fact, I have a seminary degree myself, and can never seem to resist adding a new Scripture reference book to the hundreds already littering my shelves. But most of that stuff is written for somebody else—still intended just for "clergy and the educated elite."

Somebody should do something about that, I told myself from time to time. Then one day I thought, *Maybe I should do something about that.*

So I created *Bible-Smart*.

First, I asked a group of Facebook friends to read chapters from the gospel of Matthew and send me any questions that came to mind. Next,

I did the same myself, compiling and curating questions into a long list of chapter-by-chapter, passage-by-passage sections. Then came the fun part. I spent more than a year immersed in Bible study, digging for answers to the questions on my list, writing "coffee-shop theology" segments about them, and creating a new kind of Q&A commentary for today's generation.

In other words, *Bible-Smart: Matthew* ain't your grandpappy's stuffy, old commentary book. This is a twenty-first-century spiritual-growth experience created just for you and me—a relaxed conversation for everyday pew-sitters who just want to discover more of Jesus as revealed in God's Word. No seminary degree necessary.

If your spirit is hungry, then *here's where you get fed*. When you read through this book, this is what I promise:

> ❯ You'll explore deep Bible knowledge from a nondenominational perspective—written for normal Christian people. (Seminary NOT required.)

> ❯ You'll find reliable, trustworthy answers to questions that you—and people like you—have asked about specific passages of Scripture.

> ❯ You'll gain everyday access to more than a dozen Bible-exposition styles, including archaeological insights, Bible difficulties, cross-reference comparisons, cultural commentary, factual info, geographical backgrounds, historical context, inductive studies, literary influences, personality and character studies, rhetorical influences, symbolic meanings, theological commentary, and word studies.

> ❯ You'll build a new breadth of knowledge and practical understanding of your Bible.

> ❯ You'll discover a safe space to meditate on, and discuss with others, timeless issues of the Christian faith.

> ❯ You'll draw closer to Jesus as you develop a greater understanding of God's Word—and awaken to the difference that makes in your day-to-day life.

So relax.

Imagine each entry in this book as a conversation taking place over hot beverages, with give-and-take, mutual respect, and ambient coffee-house noise in the background. You and I just hanging out, looking at Scripture together, discussing it as a real-life activity and not a theological term paper or long-winded sermon. (Yeah, it's pretty cool.)

Some like to start this book at the beginning and read consecutively to the end. Others like to pick and choose, moving around from passage to passage in no particular order—and that works too. Some use this book as a reference when preparing a small group study or a short talk on Scripture. Parents often like to read aloud a Bible passage to the family, then follow up with the appropriate sections in this book as a family devotion. And, believe it or not, many, many people like to meet a friend at a coffee shop, open a Bible and this book, and just ... talk about it (without making it weird).

As for you? Do whatever works best within the parameters of your current life, interests, and opportunities. I feel confident that no matter how or where you use this book, you'll find yourself engaged, inspired—and changed for the better when you're done.

When you're ready, you can just set your Bible beside this book and dive on in.

Now ... welcome to *Bible-Smart*. May you discover Christ in new and exciting ways through the pages that follow. See you inside.

About Source Citations

Grateful acknowledgment goes out to the authors and publishers of 170+ works that were consulted in the research for *Bible-Smart: Matthew*. In consideration of the reader's experience, I chose not to use traditional, often interruptive, academic-style citation methods like footnotes or in-text notes. Instead, this book employs a non-intrusive, "adapted MLA" style for source citations. Here's how it works:

> First, there's a full bibliography of sources at the back of this book.

> Each title in the bibliography is assigned a short abbreviation. For instance, *The Abingdon Bible Commentary* is abbreviated as "ABC."

> At the end of each commentary segment within *Bible-Smart: Matthew*, I've provided a list of source abbreviations that were used for that particular segment, along with the specific page numbers referenced from each source.

So, for instance, after one of the Matthew 17 commentary segments there's a source listing that looks like this:

Sources: IMT 201–202; BTC 216; REC2 119

Those of you who don't care about checking citations can just skip over that because it's short and unobtrusive. At the same time, readers who do want to check my sources can flip to the bibliography and see that I utilized the following in my research for that segment:

IMT   *Interpretation: A Bible Commentary for Teaching and Preaching, Matthew,* by Douglas R. A. Hare (Louisville, KY: John Knox Press, 1993).

BTC   *Belief: A Theological Commentary on the Bible, Matthew,* by Anna Case-Winters (Louisville, KY: Westminster John Knox Press, 2015).

REC2   *Reformed Exposition Commentary: Matthew, Vol. 2,* by Daniel M. Doriani (Phillipsburg, NJ: P&R Publishing, 2008).

Again, grateful thanks to all the very helpful people who created these resources and made them available for me to use in the research for this book!

Matthew
A Brief Overview

"All of this occurred to fulfill the Lord's
message through his prophet ..."
Matthew 1:22

The gospel of Matthew is an eyewitness account of Jesus' life, death, and resurrection, written by one of the twelve disciples in Christ's inner circle. Matthew (also called Levi) was a despised tax collector and "sinner" before Jesus found him. When Christ came calling, he literally left it all behind, making an instant decision to follow Jesus (see Luke 5:27–28).

Obviously, Matthew wasn't present at Jesus' birth or during his childhood, but he did have access to Jesus' mother, Mary, and to Jesus himself to learn about those times. And from early on in Jesus' ministry, the former tax collector was not only a witness to, but also an active participant in God's redemptive story on Earth. That gave him a unique perspective to be able to tell the world what happened when Christ first came.

Matthew's biblical account is also uniquely Hebrew in the historical sense. He emphasizes Jesus as Messiah and King for a primarily Jewish audience. As a result, Bible scholar L. M. Peterson reports, "The [Old Testament] casts a long shadow over Matthew's gospel. No other evangelist or [New Testament] writer, including Paul or the author of Hebrews, drew upon the Old Testament writings as Matthew did." In fact, Matthew included over fifty clear quotations from Old Testament texts in his book (plus numerous allusions and echoed phrasings). He couched nearly every moment of Jesus' life in terms of Old Testament prophecies and promises about the coming Messiah. The first time this occurs is in Matthew 1:22–23, where the gospel writer points out that Jesus' birth was a glorious fulfillment of Isaiah 7:14, the Messianic prophecy that promised:

The virgin will conceive a child...

Regardless of our own heritage, we all can gain much from Matthew's distinctly Jewish perspective in this gospel. In here we discover anew that Jesus is *our* Messiah—for both Jews and non-Jews—and the redeeming King for us all. He is indeed the One who has come, at last, to save his people from their sins.

The "When and Where" Questions

It's generally accepted that Matthew wrote his gospel about twenty-five or so years after Jesus' death, burial, resurrection, and ascension—with best guesses landing somewhere between AD 55 and AD 85. It's thought that the gospel of Matthew as a distinct book was the second gospel written, with Mark's being the first.

As for where events in Matthew's book take place, my friend Dave Branon sums it up well. "You almost need a GPS to keep track of the locations in Matthew," he says.

You can start in the Sea of Galilee area, where Mary and Joseph lived before they traveled south to Bethlehem for Jesus' birth. Then it was off to Egypt to escape Herod's wrath. The family returned to Nazareth, where Jesus grew up. He was baptized in the Jordan River, faced temptation in the wilderness, and then moved to Capernaum where much of His ministry took place. He and His disciples journeyed north to Caesarea-Philippi, and then it was south to Jerusalem to face His crucifixion.

Matthew at a Glance

And finally, here's a quick outline of what happens in the gospel of Matthew:

> ❯ **Chapters 1–2** Jesus' Birth and Childhood: *Genealogy, Visit of the Magi, and Escape to Egypt*

> ❯ **Chapters 3–8** Jesus' Early Ministry: *Baptism, Temptation, and Sermon on the Mount*

> ❯ **Chapters 9–14** Miracles, Parables, and Teachings: *Calling of Matthew (Levi), Disciples Sent Out, John the Baptist Beheaded, and Feeding of the Five Thousand*

> **Chapters 15–20** Jesus' Later Ministry: *Transfiguration, Parables of the Unforgiving Debtor, Lost Sheep, and Vineyard; and Jesus Predicts His Death*

> **Chapter 21–27** Jesus' Last Week (Passion Week): *Triumphal Entry, Arrest, Crucifixion, and Burial*

> **Chapter 28** The Resurrection: *Empty Tomb and Great Commission*

Now ... let's dive in!

Sources: CGB 300–301; WBH 520–521; ZP4 132–133; BSB 173; ADV 35

Jesus' Birth and Childhood

The Ancestors of Jesus the Messiah
Matthew 1:1–17

Why in the world would Matthew begin the story of Jesus with a tedious recitation of family genealogies?

It seems that Matthew had one main purpose in mind with his tracing of Jesus' earthly family line: To show proof that Jesus, as the adopted son of Joseph, could legally be considered a descendant of King David. This was important in light of the messianic prophecy recorded in Isaiah 16:5 in the Old Testament:

> In love a throne will be established; in faithfulness a man will sit on it—one from the house of David—one who in judging seeks justice and speeds the cause of righteousness.

God guaranteed that the Jewish Messiah would be "from the house of David"—from the lineage of Israel's greatest king. Any would-be Messiah (a.k.a. "Christ") simply had to fulfill that prophecy. A man who wasn't a "Son of David" just wasn't qualified to be the Messiah.

Since Matthew was writing to Jewish readers, he got this issue out of the way right from the start. He pointed immediately to Christ's ancestry as the first proof of many that Jesus is indeed God's promised Messiah and King.

Source: BKN 18

Wait a minute. Both Matthew and Luke claim to give a "genealogy" of Jesus, but their lists of ancestors don't match. So who was wrong?

Yes, you are correct. Read Matthew 1:1–17 and Luke 3:23–38 side by side and you'll notice a problem: The two genealogies aren't identical. Some have decided that this means the biblical accounts of Jesus are untrustworthy, but many Bible scholars, including Dr. Larry Richards, finds that to be a shortsighted view. He points to other possible explanations. For instance, some believe that Matthew's genealogy focuses primarily on the family tree of Jesus' adopted father, Joseph, while Luke's highlights the lineage of his mother, Mary. Another theory suggests that Matthew's history focuses on King David's "throne-succession" line which then jumps to Joseph's physical family line because the descendants of David's son, Solomon, died out.

Though we can't be sure which theories are correct, the fact is there *are* various theories that could legitimately explain the discrepancies between the Matthew and Luke genealogies. This means that some people may be too quick to assume that these non-identical genealogies necessarily discredit each other. It's both possible and likely that there's more to this supposed "problem" than we fully understand today.

Source: BAH 263-264

Why are so few women included in Matthew's genealogy of Jesus?

In the intensely patriarchal Jewish society of Jesus' time, it was unusual for *any* woman to be heralded in this way, let alone five of them. The deliberate identification of four Old Testament women plus Mary in Jesus' family tree is actually one of the unexpected—and culturally controversial— aspects of Matthew's genealogy.

What's more, the Old Testament women Matthew chose all had questionable reputations in Hebrew history. Tamar acted as a prostitute and engaged in illicit sex with Judah to trick him into fathering a child. Rahab was also a prostitute. Ruth was a foreigner of Moabite heritage. Uriah's wife, Bathsheba, was also likely a foreigner, of Hittite heritage, who committed adultery with King David. Why include these women right at the start of your supposedly evangelistic gospel of Christ?

One obvious explanation is that God values women just as he values men, and their inclusion in this genealogy is Matthew's way of emphasizing that truth. In addition, theologian Craig Evans suggests a possible second line of reasoning:

> In all four cases, God acted in an extraordinary and unexpected way—just as he did with Mary.... [Matthew] is suggesting that Mary is the fifth woman in the messianic line that for one reason or another was vulnerable to accusation but was vindicated.

Sources: SBW 1235; MAT 35-36

The Birth of Jesus the Messiah
Matthew 1:18-24

No one seems to know much about Mary's husband, Joseph—why is that?

Well, the Bible actually says very little about Jesus' adoptive father. Much of the traditional history of Joseph is also vague at best. Here's what we do know:

> Joseph was a carpenter by trade (Matthew 13:55), which meant working in wood, stone, or metal.

> He had a reputation as "a just man" (Matthew 1:19 ESV), likely referring to his devout, religious character.

> He was compassionate, as seen by his unwillingness to subject Mary to public shame when he found out she was pregnant before they were married (Matthew 1:19).

> He was able to recognize when God spoke to him in dreams (Matthew 1:20–23; 2:13, 19–20).

> He was immediately obedient to God's instructions (Matthew 1:24; 2:14, 21).

> He followed Jewish religious customs such as having his son circumcised on the eighth day, consecrating baby Jesus at the temple, and traveling to Jerusalem for the Feast of the Passover each year (Luke 2:21–41).

> He had other children besides Jesus (Matthew 13:55–56).

Beyond that, some have guessed that he may have been an older man and a widower when he married Mary, and that he died not long after Jesus visited the temple as a twelve-year-old. That theory could explain why he's never mentioned in the Bible after Jesus' twelfth year (even though Mary and his other children are) and why he wasn't present at Jesus' crucifixion. It could also account for why Jesus commanded his disciple, John, to care for Mary. Still, there's nothing in the Bible that indicates what happened to Joseph, so it's probably wise to consider this theory as speculation at best.

Source: WWB 244-246

Visitors from the East
Matthew 2:1-12

Exactly who were those mysterious Magi that visited Jesus?

No one knows for sure who the Magi (or "wise men") were who brought gifts to the baby Jesus, or exactly what their country of origin was, or how many there were. Matthew simply says they came "from the east," first going to Jerusalem and then on to Bethlehem, probably arriving sometime before Jesus' second birthday. Still, generally speaking, the consensus is that these "wise men" came from one of three places in the ancient world: Persia, Babylon, or the desert areas east of the land of ancient Israel.

Interestingly, Magi at that time weren't followers of the Hebrew God. They were disciples of Zoroaster, a Persian spiritual leader who taught that there was only one supreme god. Magi were known as studied in the "science" of astrology, and as experts in magic.

Given Old Testament prohibitions against sorcery, it's surprising that Matthew included these wise men as part of the history of Christ; they could be viewed negatively in the eyes of his Jewish readers. The only real reason for Matthew to include them in his account, it seems, is simply because they were actually there, regardless of what people would think of that fact.

Source: JHT 27, 29

Why did the Magi bring such unusual gifts to Jesus?

The Magi gave to baby Jesus gifts of gold, frankincense, and myrrh. Those gifts fulfilled a prophecy of the Messiah found in Isaiah 60:6 which promised, "All from Sheba will come bearing gold and incense and proclaiming the praise of the LORD."

Additionally, the gifts of the Magi communicated symbolic meaning. Gold in the ancient Middle East was associated with "noble purposes," as well as "immense worth and indestructibility." Incense was an element of worship, and "from the revelations of both Isaiah and John, we understand that incense signals the everlasting worship of Yahweh [God]." Frankincense specifically was used in an altar sacrifice at the temple. Finally, myrrh was a rare, aromatic substance used to perfume clothing and dead bodies during the embalming process.

Taken together, these three gifts can symbolize Jesus' place as the eternal King, the divine Messiah, and our suffering Savior.

Sources: DBI 341, 419; HBD 322, 672

The Escape to Egypt
Matthew 2:13-18

How could any king get away with ordering the mass murder of toddlers without sparking a revolt? Was this detail maybe an exaggeration on Matthew's part?

Matthew reports that Herod was the bloodthirsty king who ordered the mass murder of all boys aged two and under in Bethlehem and the surrounding area. History knows this king as "Herod the Great," though "great" seems a stretch for this man.

He reigned as a Roman appointee over the conquered Jewish people from roughly 37 BC until his death in 4 BC. As a politician, he was very astute, avoiding assassination, imposing peace, creating alliances, and overseeing magnificent construction projects that included palaces, the fortress Masada, the harbor at Caesarea, and even the temple in Jerusalem. As a person, Herod the Great was a murderous, emotionally disturbed, maniacally paranoid, possibly insane man.

So yes, it seems realistic to assume that Matthew told the truth about Herod's order to murder all boys under the age of two in the region of Bethlehem.

Roman emperor Caesar Augustus once said, it was "better to be Herod's pig than his son," and he was right. Because the Jewish king didn't eat pork, pigs in his household were never butchered. The same couldn't be said for Herod's family members. Herod "the Great" executed two of his sons for suspected treason, along with his wife and many others in his court and extended family. He brutally tortured and often killed anyone who even hinted at being a threat to him. Worried that people would rejoice at his death, he gave instructions (thankfully unfulfilled) for Jewish leaders in every town to be killed when he died, so people would have reason to mourn. Herod the Great died in 4 BC, after long illness and in excruciating pain, suffering from internal ulceration and decay.

Sources: WOB 136-138; HER 18-19; WEC 21

Was "Rachel, weeping for her children" a real person?

When Matthew quotes the phrase about "Rachel weeping for her children," it's a reference to Jeremiah 31:15. He points to this as a prophecy fulfilled by Herod's slaughter of the innocents in Bethlehem. While it's certainly *possible* that Rachel was a real mother who suffered the devastating loss of a child during Herod's cruel purge, the Bible gives no indication of that.

That Old Testament passage from Jeremiah originally prophesied about mourning that would accompany the conquering of the Jewish kingdom of Judah by the ancient Babylonian armies. After that conquest, Babylon would eliminate from history any remnants of an independent Jewish nation and disperse the Jewish people as slaves in exile. In this context, "Rachel" was a collective personification of all the mothers in Israel, grieving for their lost nation and exiled children.

Matthew, however, showed a dual meaning to this Jeremiah prophecy. One was in reference to the ancient exile, and the other was a collective reference to the mothers of Bethlehem weeping for the children murdered by Herod. That collective symbolism is the more accepted understanding of Matthew's reference here.

Source: ESB 1823

The Return to Nazareth
Matthew 2:19-23

Why choose Egypt and Nazareth as hiding places?

At the time when Joseph took Mary and Jesus and fled from King Herod, Egypt had become a kind of safe haven for Jews forced to leave their home country. Egypt (like Herod's Judea) was under Roman control but was outside of King Herod's authority. A Jewish philosopher named Philo (15 BC–AD 50) lived during that time. He reported that, within the Egyptian city of Alexandria alone, about one million Jews lived in relative safety.

Although Egypt wasn't exactly close for Joseph and Mary, it wasn't too far either. The border between Judea and Egypt was about eighty miles away from their home in Bethlehem—a distance that could be covered within several days. Because of its heavy Jewish population, accessible walking distance, and its peaceful coexistence with Judea as part of the Roman Empire, Egypt was an ideal place for Joseph to hide his family from Herod's murderous intent.

As for Nazareth, when it came time to return to Israel after Herod's death, that place was a tiny, backwater village situated in foothills on the southern edge of what was known as "Lower Galilee." It was dwarfed by larger towns nearby. With a population estimated by some to be as low as one hundred people, Nazareth was insignificant—and thus also a great place for a Messiah to be overlooked while growing into manhood. It was there that Jesus' earthly father, Joseph, settled his family and set up his carpenter's shop.

Nazareth was also only about four miles (roughly a fifty-minute walk) from Sepphoris (or Sepphora), a large city that had recently been razed by Roman armies to put down a Jewish uprising. In spite of the ruins, Herod Antipas (one of Herod the Great's sons) insisted on immediately rebuilding Sepphoris, making it the capital city of rule over Galilee.

"This means," Bible historian Peter Walker has theorized, "that throughout Jesus' young life and into his teenage years, Sepphora would've been a major building site—the perfect place of employment for someone like Joseph." He adds, "The family's move north to Nazareth may also have been inspired by some other considerations—good employment prospects."

Sources: ZB1 17; ISJ 31-33

Why did learning that Archelaus was in charge in Judea make Joseph afraid to go there?

Matthew reports that Joseph was afraid to live in Judea under the rule of Herod's son, Archelaus—and apparently with good reason.

After Herod the Great died, there was a power struggle among his sons over who would inherent his kingdom. Archelaus had first assumed kingship over the objections of his brothers. Meanwhile, revolutionaries stirred up opposition and threatened to derail Archelaus's bid to rule. He responded as his father would have, sending in the Roman army and massacring roughly three thousand people during the Passover holiday. That's just about the same number who were killed in America on 9/11, so you can imagine the horrifying effect that had on Archelaus's ancient subjects.

Fresh off that gruesome "victory," he went with his brother to Rome to make a case for his kingship to the emperor. After much deliberation, Caesar Augustus made a compromise. He appointed Archelaus as "ethnarch" over Idumea, Judea, and Samaria, with a promise that he would be made king if he proved worthy. His brother Antipas was installed as "tetrarch" over Galilee and Perea, while Philip was also named tetrarch over other territories in the area.

When Archelaus returned to Judea, he ruled both the Jews in the south and the Samaritans in the north with great brutality. It was so bad, in fact, that Augustus deposed and banished Archelaus only two years later, around AD 6.

So Joseph obviously knew something of Archelaus's reputation—and that caused him enough concern that he opted to go north of Samaria to Nazareth. There Joseph, Mary, and their precious family would avoid even the chance of being yet another victim to that viciously cruel king.

Source: ZP3 138

Jesus' Early Ministry

John the Baptist Prepares the Way
Matthew 3:1-12

Was there anyone in the history of the Bible that was like John the Baptist?

John the Baptist was an extraordinary figure. He shows up in both Bible history and Roman historical records from the time of Jesus. Here's what we know about him:

His father Zechariah was a temple priest, and his mother Elizabeth was a relative of Jesus' mother, Mary. In that sense, John and Jesus may have been cousins of some sort. He was miraculously born to elderly parents who had been previously unable to have kids, linking him symbolically to Old Testament heroes like Isaac, Samson, and Samuel. His impending birth was announced to Zechariah by the angel Gabriel, the same angel who announced Jesus' coming to Mary. He lived like a monk in the Judean desert along the Dead Sea, dressed in rough, camel-hair clothing, and ate mostly bugs (locusts similar to grasshoppers) and honey from wild bees.

So, was there anyone in the history of the Bible that was like John the Baptist? Yes.

In addition to his symbolic association with Isaac, Samson, and Samuel, John also conducted himself in the mold of Old Testament prophets, preaching for people to repent of their sins. Like prophets such as Jonah, Elijah, Elisha, and others, he spoke to large crowds and also called individuals to account. He angered political and religious leaders, who eventually conspired to kill him.

Most importantly, John served as the prophesied "forerunner" who announced the coming of the Messiah to the world (see Malachi 3:1 and Isaiah 40:3). In this way, Jesus linked John to the prophet Elijah as well.

John the Baptist was eventually executed by Herod Antipas, who ruled Galilee during the time of Jesus.

Source: WWA 216–218

Why did John the Baptist rebuke religious leaders who were seeking baptism? Weren't they doing the right thing?

John the Baptist apparently preached the same message over and over: "Repent, for the kingdom of heaven has come near." As a symbol of repentance, he urged people to be baptized—a ritual he adapted from the Jewish religious practice of a purifying bath before worship. In spite of that, "when he saw many of the Pharisees and Sadducees coming to where he was baptizing," he castigated them harshly.

It's noteworthy that John insulted the Pharisees and Sadducees by calling them a "brood of vipers," which basically meant he viewed them as poisonous children of snakes. In the ancient world this was an especially contemptuous insult because of a folk belief about viper births. Many thought that some breeds of viper babies ate their way out of the stomach of their mother, killing the mother in the process. In that context, John's insult is a horrifying characterization of the religious elite.

The situation here suggests that those religious leaders weren't there to be baptized, but to assess an enemy, because John's preaching threatened their place as the spiritual authorities in Israel. Additionally, "The Jew who accepted baptism from John," explains Dr. Larry Richards, "confessed his sins and expressed determination to live a righteous life." Pharisees and Sadducees wouldn't have seen themselves in need of that repentance— or John's baptism—because they pridefully assumed they were blameless regarding God's Old Testament laws.

Sources: WWA 216–218; IBB 52; BAH 267–268

The Baptism of Jesus
Matthew 3:13–17

If John's baptism was for repentance, did that mean Jesus needed to repent?

Both Christ and his disciples taught that Jesus never sinned (John 8:46; 2 Corinthians 5:21; 1 Peter 2:22; 1 John 3:5). Therefore, Jesus would have no need of repentance. You won't be surprised to learn, then, that Jesus' request to be baptized caused unique intellectual problems, both for John the Baptist and for Christians who came later.

Dr. Craig Evans reports that "There is evidence that some early Christians found Jesus' baptism somewhat embarrassing, either because it implied that Jesus, like his fellow Israelites, needed to repent, or because it implied that Jesus was in some sense subordinate to John." The Baptist himself seems to have had a similar intellectual conflict when Jesus showed up at the Jordan River—to the point where John actually tried to talk Jesus out of the baptismal request.

In spite of all that, Jesus shrugged off John's objection—and any embarrassing implications associated with it—and insisted on being baptized. Although we can't know for sure his full motivation, most assume the baptismal act was a demonstration of Christ's ritual obedience to God's will, setting an example for others to follow.

Source: BKB 79, 81

What was significant about the Holy Spirit coming upon Jesus?

The baptism of Jesus was a defining moment, one that "marks both His inauguration as the servant Messiah and the dawning of a new age of the Spirit." In that context, it's significant that Matthew records the physical manifestation of all three Persons of the Trinity as being present:

> God the Father speaks from the heavens.

> God the Son stands, dripping wet, beside the Jordan River.

> God the Holy Spirit descends in the form of a dove and rests on the Son.

This triune appearance of divinity is never again repeated in the gospel accounts. As such, theologian H. Wayne House theorizes that this inaugural moment of baptism carried immense significance for three reasons. It symbolized that: "1) Jesus joined with the believing remnant of Israel who had been baptized by John; 2) He confirmed the ministry of John; and 3) He fulfilled the Father's will."

Source: NNI 1143–1145

The Temptation of Jesus
Matthew 4:1-11

Is the temptation of Jesus a comparison to Adam being tempted in the garden of Eden (Genesis 3)?

It's possible—and that view would be consistent with the apostle Paul's symbolic comparison of Adam and Christ. Notably, Paul makes this connection twice: Once in his letter to the Corinthians (1 Corinthians 15:12–21) and also in his letter to the Roman church (Romans 5:21–24). Romans 5:19 sums up this view particularly well:

> Because one person [Adam] disobeyed God, many became sinners. But because one other person [Jesus Christ] obeyed God, many will be made righteous.

Sources: Romans 5:12-21; 1 Corinthians 15:21-24

Why did the devil say, "If you are the Son of God"? Was this meant as a challenge?

It's impossible to fully intuit why Satan says or does anything, but if I were to guess, I'd say that yes, the statement, "If you are the Son of God, then…" could be interpreted as a challenge. And if it was, then it's interesting to see that Christ was unwilling to take the bait.

Have you ever noticed that only Satan worked miracles during this temptation of Christ?

The devil first appeared out of nowhere. Then he miraculously transported Jesus to the highest point of the Jerusalem temple. Lastly, he transported Jesus to a high mountain and gave him a supernatural vision of "all the kingdoms of the world" (verse 8).

It seems significant that God's miracle-working Messiah, Jesus Christ himself, didn't perform a single miracle in his defense during this time of temptation. Despite the devil's repeated insistence, Jesus refused to overrule the laws of nature on his own behalf—even though history has shown he had that power. As noted twentieth-century pastor, Herschel Hobbs, commented:

> Jesus called upon no power that is not available to any man as he faces temptation. His only weapon was the Scripture, the Sword of the Spirit, and He wielded it within the center of the will of God.

Source: ILJ 57

The Ministry of Jesus Begins
Matthew 4:12–17

Did Jesus own a home in Capernaum?

Capernaum (pronounced kuh-PUHR-nay-uhm) in Galilee was the headquarters of Jesus' ministry and the home of his disciple, Simon Peter. In that day, it was a bustling city of about six thousand people (both Jews and gentiles) and was situated on a major trade route that connected Damascus and Alexandria. Located beside the Sea of Galilee, fishing was a prominent trade there.

Luke 9:58 records Jesus saying he had "no place even to lay his head," so it's unlikely that Christ owned a home anywhere. Archaeology professor Dr. John McRay tells us that the common view is that Jesus probably lived with Peter when in Capernaum, not in a place of his own.

Interestingly, archaeologists think they've found remains of both Peter's ancient home and the synagogue where Jesus taught in Capernaum. The house lies about eighty-plus feet away from the synagogue and was discovered under the ruins of a fourth-century church. Today, you can actually visit there. The location is marked by a modern Franciscan church in what's known as Capernaum National Park.

Sources: TEF 49; JHT 228, 229, 232; ANT 162, 164; FOD 393

What did Jesus mean when he said, "the Kingdom of Heaven is near"? Was he referring to himself?

The phrase, "kingdom of heaven" appears only in Matthew's gospel, but it's used synonymously with "kingdom of God" found elsewhere in Matthew and in the other gospels. Bible expert James Stuart Bell defines this term as meaning, "the spiritual rule of God in the hearts of believers," and another says it "describes the life of those who follow God here on our fallen planet." While both of those observations are technically accurate, as definitions they fall short of the urgency and power with which Jesus used the phrase.

Christ's teaching on the kingdom emphasized that it was physically near (or literally, "has drawn near") because he, God's Son, had come. The kingdom in this sense is both a present, intangible reality (that is, "rule of God in the hearts of believers") and also the promise of a future, physical reality (God's rule on earth) that was beginning to show itself through Christ's presence.

"The kingdom is the sum of all gifts," twentieth-century Bible scholar Sherman E. Johnson wrote in a commentary on this passage—and that rings true. I think he sums up the rest well:

> Though it will come in its complete glory only in the future, it is already beginning to manifest itself in the events connected with Jesus' ministry … the dawning of the kingdom, the appearance of its first fruits, the combination of thanksgiving for present bliss with the most poignant expectation of glory in the near future—these features run through the whole New Testament.

Sources: TTW 205–206; BAB 107; IB7 275

The First Disciples
Matthew 4:18–22

What was appealing about Jesus' call to be "fishers of men"?

Jesus told Simon Peter and Andrew that he would make them "fishers of men" (verse 19 KJV). I think a little historical background will help us understand why that would appeal to them. The image in that call was grounded in the commercial fisherman's trade on the Sea of Galilee. Unlike our modern picture of a single person casting a line off a flexible pole to catch a single fish, Jesus' reference was to "net fishing" that was usually conducted in teams.

Galilee fishermen in that day typically used three types of nets to catch their prey.

> A cast net was circular, about twenty-five feet in diameter, weighted with lead sinkers on the edge. It was tossed over the side of a boat where it floated to the bottom like an opened parachute, trapping fish inside.

> A seine net was long and narrow, with weights on one end and floats on the other. It would hang vertically beside the boat, one end at the surface, and the other deep into the water. Fishermen could then capture entire schools of fish by using ropes to pull the net up into a U-shape.

> A trammel net was the largest, stretching nearly two hundred yards. Reinforced by three layers of netting, it was typically spread between two boats on the water. Rowing the boats forward trapped fish in the huge net. When it was full, the fishermen would simply pull up the trammel to harvest their catch.

With that kind of background, Jesus' call to become fishers of men would've been understood as an invitation for Peter and Andrew to become VIPs—very important people. It would've been seen as a promise of large crowds of followers and association with a prominent rabbi already making a name for himself in their hometown.

Source: JOB 127

Who was Zebedee, and why was it important that he be mentioned here?

Much has been written about Peter, Andrew, James, and John—but what of Zebedee, the father they left behind to follow Jesus? Here's what we know:

Zebedee was a successful businessman, running a fishing operation on the Sea of Galilee. He employed his sons, their partners (Peter and Andrew) as well as other hired hands (Mark 1:19–20). He also owned at least one large fishing boat, so he was apparently a man of some financial means.

He was married to a woman named Salome, and after the crucifixion he allowed his wife to use their money to buy burial spices for Jesus (Mark 16:1). Through Salome, his sons, or directly, he may have also supported Jesus' ministry with monetary contributions from time to time.

Some think that, like his sons, he may have been a disciple of John the Baptist first, and then became a follower of Jesus (from a distance) as well.

Bible historian Ronald Brownrigg also speculates that Zebedee had been contracted to supply fish for the high priest's palace in Jerusalem. That would explain, the thinking goes, why his son John was known and welcomed into the high priest's courtyard during the trial of Jesus (John 18:15–16).

As for why he was mentioned here in Matthew's gospel? The most likely reason is that Matthew knew him, and in that paternal society, it was simply natural to mention his name when talking about his sons.

Source: WWB 444–445

Crowds Follow Jesus
Matthew 4:23-25

What was the Decapolis?

The Decapolis, or "Ten Towns," was not a single city or country. Much as we collectively refer to the northeastern states of Maine, Massachusetts, New Hampshire, Vermont, Rhode Island, and Connecticut as "New England," people in Jesus' day used Decapolis as a collective reference to a political league of ten predominately Greek towns in the eastern portion of the land of ancient Israel. Those communities were Damascus, Raphana, Kanatha, Gerasa, Pella, Scythopolis, Gadara, Dion, Hippos, and Philadelphia (no, not the one in Pennsylvania!).

The town of Hippos was just across the Sea of Galilee from Capernaum, Christ's home base. It was probably a place where fishermen like Peter and John sold fish. Additionally, the man suffering from a "Legion" of demons was from Gadara in the Decapolis, and thus was the first to spread the news of Christ into the gentile world (Mark 5:1–20).

Because of cultural similarities found in Jesus' parable of the prodigal son, Bible historian E. M. Blaiklock also suggests that the "far country" in that story, where the son squandered his fortune, might've been based on one or more towns found in the Decapolis.

Source: ZP2 81, 84

What did Jesus' healing ministry mean to the people of that time?

If we don't count resurrections (there were three of those), Scripture records twenty-three specific, miraculous healings performed by Jesus. Among those were supposedly incurable diseases, such as blindness, leprosy, deafness, muteness, crippling lameness, withered appendages, paralysis and more. According to Matthew, those twenty-three stunning miracles were just a small fraction of Christ's true healing ministry. He reports that Jesus "healed every disease and illness" among the large crowds that followed him (verse 23).

Why did Christ do that? Compassion, obviously, was a motivating factor for Jesus, but healing also meant more than that to those who saw it and/or experienced it. Jesus' medical miracles gave proof that his teaching was from God. They endorsed his credibility as God's Son and Israel's Messiah (John 3:2; 7:31). Miraculous healing, theologian J. M. Lower explains, "was performed not as broadcast philanthropy … but as a sign…. The purpose of the miracles was to show God was at work in a new way."

Sources: BAB 111; ZP3 55

The Sermon on the Mount: The Beatitudes
Matthew 5:1-12

What exactly does "Blessed" mean, and how are people "Blessed" in this context?

The longest recorded sermon of Jesus, the Sermon on the Mount in Matthew 5–7, begins with *blessed* as a repetitive theme word. "Blessed are the poor in spirit… Blessed are those who mourn… Blessed are the meek…" (Matthew 5:3–5 NIV). Historically, that word was understood to mean "happy"—or in the literal Hebrew translation, "how happy!" The Greek equivalent, used in Matthew's record of Jesus' sermon, is *makarios*, and it mirrors King David's use of the Hebrew term in the first psalm: "Blessed is the one who does not walk in step with the wicked" (Psalm 1:1 NIV).

Additionally, in pagan writings, *makarios* indicated a heavenly "state of happiness and well-being," and Christ seemed to communicate that meaning here as well.

Still, in the context of the Sermon on the Mount, Jesus' repetitive emphasis on the word "blessed" seems hard to understand. For instance, his exhortation in Matthew 5:4 could be literally interpreted, "How happy are those who are sad!" For his original hearers, and for us today, that kind of statement seems to make very little sense.

It appears that Christ intended a broader interpretation of what it truly means to be blessed. Being blessed by God is not simply enjoying a happy feeling based on your circumstances. Blessed, in Jesus' usage, carries many shades of meaning, all wrapped up like a gift for those with eyes to see and ears to hear. It includes the idea of "approval"—as in both the approval of God and people. It implies that one is "lucky," not so much in the sense of random luck, but in the sense that God orchestrates seemingly random coincidences to deliver happiness in a person's life. And, uniquely, it is a congratulatory term, as in "Congratulations for being chosen to endure sorrow! You will one day understand with great happiness what it means to be comforted by God."

In this sense, then, Jesus proclaimed that even in the worst of circumstances, we can be happy … approved … lucky … and congratulated. We are blessed, simply because God himself has determined to make it so, both here and in eternity to come.

Sources: IBD1 201; SOM 22

I thought God wanted to heal me and bring prosperity into my life. How does Matthew 5:11–12 fit with that?

Jesus' final beatitude differs from the earlier ones. Up to this point, Jesus has used general pronouns as the object of blessing. For instance, "blessed are those… blessed are they…"

Beginning in verse 11, though, his teaching shifts to the personal pronoun, "blessed are *you*,"—a direct reference that included his twelve apostles, each person in the large crowd of listeners and, by extension, you and me today.

It's important to note that this final beatitude promises great suffering for Jesus' followers: "God blesses you when people mock you and persecute you and lie about you and say all sorts of evil things against you because you are my followers" (verse 11).

Jesus didn't say *"if* people mock you..." but *"when* people mock you..." The message is clear: Undeserved hardship is an expected part of the Christian life. It's rare to find anyone today who'd be willing to "name and claim" this promise of God, but Jesus' followers experienced it nonetheless. Consider what happened to each of his original disciples, according to church tradition—minus Judas the betrayer, who killed himself:

> Andrew: Crucified on an X-shaped cross.

> Bartholomew: Flayed alive with knives until he died.

> James (son of Alphaeus): Sawed to pieces.

> James (son of Zebedee): Beheaded.

> John: Poisoned (but miraculously survived). Boiled in oil (but miraculously survived). Imprisoned, in his old age, on the island of Patmos, where he worked as slave labor in the marble mines.

> Matthew (Levi): Died a martyr while preaching in Ethiopia.

> Peter: Crucified upside down.

> Philip: Hanged to death.

> Simon (the Zealot): Sawed in half.

> Thaddaeus (Jude): Martyred while preaching in Persia.

> Thomas: Speared to death.

This last beatitude of Jesus, and its fulfillment in the lives of the apostles, leaves us with one question that must be answered by each follower of Christ today: What will you do with this difficult promise of God?

Sources: NAS 1277-1280; WWW 211

Teaching about Salt and Light
Matthew 5:13–16

This whole salt and light thing is so famous that I'm kind of embarrassed to say I find it confusing. But I want to know: What is Jesus getting at here?

Some Bible teachers try to mine deeply the idea that Christians are "salt and light." For them, every little aspect bears a significant application: Salt preserves, so we should be "preservatives" in our society. Light shines, so we should testify loudly all the time. Salt was used to kill vegetation on ancient footpaths, so we should … well, who knows what we should do with that. And so on.

In their zeal for application of the biblical text, these preachers often seem to confuse rhetoric (persuasive speech) with symbolism (figurative imagery in place of literal facts). In this case, Jesus doesn't appear to be speaking symbolically, but rhetorically. He employed rhetorical absurdity to emphasize a point, using extreme metaphors of salt and light to reveal natural spiritual truth to his hearers.

For instance, pure salt is a chemically stable substance. It never goes bad, has no expiration date, and can never "lose its saltiness." Thus, when Jesus said, "If the salt loses its saltiness" (verse 13 NIV) he made an over-the-top rhetorical statement that would've been easily understood as such by his audience. The image of a person lighting a lamp and then hiding it under a bowl was likewise ridiculous. Only a mentally unstable person would've done that.

The point Jesus seems to make here isn't that we're supposed to take on all the obscure characteristics of salt or light. Instead, Christ called his hearers to live out everyday expressions of faith that are similar to the run-of-the-mill existence of salt and light.

Just as it's natural for salt to be salty and natural for light to shine, it's a natural thing for God's children to daily express the goodness and glory of their heavenly Father.

Source: MAC 1381

Was Jesus talking about someplace specific when he mentioned a "city on a hilltop"?

It's definitely possible. In the literary and rhetorical contexts, Christ's reference to a "city on a hilltop" is obviously emphasizing the idea of his people living authentic faith-lives out in the open where anyone can see. But he also may have had a more literal meaning, rooted in the geography of ancient Galilee.

Theologian R. T. Kendall tells us that within the region of Galilee at the time of Jesus there was a small town called Safed. (In fact, Safed still exists today—now a few thousand years old.) This little place sits at the top of a mountain and, in fact, is part of the mountain range from which Jesus delivered this famous Sermon on the Mount.

"The city of Safed is visible day or night," Kendall reports. "Whether it is the same little city that Jesus had in mind, I don't know. But Safed is two thousand years old and certainly could have been the same city."

Perhaps, as he was teaching on salt and light, Jesus motioned toward Safed as a visual object lesson to illustrate his point, "like a city on a hilltop that cannot be hidden."

Sources: SOM 78

Teaching about the Law
Matthew 5:17–20

"Anyone who obeys God's laws ... will be called great in the Kingdom of Heaven." Is Jesus teaching legalism here?

Jesus' vehemence here about the sacredness of the Law and the Prophets seems to contradict his other teaching and actions, particularly in his flagrant disregard for Sabbath rules and his teachings on ritual purity. Does that mean he was lying, or worse, simply placating his Pharisaical opponents with some kind of politically correct statement? Most Christian scholars would say no—and they'd point to the distinctions Christ makes between Scripture and tradition as the reason why.

In Jewish understanding, "the Law" consisted of the first five books of the Old Testament: Genesis, Exodus, Leviticus, Numbers, and Deuteronomy.

"The Prophets" encompassed the rest of the Old Testament, all of which was assumed to have been written by God's prophets. Jesus clearly viewed all of these texts as divinely inspired and eternal—and he said just that. What he didn't endorse was every human tradition and interpretation of the Law and the Prophets that had arisen among the Jewish people over the centuries. Those human traditions often elevated outward expressions over inward character, and thus they frequently negated the loving spirit of the law while obeying the harsh letter of the law.

Jesus' teaching here, and life as a whole, helped his listeners better understand and prioritize the true nature of God's desires for humanity in practical, daily life. He alone became our living example of One who obeyed both the spirit and the letter of the Law. As twentieth-century theologian Sherman E. Johnson explained, "He made the ritual commandments subordinate to moral duties, opposed the development of purity laws, and went further than the Pharisees in relaxing the Sabbath laws to meet human needs." In other words, as he said himself, Jesus came to *accomplish the purpose* of the Law and the Prophets—not to abolish them.

Sources: ESB 1828; IB7 291

Teaching about Anger
Matthew 5:21–26

This Scripture seems to say that any angry outburst will send me straight to the "fires of hell," regardless of whether I'm Christian or not. What am I supposed to do with that?

Verse 22 does quote Jesus as saying that anyone who is angry toward another has committed a sin equivalent to murder and is "in danger of the fires of hell." This seems extreme and is difficult to reconcile with other statements of grace and forgiveness that Jesus made. I myself don't know the full measure of this teaching, but Bible scholar and teacher Warren Wiersbe offered this insight:

There is a holy anger against sin (Ephesians 4:26), but Jesus talked about an unholy anger against people. The word He used in Matthew 5:22 means 'a settled anger, malice that is nursed inwardly.'

Others see Jesus making a reference here to humanity's first murder—Cain's killing of his brother, Abel, as recorded in Genesis 4. Cain's criminal actions weren't simply preceded by his jealous anger toward his brother—that is to say, his anger didn't simply lead to the act of murder. Rather, the act of murder was actually begun in Cain's sin of "malice that is nursed inwardly." The killing of Abel itself was the final, outward expression of the murderous intent that Cain had already been nurturing within himself, out of public view.

It may be that it's in this sense that anger, unchecked, becomes equivalent to murder. Just as the seed of a rose contains all the DNA of a full-grown rose bush, it's possible that anger is the sinful seed that contains all the DNA of murder. Jesus thus strongly encourages his hearers to deal immediately with anger toward others—pursuing reconciliation and forgiveness without delay. In this peaceful pursuit, the sinful seeds of anger are rooted out and rendered ineffective in a person's life.

Sources: BEC 23; BKB 115

Why did Jesus say "You have heard ... but I say" when teaching about anger? That seems a little odd to my ear.

It is somewhat odd to our ears today, but in Israel at that time his statement would've been downright alarming. In those days, all teachers of Scripture used "borrowed authority" as the means of justifying their teachings. Rabbis quoted the Law and the Prophets, and they cited esteemed rabbinical leaders of the past to support their opinions. Prophets spoke as ambassadors of God, couching their every message in phrases like, "Thus says the Lord." Had Jesus been simply another teacher or prophet of that kind, he would've done the same.

But he didn't.

Jesus declared, "You have heard that it was said ... but I tell you ..." to emphasize his total authority as the human incarnation of the divine. The "I" in this phrase is rendered as an emphatic utterance, which could almost be interpreted as an exclamatory "*I!*" As classic theologian A. Lukyn Williams explained, "Christ claims for his words the same authority, and more than the same authority, as for those once spoken by God." That was, and still is, a very serious claim.

Jesus saw no need to appeal to any other authority but himself while teaching the true meaning of God's Word. He apparently considered himself to be God who authored that Word. Depending on your perspective, that's either frightening … or fantastic.

Sources: IB7 295; PCXV 159

Teaching about Adultery
Matthew 5:27–30

Who's responsible for the sin of lust in this context—the man or the woman?

"Anyone who even looks at a woman with lust has already committed adultery with her in his heart," Christ said in his Sermon on the Mount. Some have interpreted this statement to mean that, outside of marriage, any acknowledgment of feminine beauty by a man is adultery—the assumption being that noticing a woman's attractiveness automatically coincides with sexual desire. As a result, they often demand that women are responsible to prevent men from being tempted to sin over their bodies, perhaps by covering themselves physically from neck to foot (and sometimes veiling faces), by refusing to wear make-up, by avoiding modern clothing styles deemed "revealing," and so on. Though popular in some circles, that perspective seems to be a mistake in thinking of Pharisaical proportions.

The Greek word translated as "lustfully" or "with lust" is a variation on the term *epithymia,* which means "strong desire." In this context it clearly refers to a thought-life of the viewer that's well beyond simple appreciation or acknowledgment of God-given beauty in a feminine form. *Epithymia* here speaks of a "strong desire" to consume God's beautiful creation through intentional, inappropriate action at the expense of that creation. *It is an act of will, not of accident.* Bible scholar Lawrence O. Richards explains it this way: "A sexual desire stimulated by the sin nature—a desire that seeks to possess and use persons who are not rightly objects of desire." In other words, if your imagination is using a woman as a pornographic tool for mental sexual stimulation, that's equal to adultery—and it's *your* sin, not hers.

Acknowledging and appreciating God-given beauty in a woman, however, is not adultery, and shouldn't be conflated as such.

Source: EDB 423

Teaching about Divorce
Matthew 5:31-32

If a woman had no choice in the divorce, why was it "adultery" for her to marry someone new but not "adultery" for her husband who divorced her?

In the time of Jesus, it was husbands, not wives, who could instigate a divorce and issue their spouse a "written notice of divorce" (verse 31). But a divorce certificate according to man's laws, as Christ explains in this teaching, falls far short of God's standards. In fact, Jesus makes the bold claim that the divorcing husband "makes [his wife] commit adultery" (verse 32). In that patriarchal society, it was very difficult for a woman to survive without a husband or father as a caretaker. That meant, in order to eat and gain shelter, a divorced woman would almost certainly have to remarry.

So if remarriage in God's eyes was adultery for the divorced woman, why didn't Christ also say divorcing her was "adultery" for the man?

Theologian Craig Keener suggests that the omission of the husband here was cultural in its application, not eternal in its view. "Under Jewish law," he says, "'adultery' referred only to the wife's misbehavior, not the husband's. Matthew does not agree with this view (Matthew 5:28), but because his readers must obey the law of their communities, he deals only with the issues of the wife."

Additionally, although Jesus doesn't state it plainly, it can be inferred that he considered the divorcing husband to be guilty of perhaps a worse offense: causing another person—his wife—to commit sin (see Mark 9:42; Luke 17:1; 1 Corinthians 8:12–13). Thus, by divorcing his wife without true justification, the man became the catalyst that "causes her to commit adultery."

Sources: IBB 59; IBC 1125

Why is Jesus so opposed to divorce?

You may be surprised to discover that Old Testament law did not codify the practice of divorce. In fact, biblical history indicates that divorce predated the time of Moses. As such, it was acknowledged by the Old Testament law, but not created by it (Deuteronomy 24:1). Jesus, though, was not as tolerant. Looking at Matthew 5:31–32, Jewish theologian Aaron M. Gale comments wryly, "Jesus' sexual ethics are stricter than found in most branches of early Judaism."

Jesus' intolerance for the practice of divorce, as displayed in his Sermon on the Mount, takes on new meaning when viewed through a symbolic lens.

Consider this: Throughout the New Testament, Christ is presented figuratively as a bridegroom, and all his followers throughout the ages (the church) are collectively seen as his bride (John 3:29; 2 Corinthians 11:2; Ephesians 5:25–27; Revelation 19:6–9), or as theologian John F. Walvoord describes it, "a bride not yet joined to her Husband." In this spiritual relationship, Christ is the betrothed husband who has already paid the "dowry" through his death and resurrection (John 3:16–17; 1 Corinthians 6:17–20; Hebrews 13:12). He is now preparing a place for his bride (John 14:2)—and preparing his bride for an eternal "marriage" to him (Ephesians 5:25–27; Revelation 19:6–9).

In this context, Jesus' stringent teaching on divorce in Matthew 5:31–32 carries wonderful new significance. *Jesus Christ, our eternal Bridegroom, hates divorce.* He is therefore unequivocally, relentlessly committed to love and care for his church (you and me) through any obstacle, in spite of any sin, and beyond the reaches of time itself. *Amen!*

Sources: JAN 21; JCL 250-253

Teaching about Vows
Matthew 5:33-37

Why can't I find the Scripture Jesus quoted in Matthew 5:33 in the Old Testament?

Well, the simple answer is because it's not Scripture, and it's not in the Bible. Verse 33 records Jesus as saying, "You have also heard that our ancestors were told, 'You must not break your vows; you must carry out the vows you make to the Lord." The assumption would be that he was quoting the Old Testament, but he wasn't. At least not exactly.

Dr. Craig Evans represents many Bible scholars in his thinking that this point in Christ's Sermon on the Mount was instead a kind of summary of several scriptures, lumped into a saying that Jesus' hearers would've easily recognized (that is, "You have heard..."). The first part of his statement might have been a reference to the command of Leviticus 19:12, "Do not bring shame on the name of your God by using it to swear falsely." The second part is less obvious but probably related to Psalm 50:14, which says, "Keep the vows you made to the Most High."

In light of this "creative paraphrasing" of Scripture, some question why Jesus opted to misquote the Old Testament here. Did he simply forget the exact phrasing? Was he unconcerned about textual accuracy, or implying that the original language was unreliable? Was he not quoting Scripture at all, but referencing some other source instead?

Given the context of his broader teaching here, that last option seems most likely. It's very possible his phrasing in Matthew 5:33 quoted familiar rabbinical teachings rather than the Bible itself. That choice would've highlighted for listeners, at least subtly, how extra-biblical traditions had become so prevalent and revered that they were often regarded on par with God's Word—and used in place of the actual words of Scripture.

In essence, by quoting what his audience had been taught instead of what was accurate according to Old Testament texts, he may have been suggesting to his listeners, "What you've heard all your lives—and the way you've heard it—isn't exactly what's true."

Similar to religious leaders of ancient Israel, we modern Christians have had copious amounts of church teaching between Jesus' time and ours. One has to wonder where we, too, are susceptible to allowing our familiar, accepted traditions to overshadow God's original truth.

Source: BKB 117

Jesus seems pretty upset by the "oaths" he mentions—but they all seem fairly trivial to me. What am I missing?

In ancient Israel, an oath was both a ritual act and a binding promise. Oaths were invoked in court cases to (supposedly) ensure that witnesses would tell the truth. They were also given as proof of an unbreakable pledge of loyalty, or as a guarantee that a person would fulfill some obligation, such as a promise to repay a loan. People swore oaths by that which was valuable to them, such as families or personal wealth and security, and even their own lives (swearing "by my head"). The assumption was that failure to keep such an oath would either bring shame or personal loss. The highest, most binding ritual oath was one that brought God into the transaction because, it was assumed, God himself would inflict a curse upon any who failed to fulfill an oath made in his name.

By the time of Jesus, though, the Pharisees had used an array of semantics to skillfully excuse themselves from the duty to keep most oaths. In much the same ways that disreputable lawyers today appeal to the "fine print" to get out of obvious obligations, Pharisees were experts at dissecting the oath ritual in order to find loopholes that justified their dishonest promises. For instance, in their reasoning, an oath sworn "by the temple!" in Jerusalem could be considered frivolous and assumed to mean nothing. A promise made "by the gold of the temple," however, was binding and failure to fulfill that would incur punishment (see Matthew 23:16).

When Jesus preached against making oaths in the Sermon on the Mount, he was also indicting this kind of Pharisaical hypocrisy—and calling all God followers to a higher standard of authenticity and integrity. As Dr. Lawrence O. Richards describes it, "Christ teaches that form is irrelevant.... In the fellowship of honest people, a person's word is as binding as a sacred oath."

Sources: HBD 716; RBD 742–743

Teaching about Revenge
Matthew 5:38–42

Where did "an eye for an eye and a tooth for a tooth" come from?

What you're referring to here is known as *lex talionis*, "law of retaliation." This practice was well established in Jewish history and in the law of Moses.

The "eye for an eye" concept first appears in Genesis 9:6, just after the Great Flood when God told Noah, "If anyone takes a human life, that person's life will also be taken by human hands. For God made human beings in his own image." It was a deterrent to violent crime, and more clearly spelled out in Exodus 21:22–24 as the judicial penalty for one who caused serious injury to a pregnant woman and/or her unborn child. Leviticus 24:19–20 expands the judicial scope of both the laws in Genesis and Exodus to include "Whatever anyone does to injure another person."

Interestingly, this seemingly primitive law of physical retaliation was actually progressive for its time and even well into Jesus' day. Jewish theologian W. Gunther Plaut reports that *lex talionis* "had the important function of limiting private revenge, especially family or tribal feuds. Further, the Torah treats injuries to rich and poor, male and female, completely alike."

It's also significant to note that, despite its Scriptural and historical endorsement, the Bible doesn't record a single instance in which someone was actually maimed or blinded under the justification of *lex talionis*. Why? Plaut notes that legal and religious authorities in ancient Israel interpreted *talionis* as meaning that "financial compensation, and not literal, physical *talion*, was the intent of the law."

Thus in common practice, Plaut says, "compensation [was] scaled to the degree of the injury: the value of an eye for the loss of an eye, the value of a limb for its loss, and so forth." To that end, Jewish law had encoded "detailed stipulations for monetary compensation, much as modern insurance contracts are wont to do."

Sources: BKN 31; TOR 571–572

It seems to me that a person is most likely to be slapped on the left cheek. Why would Jesus mention the right cheek specifically?

The answer to this question probably lies in the social norms of that time in ancient Israel. In Western society today, one person spitting on another is an especially contemptuous insult. In the time of Jesus, being slapped on the right cheek was similarly offensive. The average person was assumed to be right-handed, thus the perception was that striking a person on the right cheek required a backhanded slap. That action communicated utter contempt toward someone considered inferior. In fact, it was such a serious offense that both Jewish and Roman law allowed a victim of this kind of slap to take his abuser to court and demand restitution.

"If someone slaps you on the right cheek," Jesus said, "offer the other cheek also."

In this instance, Christ wasn't simply speaking of cultivating a nonviolent attitude. Within that cultural setting, he was insisting that his followers instantly forgive—and refuse to retaliate—when others acted contemptibly toward them. Perhaps because this seems to be such an impossible demand for people like us, he later demonstrated this exact ideal during the hours leading up to his awful, humiliating, contemptible crucifixion and death.

Sources: WEC 42; IBB 60

Teaching about Love for Enemies
Matthew 5:43-48

Who taught to "hate your enemy"? And why didn't Jesus teach that?

"You have heard the law that says, 'Love your neighbor' and hate your enemy." This quote from Matthew 5:43 reveals—again—how religious leaders in Jesus' time had unwittingly distorted the Mosaic law they claimed to hold supreme. The distortion was not likely intentional or arbitrary. Scribes and Pharisees were genuinely trying to discern and fulfill God's law. It was just that in their determination to understand truth, they sometimes reached false conclusions, with devastating results. Case in point was God's sacred command to love our neighbors. In this case, Jesus decided to publicly correct that error.

In the first part of verse 43, when Christ said, "Love your neighbor," he pulled a direct quote from Leviticus 19:18, which reads in full, "Do not seek revenge or bear a grudge against a fellow Israelite, but love your neighbor as yourself. I am the LORD."

Notice anything missing?

Yep, it's the second part of the common saying Jesus quoted: "...and hate your enemy." Religious leaders over the centuries had added that little phrase and taught it for generations until it eventually came to be accepted as truth on par with God's Word.

Fact is, the law didn't command anyone to hate an enemy, and it specifically forbade hating any "enemy" who might also be a fellow Israelite (Leviticus 19:17). What's more, the wisdom of King Solomon instructed kindness and generosity toward adversaries: "If your enemy is hungry, give him food to eat; if he is thirsty, give him water to drink. In doing this, you will heap burning coals on his head, and the LORD will reward you" (Proverbs 25:21–22).

Still, among Jewish thinkers in ancient times, it was a natural progression of thought to assume that the command to love your neighbor included the flip-side command of hating an enemy. It may have been a well-intentioned application of simple logic. But it was simply, heartbreakingly, wrong.

Source: NNI 1150

There's absolutely no way I can "be perfect" as my Father in heaven is perfect. Nobody can—it's an impossible standard, and Jesus knew that. So why would he put that kind of guilt on us?

"Be perfect," Jesus is quoted as saying in Matthew 5:48, "even as your Father in heaven is perfect." So what does that mean?

First, we must remember that this command was given as part of Jesus' teaching about love for an enemy. Too often verse 48 is divorced from the five verses that come before it, and then twisted to apply to whatever pet peeve suits our fancy at the moment. But getting to an authentic understanding of this teaching comes only by considering its obvious context: "Love your enemies! Pray for those who persecute you! In that way, you will be acting as true children of your Father" (verses 44–45).

Second, it's helpful to understand the meaning and usage of the word "perfect" in verse 48. In our twenty-first century experience, we tend to define "perfect" as meaning "flawless," or without any kind of shortcoming. "That diamond solitaire is perfect," we say, "without any inclusion to mar its clarity or brilliance." But that's not an appropriate view when it comes to Christ's command here. His definition was something different, particularly as he applied it to the idea of loving our enemies. The Greek term for "perfect" in this passage is *teleios*, and instead of "flawless," it means most literally, "finished" or "mature." Dr. Wayne Detzler explains, "Perfection in the New Testament is not a flawless imitation of God. Rather it is a growth into maturity which is discernible as one makes progress in the faith."

In other words, Christ's command to love our enemies is not simply that we attempt an impossible standard of behavior. It's a call for us to participate in a Holy Spirit-cultivated growth process by which we continually become more "mature" or "finished" in our ability to genuinely love our enemies.

"Be perfect," Jesus commanded. If perfection were simply a destination on the moral landscape, that would seem a cruel, unreachable demand. But it is not that. Christ's words instead are a beckoning motion, an appeal for you and me to spend our lives on a journey of perfection, continually growing and maturing in his limitless love, one unsteady step at a time.

As we pursue this kind of perfection, we begin to reflect more and more on our Father's "finished" character of love toward enemies, moving toward maturity in fulfilling God's purpose within each of us.

Sources: CWSN 16; CWDN 1372; NTW 307

Teaching about Giving to the Needy
Matthew 6:1–4

I can feel motivated by seeing someone else give. Why is it wrong to give and let people see it?

In ancient Israeli society, giving to the needy ranked among one of the highest religious duties. As such, it was a regular, ordinary part of the Jewish person's experience.

Dr. J. D. Douglas, formerly of *Christianity Today*, tells us that, "In every city there were collectors who distributed alms of two kinds, i.e. money collected in the synagogue chest every Sabbath for the poor, and food and money received in a dish." Contrary to our modern experience, it was not the government that shouldered responsibility for the welfare of the poorer and needier members of the locality. It was the religious community.

In spite of the intent of this provision, poverty was rampant in Jesus' time. "There were few middle-class Jews," Reader's Digest editor Kaari Ward reports. "If you were not rich, you were probably poor. And in the cities, divorced from the productive land, that meant that you were very poor indeed." This economic disparity, coupled with the unique circumstances of living in a Roman-conquered territory, created a large population of beggars and day laborers who woke up each morning not knowing how they'd meet the day's necessities.

It was in this setting that Jesus took to task those who viewed others' poverty and hardship as an opportunity to shine the spotlight on themselves. Although almsgiving was a basic responsibility everyone shared in that society, some demanded public praise in repayment for fulfilling this obligation. They would announce with fanfare the amount of their gifts in the synagogue or call attention to themselves when delivering a coin or a piece of bread to a beggar on the street. Generosity toward God's loved ones was irrelevant unless it also gave them better social or political standing in the community.

"Don't do your good deeds publicly," Jesus rebuked his hearers, "to be admired by others." Authentic giving, he seems to be saying, is a matter of simple compassion, and thus is best left between you and God.

Sources: IBD1 33; JHT 74–75

When Jesus said that God "sees everything," was he speaking literally or figuratively?

"Give your gifts in private, and your Father, who sees everything, will reward you." Jesus' comment gives every indication of being a statement of literal truth, not simply a figurative or symbolic expression. It's an affirmation by Christ of the related ideas that God is both everywhere and all-knowing. In seminaries and pastoral offices they call these concepts omnipresence (or immanence) and omniscience.

Omnipresence, in its most practical sense, simply means that all of God is *everywhere at all times.* Or as theologian Michael Horton says, omnipresence is "God's transcendence of time and place." It is both his necessity and his nature to exist completely in every space at any time.

We must be aware, though, that although God himself fills all of creation, *he is not spread out nor partitioned through his creation.* His immanence doesn't dictate that only parts of him are present in any particular place or space or moment or hour. Rather, "He is present in every place because he transcends spatial categories...[and] God's transcendence of time is the very presupposition of his presence in every creaturely moment." (See Jeremiah 23:23–24; Psalm 139:7–8; Proverbs 15:3; Matthew 28:20; Acts 17:27–28.)

Nor is God's omnipresence a passive or inert existence. Jesus is very clear that the Father "sees everything," indicating an active, accurate, intelligent understanding of every place and every moment in our universe. This is called "omniscience."

"By the omniscience of God," theologian Henry Thiessen explains further, "we mean that He knows Himself and all other things, whether they be actual or merely possible, whether they be past, present, or future, and that He knows them perfectly and from all eternity. He knows them immediately, simultaneously, exhaustively and truly." (See Psalm 139:1–4; Matthew 10:29–30; Hebrews 4:13.)

Thus, when Jesus reprimanded his hearers for seeking human admiration while they gave to the poor, he did more than just point out a social or religious wrong. Christ reminded us that we all (individually and collectively) are constantly, irrevocably in the intelligent, active presence of our awesome, omnipresent, omniscient Creator—and his attention should be more than enough.

Sources: CHF 255; LST 124-125

Teaching about Prayer and Fasting
Matthew 6:5-18

Why does Jesus say it's wrong to pray publicly?

Jesus' reference to public prayer was not the same as what you and I might consider it to be today. "When you pray," he said, "don't be like the hypocrites who love to pray publicly on street corners and in the synagogues where everyone can see them." He describes flamboyant, hypocritical praying that sounds a bit like grand theatre—because it probably was.

Although some Jewish prayers (such as the *Amidah*) included standing, most did not. Thus, Bible scholar Craig Evans tells us that this word picture of Christ likely hearkens to Greek-influenced performance art of the time. The Greek word we translate as "hypocrite" in verse 5 is one that was typically associated with a career actor, or more literally, a "play-actor." In Greek culture it also carried the meaning of "pretender."

This play-actor theme continued Christ's earlier sentiments about "acts of righteousness" done as performance art (see Matthew 6:1–2), and it would've been readily familiar to Jesus' audience. Only a few miles north of Nazareth, in nearby Sepphoris, Herod Antipas had built a large, Greco-Roman style theatre with seating for a whopping 2,500 people. Antipas's father, Herod the Great, had also built similar theatres in Jerusalem and Jericho.

Jesus labeled religious narcissists who stood and made their private prayers in public settings as hypocrites. His hearers would likely have pictured the theatre in Sepphoris (or Jerusalem or Jericho), and seen a vain, preening actor, standing center stage, delivering a sloppy soliloquy in hopes of applause. Prayer, according to Christ, was never meant to be that.

Source: BKB 121-122

Is the Lord's Prayer supposed to be repeated word for word, or is it a sample prayer?

The Lord's Prayer, as quoted in Matthew 6:9–13, is one of the most famous Bible passages of all time. It records Jesus' specific instructions for how to pray.

It's important to notice, that immediately before giving the Lord's Prayer, Christ warned his followers to avoid "babbling like pagans" when they prayed. Pagans at that time viewed prayer as something like a business contract that had the sole purpose of earning favor from whichever deity was its object. As a result, Greeks peppered their prayers with all types of honorifics and titles, hoping to flatter their way into heavenly favor. Other pagan prayers did the same, and also reminded the deity of all the ways the pray-er had kept their end of the blessing bargain by making sacrifices and/or defending the reputation of the so-called god.

Jesus dismissed this approach to prayer as worthless and insulting. Instead Christ offered a prayer structure based on an intimate, family relationship with our heavenly Father.

Many people today call the Lord's Prayer a "model prayer," because it demonstrates key elements of prayer for us. In Jesus' day, though, his disciples would've known it as an "index prayer."

Index prayers were common in ancient Judaism, something a rabbi would use to teach people to practice praying. These were what we might call "directed prayers," delivered in outline form. For instance, a rabbi would collect a few short sentences that each identified an item for prayer. The intent was that a person following an index prayer would start with one of those statements, but then "enlarge upon it," drawing out what it means and how it applies. They were not to simply memorize and recite each line, but to use each line as a catalyst for deeper, more personal times with God.

That's the kind of index prayer that Jesus gave in Matthew 6:9–13, and it has proved a timeless model for Christ followers ever since.

Sources: IBB 62; APB 92

What's the real point of fasting?

Jesus' instructions about fasting in Matthew 6:16–18 assume that fasting is a normal part of a life devoted to God ... but why fast? Why did (and do) people go without food and/or water as a religious observance? Here are a few reasons from Scripture:

> ❯ Once a year, as a commemorative action on the Day of Atonement (Yom Kippur). This annual observance was a solemn moment when a high priest offered a symbolic sacrifice for the collective sins of the entire nation of Israel (Leviticus 16:29; Jeremiah 36:6).

> During calls for national repentance (Nehemiah 9:1).

> In times of public or personal crisis (Judges 20:26; 2 Samuel 12:15–18).

> Four times a year as a commemorative action to remind of the destruction of Jerusalem in 586 BC (Zechariah 7:2–5; 8:19).

> As an expression of mourning (Matthew 9:14–15).

> As a means of humbling oneself before God (Isaiah 58:3–5).

> As an expression of worship (Acts 13:2).

> As a ritual of commissioning others into leadership within the church (Acts 13:2–3; 14:23).

Sources: RBD 111, 373; MAC 1384

Teaching about Money and Possessions
Matthew 6:19–34

How do things like moths and rust ruin treasure?

In the ancient world, storing valuables typically boiled down to one of these two methods: hide it or guard it (or both). There were no banks or safety deposit boxes in those days, so a man's wealth was, literally, only those valuables which he could somehow protect. (And yes, with rare exceptions, wealth was held almost exclusively by men.)

Royal wealth, including riches in the temple treasury, had to be guarded by soldiers because it was always a primary aim of any invading army. It required heavy military defenses in order to discourage enemies from attempting to plunder the nation's assets. Still, even then, it was never really safe because there was always some army that was stronger lurking nearby.

Personal wealth could be used to buy luxury and power, sure, but it was also a constant target for lawless men, bands of robbers, and even enemy armies. Since people with personal wealth didn't typically possess soldiers to guard their treasure, they most frequently resorted to hiding their riches: underneath a house, buried in a field, in a cave, or in some other secret place near their homes. The trouble with hiding treasure was that natural elements—rust, insects (like moths), wild animals, water and natural disasters—could "invade" and destroy it. And, of course, robbers could find it and steal it away.

So, despite its obvious advantages, wealth in Jesus' time was always a precarious thing—easily taken or destroyed. Jesus advises against letting your life be about the acquisition and holding of earthly wealth. A better investment for your life, he says, is to "store your treasures in heaven" (verse 20).

Source: ZP5 807–809

What is Jesus getting at when he says, "When your eye is healthy, your whole body is filled with light"?

Jesus employs two familiar symbols for his audience in this teaching: eyes and light.

In the ancient Jewish world, a person's eyes were considered "windows" through which truth filled the mind and body. "The figure," notes Sherman E. Johnson "is that of the one-room Palestinian house." If the window to the house was clean and well maintained, sunlight could fill the whole house with warmth and light and possibility.

Light was (and still is) a common metaphor for God's truth, God's presence, and the blessings of experiencing God firsthand (Psalm 119:105; Isaiah 60:19; 1 John 1:5; Revelation 21:23–24). So the idea was to keep one's spiritual eyes in good condition to receive and understand God's light of truth in a life.

It's important to note that Christ's symbolic promise here is not a guarantee of external, earthly comfort and success. (Remember what he just said about where to store your treasures?) Rather, it's an internal pledge of God's presence, truth, and blessing within each of us—in both harsh and helpful circumstances.

Thus, Christ's promise is essentially this: If your spiritual eye is in good shape—that is, if your heart and mind are focused on the pursuit of his treasures of heaven—then the light of God's presence and truth will fill your soul with health and understanding and strength to face any and all situations in your life.

Sources: IB7 318; DBI 510-511

Jesus' main teaching on worry is fairly well known. Are there any interesting aspects of it that may not be so well known?

OK, you asked, so here are a few random thoughts about verses 25–34 that I find interesting:

> In Jesus' time, poverty was the norm, not the exception. Add to that the unpredictability of crops and crime and war and more, and you can see why people would worry about what they would eat or drink or wear from day to day.

> Most laborers worked on a day-to-day basis, earning wages one day at a time and starting each new morning freshly unemployed. There was no such thing as vacation pay or sick days. Provision of basic necessities (food, water, clothing) for tomorrow was always uncertain.

> Jesus' statement, "add a single moment to your life" is actually an idiomatic expression in Greek that's hard to understand with exactness. The literal translation is "add one forearm length [cubit] to his age." In other words, Jesus basically said, "Worrying can't add eighteen inches to your lifespan." *What?*

> During his Sermon on the Mount, when Jesus said, "Look at the lilies of the field and how they grow," it's likely that lilies were actually growing all around him and his audience at that exact moment. (Kind of cool, if you ask me.)

> When Jesus spoke about wildflowers (or grass, in some translations) being thrown into the fire, that was a reference to common frugality among ancient Israelites. Unlike today, cut grass and overgrowth at that time was a useful source of fuel for many homes. People would cut the green growth of spring, let it dry, then wrap it into bundles—kind of like little logs. They'd burn those bundles in fire ovens for cooking and heating. Pretty smart!

> Jesus' observation that "each day has enough trouble of its own" was apparently a maxim he invented. There is no exact parallel to this statement recorded before he said it.

Sources: ZP1 49–50; JHT 75

Do Not Judge Others
Matthew 7:1-6

Matthew 7 begins, "Do not judge." Then as it goes on, I am presented with scenarios that I have to make judgments about: my brother's eye speck, whether someone is worthy of my pearl, whether a prophet is false, and so on. How do I reconcile what seems to be a contradiction here?

These words of Jesus have been a source of confusion—and antagonism—for centuries. The problem seems to be that many of us misunderstand the distinctions between similar Greek terms that mean different things.

Anakrinō ("to discern") is a general term that means to investigate, examine, scrutinize, or question. It's a verb that happens outside of a courtroom, a search for truth that may be in preparation for a trial, but also happens when no formal, legal proceeding is in sight. This type of discerning effort is lauded in the Bible. For instance, Paul prayed for Christians in Philippi to grow "in knowledge and depth of insight, so that you may be able to discern [*anakrinō*] what is best" (Philippians 1:9–10 NIV). Additionally, Acts 17:11 praises the people of Berea because they "examined [*anakrinō*] the Scriptures every day to see if what Paul said was true" (NIV). Unsurprisingly, then, *anakrinō* is NOT the term recorded in the text of Matthew 7:1.

Krinō ("to judge") is the word attributed to Jesus in Matthew 7. This is a verb that means "to pronounce judgment" and "to assume the office of a judge." It's a specific term that refers to a courtroom-style setting where a defendant is either convicted or exonerated. It carries with it both the ability to act ("pronounce judgment") and the legal authority to enforce the action ("the office of a judge"). In Jesus' context, it refers to the coming eternal judgment of a person's soul.

Speaking primarily to the practices of Pharisees and overbearing religious leaders, Jesus condemned a hypocritical attitude of judgment (*krinō*) toward others that exceeded the otherwise praiseworthy attempts at discernment (*anakrinō*). He railed against anyone presuming to have authority to "assume the office" of Judge over the souls of his creation. As God incarnate, Christ alone holds that authority—and he intends to keep it.

In practical terms, then, we are to *anakrinō* our hearts out, seeking to know and understand truth as it relates to our daily lives of service, but we are never to assume that gives us the right to *krinō* our fellow sinners to hell or other spiritual punishment. We'd be wise to follow the apostle Paul's example in 1 Corinthians 4:4–5:

> My conscience is clear, but that doesn't prove I'm right. It is the Lord himself who will examine me and decide. So don't make judgments about anyone ahead of time—before the Lord returns. For he will bring our darkest secrets to light and will reveal our private motives. Then God will give to each one whatever praise is due.

Sources: VCEN 171, 336

Effective Prayer
Matthew 7:7-11

Jesus clearly promises "you will receive what you ask for" in prayer. So why do so many of my prayers go unanswered?

Christ's exhortation to "keep on asking … seeking … knocking" in prayer appears to be a *carte blanche* promise that God will give anything you or I ask for. The normal Christian life, on the other hand, seems to discredit this promise on a daily basis.

So what gives? Was Jesus lying, or mistaken, or exaggerating for effect? Are we doing something wrong in the ways we "ask, seek, and knock"?

Perhaps the problem lies in a twenty-first-century perception that we're entitled to immediate gratification, and in our assumption that God will override his good, eternal desires for us in response to the selfish, shortsighted desires we have for ourselves. Here's how theologian Lawrence O. Richards explains it:

> Jesus describes prayer as asking, seeking, and knocking. "Ask" is the act of prayer in its simplest form. "Seek" conveys intensity, and "earnest sincerity." And "knock" pictures persistence. We knock on the door of heaven and keep on knocking! It is important not to mistake what Jesus is saying as laying down conditions which, if met, will move God

to respond to us. Jesus is not saying if you ask ardently enough, then God will answer your prayer. He is simply saying that when we feel a need so intensely that it drives us to the Lord again and again, we need not be discouraged even if the answer is delayed. God really does care about those things that matter to His children. And God responds to our requests by giving us good gifts.

Jesus promised that if we "keep on asking … seeking … knocking" then our heavenly Father will respond with "good gifts" (verse 11). Our job, then, is to keep asking with sincerity and persistence—and let him worry about when he answers and which good gifts he delivers in response.

Source: NTL 41

The Golden Rule
Matthew 7:12

Why does Jesus' Golden Rule seem out of place in the Sermon on the Mount? Was it added to Matthew's gospel after the fact?

The Golden Rule does seem to be awkwardly placed in the Sermon on the Mount—but no, there's no evidence it was inserted at a later time. In modern Bibles, it's lumped in with Matthew 7:7–11, appearing as the final sentence in this section of Jesus' Sermon on the Mount. This is particularly perplexing because verse 12 in some translations begins with "So…" or "Therefore…" indicating that this Golden Rule is understood to be the natural outcome of what Christ has just said before it. The problem is that verses 7–11 are all about God's promise of provision in answer to prayer—not about social behavior.

So why the abrupt change of subject? Why go directly from "good gifts" from your heavenly Father to, "do to others…"?

The confusion, it seems, stems from our modern need for paragraph and subheading breaks. Recall, the gospel of Matthew, as originally written, was not divided into chapters, subchapters, and verses. When this section of Scripture was formatted for more modern eyes, Christ's Golden Rule was placed in direct context with verses 7–11 when it likely should have stood on its own as an independent, albeit short, section.

Bible scholar Craig Evans explains:

Matthew's therefore may well sum up the whole of the Sermon on the Mount, especially harking back to the thesis statement in Matthew 5:17–20. In Matt 5:17, Jesus declares that he has come 'to fulfill' the Law and the Prophets. What follows (in Matt 5:21–7:12) shows how he understands this fulfillment to take place, ending with the Golden Rule, which sums up the whole of the Law.

Understood in the context of the entire Sermon on the Mount, the placement of the Golden Rule makes much more sense. It was apparently used by Jesus to summarize his whole sermon to this point, and to lead into his concluding illustrations which appear in Matthew 7:13–27.

Source: MAT 169

The Narrow Gate
Matthew 7:13–14

Was Jesus referencing a particular road or gate when he said, "The highway to hell is broad, and its gate is wide"?

Well, we can't know for sure, but as it is with other references in his Sermon on the Mount, it's quite possible that Jesus used a literal, visual cue as a symbolic example when he made that statement.

In a general sense, most roads in the land of ancient Israel were common traveling paths, worn smooth over the years from travelers and their livestock walking the shortest distances between towns, cities, and nations. "Narrow roads" were different; they typically referred to difficult-to-traverse mountain pathways used by local travelers instead of more well-traveled roads used by outsiders.

Meanwhile, the Romans of Jesus' time had created and maintained an impressive series of international trade routes that could accommodate all kinds of merchant and tourist traffic—and even legions of soldiers. These "broad roads" were well traveled, well kept, and commonly known to anyone living in Israel. One of these Roman trade routes was laid out over the coastal plains and valleys of the Middle East, connecting Israel to Africa, Asia, and Europe.

A section of that Roman highway, situated in the plain of Magdala, would've been visible to Jesus and his hearers at the time when he delivered his Sermon on the Mount. When he said, "The highway to hell is broad," Jesus may have gestured toward that Roman road for visual emphasis.

Sources: VGG 64-65

What would the mention of a "narrow gate" have meant to Jesus' hearers of the Sermon on the Mount?

When we read about Jesus contrasting the wide and narrow gates, the modern assumption is to picture two separate gates at the end of separate roads. Historically speaking, that image is probably incorrect.

In Jesus' time, city gates were large and multi-layered. The broad, tall, wide gate opened during the day to allow entry of large caravans, livestock, groups of people, and so on. It was a bustling, busy, place where anyone, such as thieves or other criminals, could hide undetected within a crowd. Just inside that gate, or sometimes inset into the broad gate, was a smaller opening that allowed only one or two people, or a single donkey to pass through. This was typically guarded. No one could pass through here anonymously.

This type of city-gate setup was similarly true in wealthy homes and estates, and that seems to be Jesus' reference point in the parallel passage of Luke 13:24. These large homes typically featured a walled-in courtyard with a large entryway that was opened to allow carts and animals to pass through during the day. Inset into that large door would have been a smaller door which individual family members used to enter and exit in either day or night.

Thus, to "enter through the narrow gate," could have been understood to mean entering God's kingdom without anonymity, without any possibility of hiding anything about who you are—and to enter as a recognized member of God's family.

Sources: ZP2 645-646; SLU 359

The Tree and Its Fruit
Matthew 7:15-20

How would ancient Israelites have understood Jesus' reference to wolves disguised as sheep?

Jesus' symbolic warning here would've been clear and the threat of "wolves" familiar to those listening to him teach: Christ's followers are vulnerable sheep, and false prophets are the hungry predators who will harm them.

In biblical use, in both Old and New Testaments, the term "wolf" or "wolves" is almost always a symbolic image. Only rarely, such as in Isaiah 11:6 and 65:25, and once in John's gospel (John 10:12) does the term refer to a literal, physical animal—and even then, the wolf is a representative icon.

In most other uses (including Matthew 7:15), the wolf represents only the worst, and most dangerous, aspects of people and life. It's a depiction of callous, insatiable hunger (Genesis 49:27), of destruction (Jeremiah 5:6), and of vicious, deadly abuse of the innocent (Ezekiel 22:27; Habakkuk 1:8; Zephaniah 3:3; Matthew 10:16; Luke 10:3; Acts 20:29).

Bible scholar J. D. Davis informs us that in the land of ancient Israel, "Owing to the ease with which food is obtained, and the mildness of the winter, they [wolves] do not hunt in packs, as in the colder north, but prowl alone." So Jesus' warning could apply to either a "lone wolf" false prophet or a group of them hidden among his followers. The result of either of those situations is deadly.

Sources: HBD 1138; DOB 822

What kind of fruit is supposed to tip us off to false prophets?

Speaking against the threat of false prophets in verses 15–20, Jesus makes this statement, "You can identify them by their fruit."

So what "fruit" is he talking about?

Jeremiah 14:14 offers us help to understand—it's a passage where God himself describes five activities of false prophets. Let's break that verse down into bullet points to help us see it more clearly.

In Jeremiah's proclamation, the Lord says:

> ❯ "The prophets are *prophesying lies* in my name. I have not sent them …

> ❯ They are prophesying to you *false visions,*

> ❯ divinations,

> ❯ idolatries and

> ❯ the delusions of their own minds." (italics mine, NIV)

With this verse in view, we can draw the following conclusions:

Anyone who presents untruth as God's truth ("prophesying lies in my name") should be considered a false prophet. This would apply to preachers and teachers who distort or disavow the Bible's teachings in order to accommodate their own preferences or current societal norms.

Likewise, claiming to have new, personal revelation of God's plans that conflicts with, or contradicts God's truth in Scripture ("prophesying false visions") would be considered bad fruit from a false prophet.

People who attempt to predict the future by supernatural means, even misusing Scripture to support their predictions (such as when preachers announce the date of Christ's return) would be guilty of "false divinations"—and that's bad fruit which is evidence of a false prophet.

Also, teachers who allow any other thing—such as piety, money, prestige, other prophets, social concerns, and so on—to be placed in higher authority than Christ himself ("idolatries") would be guilty of producing bad fruit.

Last but not least, church leaders who begin to invent new standards of truth and behavior for themselves, who assume that their ideas somehow supersede the truth of Scripture, or that they are somehow not subject to the same standards as other Christians, are guilty of prophesying "the delusions of their own minds." That's bad fruit and is more evidence of a false prophet.

Now the question arises: Do you follow any church leaders who are producing this kind of bad fruit? If so, what will you do about it?

Source: BKB 145

True Disciples
Matthew 7:21-23

What am I to make of Jesus' description of the final judgment?

Matthew 7:21–23 is a sobering text, and it contains probably the most tragic truth revealed in all of Scripture. Jesus says, "Not everyone who calls out to me, 'Lord! Lord!' will enter the Kingdom of Heaven." I have three observations on this passage:

First, some skeptics assert loudly that Jesus never claimed to be God, but his statements here in these verses make that a laughable, indefensible position. Consider: Jesus called himself by a title ascribed to God ("Lord, Lord"); Jesus claimed to have sole authority over who enters the kingdom of heaven—God's eternal realm; Jesus insisted that he will preside over the final judgment of humanity—a judgeship reserved solely for God himself; and Jesus claimed to have authority to send evildoers to eternal punishment— also something reserved only for God himself. If Jesus is not God, then he was a blaspheming pretender to deity, and Matthew 7:21–23 is proof of that.

Second, it's possible for some to mimic God's miracles, yet not be followers of him at all. Remember the magicians in Pharaoh's court? They replicated God's miracles in a failed attempt to discredit his authority (Exodus 7). In Jesus' time and during the days of the early church, others appropriated Jesus' authority to work miracles and cast out demons—and sometimes succeeded (Mark 9:38; Acts 19:13–16). Thus, a miracle itself is not proof of God. In fact, Old Testament law specifically warned against following a miracle-worker if his teaching led away from the one true God (Deuteronomy 13). This situation seems to be what Jesus is describing in Matthew 7:21–23.

Third, at the final judgment, false prophets will appeal to their religion for salvation, while Jesus will emphasize a relationship with him. They'll point to their resumé of good works as evidence they belong in heaven: prophesying in Jesus' name, driving out demons, and performing miracles. Christ, in response, will point to their lack of a personal relationship with him, saying, "I never knew you." This lends credence to the apostle Paul's theology later expounded in his letter to the Ephesians, that grace—not works—is the essential component of salvation (Ephesians 2:8–9). Heaven awaits those who, by grace, enter a personal friendship with Jesus—not those who try to earn their way into his favor.

Source: MAT 178–179

Building on a Solid Foundation
Matthew 7:24–29

In Jesus' time, where would a house be built on a rock, and why would anyone build a house on sand?

It's natural to think that the house on solid rock and the house on sand in Jesus' parable refer to houses in different locations, but the geography of the land of ancient Israel leads historians at Gordon-Conwell Theological Seminary to think otherwise. In fact, they say, Jesus was probably referring to two houses built side by side, on the banks of the Sea of Galilee.

In this familiar first-century location during the hot summer, the sand around the lake was as hard as rock. Thus, the temptation for a foolish builder would be to build a house on that sand, assuming it would stay rock-hard all year long. A wiser person, though, would understand the changes of the seasons and, regardless of outward appearances in summer, would dig through the sand until reaching bedrock (about ten feet below) for the foundation.

The house anchored to the bedrock would last for decades, through stormy weather, high winds, and flooding. The one built on summertime's rock-like sand would probably fall before a year passed. That sandy foundation would moisten and crumble during rough weather seasons, causing a spectacular collapse.

Source: ASB 1570

What does Matthew mean when he says that Jesus "taught with real authority"?

In his exposition of Matthew 7:28–29, theologian Sherman E. Johnson has commented, "People listened to Jesus, and then said: 'That is what I have always known deep down, even though I have no words to say it.'"

This, Buttrick explains, is something of what Matthew means when he says that Christ "taught as one who had authority."

Of course that's true, but Matthew also seems to be doing more than simply saying people were impressed by Jesus' teaching. Looking at this gospel as a whole, it seems that Matthew intended this to be both the conclusion of Christ's Sermon on the Mount and a thesis statement for Matthew's upcoming "argument by example" that Jesus held all the authority of God in human flesh.

From this point on in Matthew's narrative, the gospel writer presents overwhelming evidence, time and again, of Jesus' heavenly authority expressed in human affairs. Consider chapter 8 alone and you'll see:

> Christ demonstrates divine authority over a devastating sickness (leprosy) that humanity cannot tame (Matthew 8:1–4).

> Christ demonstrates omnipresent authority over time and distance, and over gentile inclusion in the Jewish kingdom of God (Matthew 8:5–13).

> Christ demonstrates the Creator's full authority and ownership over the human body, healing Peter's mother, driving demons out of people, and healing the sick (Matthew 8:14–17).

> Christ demonstrates authority over a person's family obligations and the choices of a would-be follower (Matthew 8:18–22).

> Christ demonstrates full authority over nature, deflating a storm with just a verbal command (Matthew 8:23–27).

> Christ demonstrates absolute, kingly authority over the spiritual realm by subduing and exiling an army of demons (Matthew 8:28–34).

So when Matthew makes the comment that Christ "taught with real authority," the gospel writer seems also to put forth a claim of deity about Jesus—one that he then goes on to support with testimony proving to his readers that Jesus is indeed the all-powerful, incarnate Son of God.

Source: IB7 335-336

Jesus Heals a Man with Leprosy
Matthew 8:1-4

What was it like to live with leprosy in Jesus' time?

Matthew 8:1–4 gives no obvious reason for Jesus' decision to heal, except that the man with leprosy asked. However, Matthew indicates elsewhere that compassion was Christ's ongoing motivation for healing (see Matthew 9:35–36; 14:14; 15:32–38; 20:29–34). That compassion was justified, especially considering these awful facts about living with leprosy in those days:

> The term used for leprosy in the New Testament was a general reference to seemingly incurable skin infections. It could have included the formal affliction, which we now call Hansen's Disease, or any other severe skin disease with inflammation.

> By Mosaic law, priests—not doctors—were charged with diagnosing leprosy in people (Leviticus 13:2). Sometimes they tried to treat the disease with various baths, ointments, and mixtures of herbs and oils applied to the skin.

> The process for diagnosing leprosy went something like this: A person with serious skin infections such as tissue-crusts on the skin, severe rashes, or "whitish-red swollen" spots would go to a temple priest to be examined. The priest would look to see if the infection had penetrated the skin, or if hair in the affected area had turned white. If so, he would declare the person "unclean" with leprosy. If not, a seven-day quarantine was instituted, with a new examination for leprosy scheduled afterward (Leviticus 13:2–8).

> Being diagnosed with leprosy was a death sentence, physically, socially, economically, and spiritually. In fact, rabbinic tradition, as Chuck Swindoll explains, "held that curing leprosy was as difficult as raising the dead, perhaps because they saw the disease as the physical manifestation of sin's consequences."

> A leper was considered physically unclean—and contagious—as well as spiritually unclean. That meant a leper was completely

shunned from normal activities of community life and banned from inclusion in worship in the temple or any synagogue. The leper couldn't hold a job, couldn't live in a home with non-lepers (including his or her own family), couldn't shop in a market, couldn't own property, couldn't touch or hug or hold hands. Nothing. The leper's only option was begging for scraps, isolation, and waiting to physically deteriorate and die.

This was the terrible situation of the man who came to Jesus, begging to be healed. Christ's response was compassion—and healing. Pastor Chuck Swindoll notes one particularly significant aspect of this miracle:

[Jesus] reached out and literally touched the man society had rejected as untouchable. In other instances, Jesus merely spoke a word and the miracle took effect. In at least one case, He healed from a distance of twenty miles (John 4:46–54). But in this situation, he chose to touch the leper's diseased skin, as if to say, "Your disease doesn't prevent me from accepting you."

Sources: JHT 161; ILJ 185-188; SLU 127-128

The Faith of a Roman Officer
Matthew 8:5-13

What kind of Roman officer asked Jesus for a miracle?

In the days when Jesus walked the earth, the Roman army ruled the land where he walked. The Roman officer who begged Jesus for a miracle in this historical event was part of that occupying army, a career military man, known as a centurion.

Rome's fighting forces were generally organized into legions, or the equivalent of about six thousand soldiers. Within each legion, the troops were again organized into sixty groups ("cohorts") of one hundred soldiers each, and each cohort was commanded by a centurion. Historian Ronald Brownrigg tells us that centurions were always promoted from within the ranks of a legion, typically leading the men who had seen them prove themselves in battle. In today's world, an army company's sergeant-major would be a comparable rank to the centurion.

The Greek historian of Rome, Polybius, described centurions as "men who can command, steady in action, and reliable … ready to hold their ground and die at their posts." No surprise, then, that centurions were well regarded and likely influential, high-ranking members of any local community.

This was the type of soldier who approached Jesus in Capernaum to beg a miracle for his servant. He is one of only two centurions mentioned in the gospel accounts of the life of Christ, the other being the centurion who presided over Jesus' execution.

It's significant that this gentile, Roman, military commander would humble himself before Christ the way that he did. Given his position, he could have demanded a miracle of Jesus (much the way King Herod later attempted to do; see Luke 23:8–12), but he didn't. Perhaps that's why Jesus complimented him by saying, "I have not found anyone in Israel with such great faith."

Source: WWB 57–58

Jesus Heals Many People
Matthew 8:14-17

This Scripture mentions Peter's mother-in-law. Do historians know anything about Peter's family, or his wife?

Matthew 8:14–17 is testimony (again) to Jesus' divinity and compassion, but it also reveals important historical background about Christ's foremost disciple, Simon Peter. Because of this Scripture (along with Mark 1:29–34; Luke 4:38–41; and 1 Corinthians 9:5), we know with certainty that Peter was married, and that he lived in a home in Capernaum as patriarch of his extended family, which was customary in ancient Israel.

So what do we know about Peter's unnamed wife?

Scripture tells us that she traveled with Peter on his preaching and teaching journeys (1 Corinthians 9:5), and that her mother lived in the house she shared with Peter and his brother Andrew's family (Mark 1:29–34). Beyond that, we have the testimony of church tradition which indicates that she was the daughter of Aristobulus, a coworker of the apostle Paul and brother to Paul's first missionary partner, Barnabas. It's also possible she was, at least in part, a role model in Peter's mind when he wrote his now-famous advice on the character and conduct of husbands and wives in marriage (1 Peter 3:1–12).

Christian tradition tells us that she was imprisoned with Peter at the time of his martyrdom—and that she was murdered just before he was. Perhaps that was intended by his captors as additional cruelty for Peter, to be forced to watch his wife painfully endure execution for her faith in Christ. Regardless, Bible historian Herbert Lockyer relates the accounts of their final moments this way:

> When death came, his [Peter's] wife was martyr[ed] first, and as she was led out to die, Peter comforted her with the words, "remember the Lord." When Peter's turn came he begged his crucifiers to crucify him head downward, feeling he was unworthy to die in exactly the same way as his Lord. In heaven, Peter and his loyal wife shine together as stars for having turned many to righteousness.

Sources: AWB 220; WWW 38

The Cost of Following Jesus
Matthew 8:18-22

What does "Son of Man" mean, and why did Jesus call himself that instead of "Son of God"?

This encounter with would-be disciples is the first instance where Matthew records Christ calling himself the "Son of Man." In all, Matthew documents thirty-two times that Jesus used this culturally charged title for himself.

The phrase "Son of Man" was not unique to Christ. In the Old Testament it mostly referred simply to one who was part of the human race (for example see the following in the ESV translation: Numbers 23:19; Job 25:6; Psalm 8:4; Isaiah 51:12 and so on). Most notably, God called the prophet Ezekiel "Son of Man" as a proper name, addressing him this way early and often (Ezekiel 2:1 and throughout the rest of that book).

However, scholars like Leland Ryken and his colleagues would agree that when Jesus called himself "Son of Man" he was identifying himself with a well-known Messianic prophecy from Daniel 7:13–14, which says in part, "As my vision continued that night, I saw someone like a son of man coming with the clouds of heaven.... He was given authority, honor, and sovereignty over all the nations of the world."

This encounter recorded in Matthew 8 must've been a confusing, ironic moment for the "teacher of the law." As someone well versed in Messianic prophesies, like the one in Daniel, the "Son of Man" reference would've been easily recognized as a claim by Jesus of sovereign power. Then, immediately after making that divine claim, Jesus says that he—the Son of Man—doesn't even have a place to lay his head.

The all-powerful Messiah is homeless and destitute? What?

We're not told how this teacher of the law responded to that mixed messaging of Christ. Perhaps he walked away confused and disappointed. Or maybe he took up the challenge to follow this homeless Messiah, even though he didn't understand it all. And maybe Matthew deliberately left out the conclusion of this man's encounter in order to prompt people like you and me to ask the question: *How will I respond to the Son of Man?*

Source: DBI 447

Jesus Calms the Storm
Matthew 8:23-27

I'm curious to know more about the Sea of Galilee. What can you tell me?

The Sea of Galilee is an important location in the history of Jesus, particularly because it was there that he once demonstrated divine mastery over creation by miraculously calming a deadly storm. Here's what we know about that body of water.

Although it's called the "Sea" of Galilee, it's actually a large, freshwater lake, so it's sometimes referred to as Lake Galilee by modern folks. Others have also called it the Lake of Gennesaret (Josephus), the Sea of Tiberias (naming it after a city on its southwestern shore), and Sea of Kinnereth (its ancient Hebrew name).

Measuring about sixteen miles from north to south, and about nine miles from east to west, the Sea of Galilee calls to mind the shape of a harp.

Perhaps that's why ancient Israelites tagged it the Sea of Kinnereth, possibly a reference to the Hebrew word *kinnor*, which means "harp."

The location of the Sea of Galilee makes it particularly susceptible to storms. It sits about six hundred and forty feet below the level of the Mediterranean Sea and is surrounded by steep hillsides along most of its shores. Ravines on the west side funnel cool air into the bowl-like basin where the sea sits. When cool air rushes into hot air rising from the valley lake, it can create sudden, fierce winds that stir up tsunami-like waves big enough to swamp a boat.

In Jesus' day, the Sea of Galilee supported a thriving fishing industry; it was where Peter, James, and John earned their living as fishermen. The great lake held three kinds of fish: Sardines, Barbels (named for the barb-like feelers on their upper lips), and a tasty Bass-like fish. The latter still lives in that lake and has been renamed "St. Peter's Fish" in honor of Jesus' famous disciple. Today, restaurants on the shores of the Sea of Galilee serve St. Peter's fish as part of their menus.

In 1986 when a drought shrunk the water levels of the Sea of Galilee for a short time, two men on a walk by the lake spotted the outline of a sunken boat in the mud. After experts excavated it, they discovered it was a fishing vessel about two thousand years old—likely from the time of Christ. The excavated boat measured about twenty-four feet long and six feet wide, large enough to hold a sleeping Jesus and all twelve of his disciples. Many theorize that Jesus calmed the storm in a boat very similar to this one.

Sources: WWA 340-341; ISJ 66–67

After all the miracles that Jesus had done, why were the disciples "amazed" by this one?

Let me start the answer to that question by telling you about Antiochus IV Epiphanes. In the second century BC, he was a Syrian Greek tyrant who ruled over the Jewish nation with an iron fist, claiming god-like power over all of nature. In the end, though, he was stricken ill and weak, prompting this pitiful epitaph from 2 Maccabees 9:8:

> Thus he who had just been thinking that he could command the waves of the sea, in his superhuman arrogance, and imagining that he could weigh the high mountains in a balance, was brought down to earth and carried in a litter, making the power of God manifest to all.

In stark contrast, when compared to the bluster of earthly rulers like Antiochus IV Epiphanes, Jesus didn't proclaim his deity by governmental decree, with military might, through political power, or propagandistic hyperbole. Christ simply exercised divine authority in daily life—like when he literally commanded a storm to be still and all of nature hurried to obey him.

It's no wonder that Matthew reports Christ's disciples "were amazed" (Matthew 8:27). Mark adds they were "absolutely terrified" (Mark 4:41). In ancient Israel, Dr. Charles Swindoll tells us, "The sea was a mysterious, dangerous place, characterized by chaos and possessing the power to kill without warning….To some biblical writers the sea acted as a symbol, 'a principle of disorder, violence, or unrest that marks the old creation' (cf. Ps. 107:25-25; Isa. 57:20; Ezekiel 28:8)." Biblically speaking, only God himself was able to tame the chaotic sea—only God could impose his will upon that uncontrollable force (Psalm 65:7; 89:9; 104:6-7).

That Jesus demonstrated God's sole and total authority over the waters—and that he did so with such enormous ease—had to be stunning for anyone to witness. As theologian Craig Evans comments, "In contrast to the Greco-Roman despots like Antiochus IV and the later Roman emperors, about whom all sorts of hyperbole were inscribed,… Jesus is the genuine article. He speaks the word, and it happens."

Amazing. And terrifying. And more wonderful than words.

Sources: MAT 196; SLU 204

Jesus Heals Two Demon-possessed Men
Matthew 8:28-34

Wait a minute. Why does Matthew say there were two demon-possessed men while Mark says there was only one?

The exorcism account of Matthew 8:28–34 is generally believed to be the same event also documented in Mark 5:1–20 and Luke 8:26–39. Matthew and Luke abbreviate the details, and thus are sometimes assumed to have drawn from Mark as the source.

The biggest difference between the account in Matthew and the accounts in Mark and Luke is in the number of demon-possessed men who are set free. Mark and Luke tell of only one demoniac living in the area of the Gadarenes, yet Matthew states clearly that there were two men in this encounter. Some see that difference as a forgivable error on Matthew's part—as if Matthew doubled Mark's number by accident or happenstance.

That view is common, but insufficient, because it assumes a lack of biographical integrity in Matthew's writing overall. This assumption is wildly inconsistent with the known history of the text of Matthew's gospel. Also, if Matthew is not to be believed in his counting of the number of demoniacs, can he then be believed when he says the demoniacs were healed? Perhaps he embellished that too?

A more likely explanation is that two demon-possessed men were actually involved in this exorcism, as Matthew indicated, and that Mark and Luke felt it necessary to focus their accounts on just one of the two. "Mark and Luke wrote of one demon-possessed man," theologians John Walvoord and Roy Zuck comment, "but they did not say only one. Presumably one of the two was more violent than the other," and therefore was highlighted in the retelling. That perspective makes sense, though there could be additional literary reasons for Mark and Luke to omit a relatively inconsequential person from their telling of this historical event.

It's possible that only one of the two men was a mouthpiece for the demons that spoke with Jesus, and so his story is told to the exclusion of the second man. Also, it's possible that only one of the two exorcised men stayed with Jesus afterward, begging to be allowed to go back across the Sea of Galilee with him (Mark 5:19–21). Thus, his details would've been highlighted while the second man could have faded into the background.

Regardless, the difference doesn't dictate that one specific version is accurate and any of the others is error. The most likely explanation is the obvious one: All three perspectives of this miracle are accurate and must be taken as a whole to tell the complete story of what actually happened.

Sources: BKB 184-185; BKN 38

What was the deal with the drowning pigs? Did the demons survive the deaths of the pigs?

When Jesus healed two demon-possessed men in the region of the Gadarenes, the demons begged to be exorcised into a nearby herd of swine. Jesus granted that request, so the demons inhabited those pigs. The whole herd then stampeded into the Sea of Galilee and drowned. This is such an odd turn of events; how do we make sense of it?

The first thing to note is the demons' manic fear of God's coming judgment. "Why are you interfering with us, Son of God? Have you come here to torture us before God's appointed time?" they ask Christ. This strongly suggests that Jesus himself will be involved in administering punishment at the end of days. The demons obviously recognized him as their future judge, even addressing him with the title, "Son of God." Theologian Craig Keener observes, "Apparently even the demons did not expect the Messiah to come in two stages, a first and second coming."

It's also important to understand that this miracle of exorcism took place in the predominately non-Jewish region of the Gadarenes, which explains the presence of swine herders and a large population of pigs. Jews regarded pigs as filthy, unclean animals worthy of nothing more than contempt. Thus when demons begged to be banished into a herd of pigs, to Jewish ears, that would've seemed a fitting punishment—a vile, disgusting habitat appropriate for evil spirits.

We're not told what the final fate of those demons was, only that the pigs they inhabited stampeded and died. Jewish tradition held that demons could be either bound or killed, and so some speculate that when the pigs they inhabited died, the demons themselves were also destroyed. Jewish folklore also held that demons were somehow tortured by, and thus afraid of, water. In one legend, King Solomon condemns a demon to captivity by surrounding it with barrels of water, therefore preventing it from escaping. Thus, when demon-possessed pigs died by drowning in the Sea of Galilee, Jews in Jesus' time could have viewed that as a way of imprisoning the demons by immersing them in water.

Still, we'll never know for sure exactly what was going on here, and perhaps that's for the best. It's enough for us to see what Jesus' disciples, the residents of Gadarenes, and those demons, all unexpectedly understood that day: *Jesus Christ is Lord of all.*

Sources: IBB 69; BKB 183, 185

Miracles, Parables, and Teachings

Jesus Heals a Paralyzed Man
Matthew 9:1-8

Does a person get sick because of sin?

The mysterious relationship between sin and sickness is a question that's brewed for hundreds of generations.

Ancient Jewish thought had settled on the assumption that every sickness was punishment for some kind of sin, thus no healing could occur until that sin had been erased. That belief was encapsulated in this rabbinical teaching: "The sick doth not recover from his sickness until all his sins be forgiven him ... if God heal his soul from its sickness ... by making atonement for his sins, then his body is healed." This view was supported by scriptures such as Psalm 103:2–3, "Praise the LORD, my soul, and forget not all his benefits—who forgives all your sins and heals all your diseases" (NIV).

So, when friends brought a paralyzed man to Jesus for healing in Matthew 9, the common assumption was that the paralyzed man was suffering punishment for some sin he'd committed.

Now, elsewhere in Scripture, while commenting on the case of a man born blind, Jesus made it very clear that sickness is not always a consequence of personal sin (John 9:1–6). But in the case of this paralyzed man, Jesus was equally clear that his sin was indeed the root cause of his infirmity. In fact, the miraculous healing he received was proof that Christ, as God incarnate, had forgiven the man's sins.

So, does a person get sick because of sin, or is physical sickness independent of spiritual and moral causes? The answer appears to be "Yes, both circumstances can be true." In the case of this healed man, though, it was his sin that caused his suffering—and Christ's generous forgiveness which redeemed both the man's body and soul.

Sources: RBD 301; PCXV 360

What would the paralyzed man have understood from Jesus' pronouncement that his sins were forgiven?

"Be encouraged, my child! Your sins are forgiven," Christ said as his precursor to healing. Here's a little deeper insight into what that simple sentence meant to first-century ears:

> "Be encouraged" (*tharséō*)—This is more than simply "cheer up!" It connotes both a promise of good outcome and a charge to marshal one's courage in the face of imminent difficulty. It's a synonym for the Greek word, *tharréō*, which means to be full of hope and confidence.

> "Child" (*téknon*)—When used as a term of address, this term implies both sympathy and common ground between the person talking and the person being spoken to.

> "Your sins" (*hamartías*)—Any offense against God, which includes the guilt, punishment, and power of sin in a person's life.

> "Are forgiven" (*aphíēmi*)—To send away; to remove the penalty of sin; to pardon completely.

That, in a nutshell, is likely what the paralyzed man would've instinctively understood from Jesus' comment.

Sources: CWSN 27; CWDN 718–719, 130, 299; PCXV 359

Jesus Calls Matthew
Matthew 9:9–13

I know Matthew wrote this gospel, and that he was a tax collector, but that's it. What else can you tell me about him?

Walking through Capernaum ("his own town," Matthew 9:1), Jesus came across Mathew sitting at a tax collector's booth. Christ plucked him out of obscurity with these two words: "Follow me." Here's what we know about that man:

> The name Matthew means "gift of Jehovah," or "gift of God."

> Matthew was also called Levi (Mark 2:13–17; Luke 5:27–28), which may have been his birth name, changed later by Jesus to Matthew; or it may have been a nickname; or it may have been a tribal designation meaning he was from the Israelite tribe of Levi; or it may have been part of his full name as in, "Matthew Levi."

> He was a known tax collector, a lucrative but despised occupation in ancient Israel. Matthew was well-acquainted with other tax collectors and "sinners," and invited them to a large party where Jesus was the guest of honor.

> Some scholars like Herbert Lockyer and Alexander Whyte think that Matthew and Jesus probably knew each other, or at least knew of each other, prior to the day when Christ called for this tax collector to follow him. The assumption is that Jesus' family would've paid taxes at Matthew's toll booth at one time or another, and also that Matthew would've heard about—or even heard firsthand—Jesus' preaching in Capernaum.

> Matthew left his career as a tax collector and became one of Christ's twelve, trusted "inner circle" disciples. He is named in every list of the twelve disciples in the New Testament.

> He's generally accepted as the author of the gospel of Matthew in the New Testament (though some dispute that). Biographer John Delaney indicates that he wrote this gospel sometime between

AD 60 and 90, and Ronald Brownrigg suggests that he probably used at least three sources (including the gospel of Mark) to compile his account of Jesus' life, death, and resurrection. In fact, about 95 percent of the gospel of Mark is included in some form in the gospel of Matthew.

> ❭ Matthew preserved for history the best, and most complete record of Jesus' teachings on various subjects, including the now-famous compilation of Christ's teaching in the Sermon on the Mount and a collection of Jesus' kingdom parables.

> ❭ Church tradition tells us that after Jesus' death and resurrection, Matthew preached as a missionary in Ethiopia and that he was martyred there, killed by either an axe or a sword.

Sources: WWB 306-308; DOS 394-395; AMB 232; JOB 134

Why all the hatred toward tax collectors in Jesus' day?

Tax collectors in Jesus' time were so reviled that their occupation (*telōnēs* in Greek) became synonymous with the word "sinner." In fact, the simple act of eating a meal with a tax collector enraged the religious leadership of that day.

Why were they so universally despised? There were two main reasons.

First, during the time of Christ, Jewish tax collectors were traitors to the nation of Israel. Living in God's promised land under the occupation of the oppressive Roman army was onerous to nearly all Jewish people. Tax collectors, though, not only accepted that circumstance; they embraced it. Pastor Chuck Swindoll explains, "Tax collectors had betrayed their people, rejected their heritage, despised their temple, and renounced their God. Tax collectors had sold themselves to foreigners, which put them on the same level as shameless harlots."

Second, at that time, tax collectors were thieves and abusers of their own countrymen. The Roman government used a system of "tax farming" to collect money from its conquered peoples. An entrepreneur would "buy" the obligation to pay taxes for a certain region, then would strong-arm people into overpaying their tax obligations to the state. The entrepreneur would pay the monthly quota owed to Rome, and then pocket the rest to amass personal wealth. These tax collectors literally had a license to steal—and they used (abused!) that power freely.

In that context, it's hard to say which was more astounding: that Jesus would dare to ask a tax collector (traitor! sinner! thief! abuser!) to be his disciple—or that a reprobate tax collector would actually follow Jesus' call.

Sources: SLU 135; BIG 269

A Discussion about Fasting
Matthew 9:14–17

When John's disciples asked about fasting, why didn't Jesus just give a straight answer? Why all the symbolism?

Christ's culturalized references to a bridegroom, cloth, and new wine all held deep spiritual significance, but they all came from practical, commonsense life that John's disciples would've easily understood. Consider these everyday insights from Bible historian Craig Keener:

> A wedding celebration, when the bridegroom was present, was an extended affair that required seven days of festivity, including a feast.

> "One was not permitted to fast or engage in other acts of mourning or difficult labor during a wedding feast. Jesus makes an analogy about the similar inappropriateness of fasting in his time."

> Old clothes would've been shrunken from washing, so putting a new, unshrunk patch on pre-shrunk clothing would've been a waste of resources. After washing, the new patch would shrink and tear away, making a bigger hole.

> Wine was usually kept in either jars or leather wineskins. "Old wineskins had already been stretched to capacity by fermenting wine within them; if they were then filled with unfermented wine, it would likewise expand, and the old wineskins, already stretched to the limit, would burst."

Source: IBB 70

Jesus Heals in Response to Faith
Matthew 9:18-26

Why was the "woman who had suffered for twelve years with constant bleeding" trying to be so sneaky about asking Jesus for healing?

The menstruating woman mentioned in this passage lived twelve years with a chronic uterine illness—but her physical suffering was not the worst part of her daily life.

Here are the facts about what this woman most likely endured for more than a decade:

> She was probably in her mid to late twenties—a young woman by our standards. According to Bible historian, Craig Keener, "[Her] ailment probably started after puberty; given an average life expectancy of about forty years and the 'twelve years' she had been ill, she may have spent half or all her adult life with this trouble."

> Because of her feminine discharge, this woman was literally shunned by everyone in her society. This was not simply a community prejudice; it grew out of an Old Testament law in Leviticus 15, where a menstruating woman was ceremonially unclean and should be avoided until she could be considered clean again.

> According to Jewish law and customs by the time of the New Testament, this unnamed woman was considered contagiously unclean, both physically *and* spiritually. She was to be confined to her home while menstruating (which, for her, was all the time).

> She was not allowed to touch *anybody*. Her family members weren't even allowed to lie on a bed or sit on a chair that she'd touched. People who touched this menstruating woman, even by accident, were considered contaminated right alongside her and had to take a bath to purify themselves, wash their clothes, and stay isolated until evening.

> She was forced away from religious gatherings, from temple worship, even from joyous annual religious feasts that consumed her Jewish culture in regular intervals.

> Gentile cultures of that time had similar rules. For instance, the Roman philosopher Pliny dictated that the touch of a menstruating woman was invisibly harmful and to be avoided.

> Some extremists forbade even speaking with a menstruating woman or making eye contact with her because they believed her breath was poisonous and her gaze was injurious.

With all that going on, you can see why this poor, ostracized woman would've wanted to stay hidden—and why she'd risk sneaking toward Jesus for a miracle.

Sources: IBB 148; BKN 124; ZB1 237

Is this "leader of a synagogue" the same person as Jairus who's mentioned in other gospels?

Matthew 9:18–26 reports how Jesus raised from death the daughter of a "leader of a synagogue" in Israel. The story is told in passing here, not even bothering to include the ruler's name. From corresponding reports in Mark 5:21–43 and Luke 8:40–56, though, we can learn that it was, in fact, Jairus—as you suspected. Here's what we know about him.

Jairus is pronounced JIGH-ruhs or JAY-uh-ruhs. His name is from the Greek word, *Iairos*, which means "he enlightens," or in the Hebrew context, "whom Jehovah enlightens." He lived somewhere in the region of Galilee, not too far from Jesus' home base in Capernaum. Although he was a leader in the synagogue, he was probably not a rabbi. Most likely he was a synagogue elder, which meant he was a layman with administrative duties. This would've given him significant authority over things like selecting who could teach, deciding what would occur during worship services, maintaining synagogue buildings, and overseeing community affairs. He would've been a very influential man in Galilee.

Ronald Brownrigg informs us that Jairus was likely the head of the local Sanhedrin or court of elders in his community. In this role he would've carried religious, political, and judicial power. It's also assumed, by his position as an elder and by the crowd of mourners that gathered outside his house (Matthew 9:23–25), that Jairus was a wealthy man.

Given his leadership position, Jairus could have come to Jesus and demanded a miracle (much like Herod did later; Luke 23:8–9). Or he could have approached Jesus as an equal, making a formal request. But he didn't do either of those things. Matthew says he "knelt before" Jesus humbly; Mark and Luke reveal that in kneeling, he "fell at his feet"—that is, he groveled like a slave before Christ and begged for a miracle.

Most importantly, *Jairus believed in Jesus.* His faith drove him to hope in Christ in the first place. When servants told him that his daughter had died, he continued to trust that Jesus could somehow overcome even that final circumstance. His faith was not in vain.

Sources: WWA 182; TEF 90; WWB 147; SLU 213

Jesus Heals the Blind
Matthew 9:27-34

What did Jesus mean when he said, "Because of your faith, it will happen"?

"Do you believe I can make you see?" Jesus asked two blind men. When they answered yes, he said, "Because of your faith, it will happen." And their sight was instantly restored. That's a lot riding on one little word: "faith." So what exactly does it mean?

Theologian Lawrence O. Richards offers insight from both the Old and New Testaments:

When we read "belief" and "faith" in the Old Testament … the original usually has the Hiphil stem of the Hebrew word `āman. The root indicates firmness and certainty; in this stem, the verb means "to be certain," "to believe in," or "to be assured."… This powerful Old Testament term, which captures the biblical meaning of faith, affirms certainty.

Pistis ("faith," "belief") and related words deal with relationships established by trust and maintained by trustworthiness…. These words are used in the New Testament in a variety of constructions. For instance, to "believe" is used with the accusative to mean, "be convinced of," or "entrust." … The most important construction is unique to the New Testament, an invention of the early church that expresses the inmost secret of our faith. That construction links faith with the preposition *eis,* "to" or "into." This is never done in secular

Greek. In the New Testament it portrays a person committing himself or herself totally to the person of Jesus Christ, for our faith is into Jesus.

With that in mind, it's interesting that Jesus didn't ask the blind men, "Do you believe *God* can do this?" but instead asked, "Do you believe that *I* am able to do this?" They responded with *certainty* of Christ's intention and placed full faith *into* his personal will (and ability) to act.

Today it seems we often try to manufacture faith out of hope that God will do our will rather than letting faith arise out of our certainty of his will. Perhaps, from these blind men, we can glimpse a little better what it really means to have rock-solid faith into Jesus—no matter what the circumstance.

Sources: EDB 113, 116-117

Exactly who is the "prince of demons" referenced in Matthew 9:34?

Jesus' enemies were pretty familiar with that guy—so much so that they felt confident accusing Christ of being his evil pawn. So who were they talking about?

The "prince of demons" was a title for a high-ranking, fallen angel derisively named "Beelzebul" by the ancient Jews. He appears in a non-biblical Jewish work, the *Testament of Solomon*, where, as the story goes, he is overpowered and imprisoned by King Solomon.

The name itself originates from the insulting Hebrew term *Baalzebub,* which referred to the false god Baal and means alternately "Lord of the flies" and "Lord of the dung heap." Some have thought Beelzebul to be another name for Satan, which could be the case, but that assumption is inconclusive; the name could also refer to a lesser demon in the service of Satan but who wields some measure of authority over the demonic realm.

In any case, this "prince of demons" is a vile, contemptible being, a force intent on wreaking evil—and the Pharisees of Jesus' day knew that. Given that knowledge, it's unlikely that their accusation of Jesus was a literal one. Beelzebul would never free people from demonic possession and captivity; it simply isn't that being's nature, nor is it consistent with the goals of the supernatural enemies of God. (Jesus made clear that obvious thinking in Matthew 12:25–29.)

It's much more likely the Pharisees' accusation was simply a desperate smear attempt by people who hated Christ. Convincing people that Jesus was associated with the infamous "prince of demons" would've been both a contemptuous personal insult (calling Jesus lower than a big pile of feces) and an attempt to discredit his reputation as a holy man and prophet.

The great irony was that, in calling Jesus a slave to Beelzebul, the Pharisees discredited themselves instead of Christ—and entrenched themselves as allies of the so-called "prince of demons" that they claimed to despise.

Sources: BKB 249; ZP1 505–506

The Need for Workers
Matthew 9:35–38

What would it have been like when Jesus traveled around and taught in synagogues?

We like to picture Jesus preaching and teaching to multitudes on mountainsides—and of course he did that. But the bulk of his speaking ministry happened indoors, in smallish venues, in local synagogues all over Galilee. So what would that have been like? Here's what we know.

Synagogues began in the homes of Jewish captives living in exile in Babylon. Since the Jerusalem temple had been destroyed, these synagogues were vital in keeping alive their faith and some forms of worship.

By the time of Jesus, "house synagogues" were common anywhere a significant population of Jews lived, even in places as far-flung as Rome, Parthia (part of Iran today), North Africa, and Asia Minor (Turkey today). In larger cities, particularly in Israel, the synagogue had also evolved into a formal assembly held in a public building—generally the tallest structure in the community. Jesus likely taught in both "house synagogues" and community synagogue buildings.

There had to be at least ten men present in a synagogue before public prayers could commence. God-fearers, or gentile men who aligned themselves with the Jewish faith, might also be in the synagogue audience.

The primary function of a synagogue was to provide lifelong education in the Law and the Prophets (the Old Testament). To that end, men read aloud and discussed Scripture, rabbis delivered oral commentary and sermons, and everyone participated in traditional expressions of worship such as prayer, singing, and almsgiving.

The synagogue also functioned as a community center of sorts. As the central gathering place of Jewish society, people would congregate here to discuss local affairs, make announcements, collect and distribute funds for charity, and occasionally share meals. Legal proceedings could also take place here, with the synagogue elders serving as judges.

During a synagogue meeting, women weren't typically allowed to speak, though they could sit in and listen. Any man over the age of thirteen could lead in prayer, or request permission to speak, or be invited to speak. When Jesus appeared at a synagogue, it was likely he was often invited to speak in this way, simply because he was so famous.

A synagogue meeting almost always ended with reciting Numbers 6:24–27 as a benediction: "May the LORD bless you and protect you. May the LORD smile on you and be gracious to you. May the LORD show you his favor and give you his peace."

Sources: NUB 358; JHT 156–159.

Why did Jesus feel sorry for the crowds of people?

Matthew 9:36 reports this of Jesus, "When he saw the crowds, he *had compassion* on them because they were confused and helpless, like sheep without a shepherd" (italics mine). This symbolized a view that the people of Israel ("sheep") were in a state of danger and distress that came from either an absence of godly leadership ("shepherd"), or a corruption of authority placed in leaders. Theologian Eduard Schweizer explains, "The image suggests a flock that is tormented and almost totally exhausted, or is at least being led astray and neglected by careless shepherds."

It's important to understand that Jesus' response to this tragic situation wasn't simply "feeling sorry" for them. In fact, the two-word phrase "had compassion" in verse 36 is actually just one word in the original Greek: *splagchnízomai*—and it means more than we might assume.

We tend to read this and think that Jesus had sympathy for others—but also that he was somehow separate from their suffering. As Ronald F. Youngblood describes it, "God's mercy on the miserable … grew out of his attitude of compassion." His divine hand, we assume, was reaching in from the outside to alleviate pain.

There's a measure of truth to that thinking, but it's not entirely correct. The more accurate interpretation of *splagchnízomai* is that Jesus not only saw and sympathized with their suffering, but that he *experienced it emotionally* within himself as well.

You see, *splagchnizomai* connotes more than just sympathy or even basic empathy; it means literally "to feel deeply or viscerally, to yearn." Synonymic meanings include "a feeling of distress from the ills of others … to suffer with another."

In other words, Jesus didn't simply "feel sorry" for those in misery, he incarnated their misery into his own being. He suffered alongside them, in both their physical and spiritual anguish. It was out of that shared suffering that he enacted his compassionate acts of healing—physical, emotional, spiritual, intellectual—that changed people forever. This is a heart-stopping, beautiful truth: Our God cares for us because he knows, personally, our pain. (See also Isaiah 53:3.)

Sources: GNM 233-234; NIB 741-742; CWDN 1306

Jesus Sends Out the Twelve Apostles
Matthew 10:1-42

So … were there really thirteen apostles of Jesus?

The New Testament gives four separate listings of Jesus' closest disciples, a group of men known as "the Twelve." The account in Matthew 10:2–4 claims to be a complete summary of "the names of the twelve apostles." That list includes:

> Simon (who is called Peter)

> Andrew

> James (son of Zebedee)

> John

> Philip

> Bartholomew

> Thomas

> Matthew (the tax collector)

> James (son of Alphaeus)

> Thaddaeus (sometimes written as Lebbaeus)

> Simon the Zealot

> Judas Iscariot (the betrayer)

Mark's list (in Mark 3:16–19) is identical to Matthew's except that the order of the names is changed. But a question arises in the lists found in Luke 6:14–16 and Acts 1:13. In these lists, eleven of the twelve are the same as those in Matthew (though Judas Iscariot is left off the list in Acts because, as we're told, he died a gruesome death; Acts 1:18). The name of Thaddeus, though, is not included by Luke in either his gospel or the book of Acts (which Luke also wrote). Additionally, another name—"Judas son of James"—is added to the list of apostles in both of Luke's books.

So what gives? Where there really thirteen apostles? Most Bible historians think the answer is no.

The literary and historical evidence suggest that, just as Simon was also called Peter, Judas son of James was also called Thaddeus—a nickname that he preferred exclusively after Christ's death and resurrection. As such, most theologians, like Michael Wilkins, believe biblical mentions of "Judas son of James" and "Thaddeus" refer to the same person. Dr. Wilkins comments, "After the name Judas became stigmatized because of the traitorous Judas Iscariot, Judas the son of James changed his name to Thaddeus. In that case, Matthew and Mark provided the safer and alternative name, while Luke stuck with the controversial name."

Source: HAC 75-76

What happened when someone was "flogged with whips in the synagogues"?

Don't gloss over Jesus' promise of flogging that's recorded in Matthew 10:17—you can be sure his disciples didn't. Here's what would've happened:

Any person—man or woman—deemed guilty of entering the temple while unclean would be subject to the punishment of flogging. For instance, after Acts 10:9–16 happened (when God lifted the ban on eating certain meats), synagogue officials would've deemed most Christians guilty of being unclean.

After the synagogue officials had passed judgment, a disciple of Jesus would've been stripped to the waist and made to lie down or crouch low to the ground. His hands would be tied to a pillar for the duration of the flogging.

Four people were required to conduct the flogging. A *hazzan* ("administrator") did the actual whipping. A second person counted the number of blows. A third person gave the commands. And while the beating took place, a fourth person read aloud Deuteronomy 28:58–59—a passage about misery and "indescribable plagues."

The *hazzan* would use a sturdy leather whip for the flogging. This was usually a whip made of four plaited thongs attached to a handle. The standard number of lashes was forty, though most often one of Jesus' disciples would've been whipped thirty-nine times (known as forty less one). This was done just in case the *hazzan* and/or the counter lost count sometime during the bloody delivery of punishment. One-third of the lashes (about thirteen) were delivered to the disciple's chest, and the remainder (about twenty-six) were delivered to the back.

If Jesus' disciple appeared near death as a result of flogging, the *hazzan* was supposed to stop. In spite of that, there are some records of people dying from a synagogue flogging.

Source: ZB1 69

Was Jesus mistaken when he promised to return for his disciples?

Matthew 10:23 quotes Jesus as saying to his disciples, "I tell you the truth, the Son of Man will return before you have reached all the towns of Israel." This appears to be a reference to the second coming of Jesus—and it clearly didn't happen.

So … how do we make sense of that? Theologians offer several theories. According to Dr. Michael Wilkins, they are:

> **THEORY #1:** Jesus was promising to appear to his disciples after he raised himself from the dead. This interpretation assumes "Jesus was promising that the disciples would witness the eschatological coming of the Son of Man … at his resurrection."

> **THEORY #2:** Jesus was promising to return to his disciples as the living presence of his invisible Holy Spirit, a promise which was fulfilled dynamically at Pentecost (Acts 2:1–13).

> **THEORY #3:** Jesus was indicating a "continuing mission" to Israel over the ages and was offering "comfort to the mission-disciples about their ultimate salvation unto the end … the mission to Israel will not conclude before the Son of Man returns. There will be a continuing mission to Israel alongside the mission to the Gentiles."

> **THEORY #4:** Jesus was referencing his future second coming, thousands of years away, but "he was not saying that the Twelve would personally see this. Rather, he means to instill a sense of urgency in the mission to Israel by stating that it will not be complete by the time of his return."

Source: HAC 78-79

Jesus and John the Baptist
Matthew 11:1–19

Where was John the Baptist held in prison?

In this account, we find out from Matthew that, while in prison, John the Baptist heard about what Jesus was doing, and wanted to know more. What Matthew didn't report was the conditions John endured as a political captive.

Dr. Michael Wilkins tells us that John the Baptist was imprisoned in the castle fortress of Machaerus, located just east of the Dead Sea in Judea. Herod Antipas (also known as Herod the tetrarch), was ruling Judea and had committed public sins of marital corruption. That prompted John the Baptist to preach against the de-facto king's immorality. Antipas exacted vengeance, locking John up indefinitely in the dungeon of his fortress (Matthew 14:3–4).

Neither history nor archaeology tell us exactly what John might have endured while imprisoned in Machaerus. Still, the Tullianum prison in Rome would've been fairly similar—and we know what that was like. Tullianum was "a conical, windowless chamber of rough-hewn tufa, the only entrance to which is a hole in the floor of the room above." According to historian and expert on Roman culture, Philip Matyszak, "Prisoners were flung through this hole into the prison, and on occasion left there to starve and rot." About a hundred years before Christ, a Numidian king named Jugurtha was imprisoned in Tullianum, and his first comment was that it was unbearably cold.

Prison in Machaerus would've been something like that Roman hellhole. John the Baptist lived there for more than a year before he was unceremoniously decapitated in his cell simply to please the whims of Antipas's cruel wife, Herodias (Matthew 14:1–12).

Sources: ZB1 71; ARF 78

John had baptized Jesus—why did he now ask if Jesus was really the Messiah?

When John the Baptist was in prison and heard that Jesus was nearby, he sent his disciples to ask of Christ: "Are you the Messiah we've been expecting, or should we keep looking for someone else?" (Matthew 11:3). Why did he ask this question?

Legendary eighteenth-century preacher John Wesley explained John the Baptist's question as a manipulative teaching exercise. John sent his disciples, Wesley taught, "Not because he doubted himself, but to confirm their faith."

Hm ...

I suppose that contrived explanation could be true; after all, Wesley's teachings have endured for generations, right? But from where I sit, I can see really only one (obvious) reason why the Baptist asked his question: *John wanted to know if Jesus was the one who was to come.*

You see, John was, in some ways, a victim of his own mistaken expectations. At that time, most Jews expected a militaristic Messiah, a political power who would rain judgment down on enemies of righteousness. John himself had preached that "He is ready to separate the chaff from the wheat with his winnowing fork. Then he will clean up the threshing area, gathering the wheat into his barn but burning the chaff with never-ending fire" (Luke 3:17).

John's Messiah was defined by the anticipation of God's wrath poured out on evildoers—especially on people like his captor, Herod Antipas, and the cruel, occupying Roman army. But Jesus didn't fit John's beliefs. Meanwhile, faithful John the Baptist rotted in prison, suffering, waiting for Christ to be the conqueror he was expected to be.

Theologian Sherman E. Johnson commented on John's dilemma by saying, "The waiting fretted his soul.... Doubt grew chiefly on the fact that Christ did not fulfill either the hope of the Messiah as nationalistically interpreted, or the picture that John himself had drawn."

Bravo for John that, instead of stewing in doubt and frustration, he decided to go directly to the source of faith to find out for himself the answer he needed. When he heard that Jesus was nearby, he sent his disciples to ask, "Are you the Messiah we've been expecting, or should we keep looking for someone else?" (Matthew 11:3).

I wonder if you and I have the courage to do the same with Jesus today.

Sources: CBC 925; IB7 379

Judgment for the Unbelievers
Matthew 11:20-24

Whatever happened to Capernaum?

It seems that the people of Capernaum had something of a love-hate relationship with Christ, and in the end, it cost that city everything. Here's what we know about that ancient location:

Capernaum was the primary headquarters for Jesus' ministry in Israel. After his baptism, Jesus moved to this village and likely lived with Simon Peter's family while teaching, healing, and working miracles in this area.

Capernaum, which in Hebrew means, "Village of Nahum," was about a day's walk (twenty miles) from Jesus' hometown of Nazareth. Located on the eastern border of Galilee, it wasn't large. Its borders covered only about fifteen acres—or about the size of three football fields by two football fields (300 yards x 200 yards). During the time of Jesus, the population of Capernaum was roughly 1,500.

Located on the coast of the Sea of Galilee, Capernaum was known mostly as a fishing village. However, it also boasted a thriving farming community and a prosperous industry in the processing of olive oil. It's no wonder, then, that many of Jesus' illustrations involve these industries.

Capernaum was also a busy border town, despite its small size. It sat on a trade route byway that connected Egypt and Arabia in the south with all the countries located north of Israel. As such, a customs station was placed in Capernaum, collecting taxes from merchants going to and from Syria.

Jesus performed a number of significant miracles in Capernaum, including the healing of a paralyzed man (Mark 2:1–12), a miraculous catch of fish that convinced his first disciples to follow him (Luke 5:1–11), healing blind men (Matthew 9:27–31), exorcising demons (Matthew 9:32–34), raising the dead (Luke 8:40–56) and many more. Despite that, the people as a whole refused to believe in him.

Jesus predicted the demise of Capernaum as punishment for their rejection of his miracle-working presence. This came to pass, at least in part, in the seventh century when Muslim invaders came into Israel. My friend and noted Bible scholar, Stephen M. Miller, tell us that the residents of Capernaum fled, abandoning their homes to the elements. Over time, this ghost town was ruined by wind and earth until it was buried and forgotten—a striking image when compared to Jesus' prophecy: "And you people of Capernaum, will you be honored in heaven? No, you will go down to the place of the dead."

Today, Capernaum exists only in ruins, cared for by a community of watchful Franciscan monks who bought the property from Arabs in 1894.

Source: WWA 64-67

If Jesus knew that a few miraculous healings would've turned the population of Sodom to repentance, renewed thousands of people into relationship with God, and saved an entire civilization, why did he choose burning annihilation instead of miracles for all those ancient people?

It's a fair question—but not one with easy answers.

Jesus pronounced plainly in Matthew 11:23 that his miracles would have brought repentance to the infamous Sodom of Genesis 19. He also revealed his loving heart for similarly wicked people when he said, "I have come to call not those who think they are righteous, but those who know they are sinners and need to repent" (Luke 5:32).

The people of Sodom would certainly fit that description. So why were they destroyed, when morally awful people after Christ have been redeemed? *Hm.*

For a time, J. I. Packer informs us, some scholars argued that Sodom never really existed. That assumption, coupled with the melodramatic demise described in Scripture lent itself to the idea that the Sodom story was symbolic myth instead of literal destruction. If true, that would've let Jesus off the hook (so to speak). However, that belief doesn't stand up under scrutiny. For starters, the Bible references Sodom (or some variant of that name) more than fifty times, and every time it's treated as a literal, historical place.

Additionally, although no ruins of Sodom have ever been found, the discovery of artifacts in the area of Tell Mardikh, Syria (Ebla, in ancient times) reveals both Sodom and Gomorrah (along with Jerusalem) as known locations in business records dating as far back as 3000 BC. So, according to Packer, the theory behind no ruins is that "a divinely-ordered earthquake … released a cloud of natural gas, which exploded … [and] the ruins of these cities were gradually covered with the water of the Dead Sea." Still, that doesn't give a clean, intellectual solution to this question; so all I can give is my best guess:

I think Sodom was destroyed for all of us who came after, a terrible sacrifice so we would have an example to warn us of the devastating, eternal consequences of sin.

Scripture seems to indicate that was at least part of the reason: "God condemned the cities of Sodom and Gomorrah and turned them into heaps of ashes. He made them an example of what will happen to ungodly people. But God also rescued Lot out of Sodom, because he was a righteous man" (2 Peter 2:6–7). Additionally, Jude 1:7 says, "And don't forget Sodom and Gomorrah and their neighboring towns…. Those cities were destroyed by fire and serve as a warning of the eternal fire of God's judgment."

My old pastor, Chuck Swindoll also helps us find a measure of comfort within the sorrow of Sodom's fall. Pointing to Peter's commentary on Lot, he says, "The judgment of the wicked [in Sodom is] an example for Christian hope. In the coming judgment, God will preserve Christians who live righteous lives in the midst of the day-to-day immorality and lawlessness of the pagan world."

Again, I don't think this is a complete, or even satisfying, answer, but it's the best I can offer you right now. I hope it's helpful in some small way.

Sources: BAL 97, 189; SJP 295

Jesus' Prayer of Thanksgiving
Matthew 11:25–30

Why would God hide knowledge, especially important truth that can impact a person's eternity, from the "wise and learned" (NIV)?

All right, to attempt an answer to this question, we'll need to break it down into its logical parts:

> First we ask: When Jesus prayed, "Lord of heaven and earth … you have hidden these things from the wise and learned, and revealed them to little children" (verse 25 NIV), was this statement communicating a universal principle of salvation, or was it specific to the situation?

> Second: Did God hide his truth from the "wise and learned"(or "wise and clever" in some translations) simply because they were wise and learned, or because that learning had somehow corrupted their character?

Looking at Question #1, when taken in context of the New Testament as a whole, it's clear that Jesus' pronouncement against the "wise and learned" was not a universal principle of salvation. A number of well-educated people were followers of Christ, including Nicodemus, a "Jewish religious leader" (John 3); Luke, a doctor who wrote the gospel of Luke and the book of Acts; and the apostle Paul (Acts 9:1–31; 22:3).

That evidence, coupled with Matthew's statement at the beginning of Matthew 11:25—"*At that time* Jesus prayed this prayer" (italics mine)—strongly suggests that he was speaking about the situation specific to Matthew 11. In that case, he would've been referring to the unbelieving "wise and learned" in the listening crowd and to those who had opposed him in the towns he had just condemned in verses 21–24 (Capernaum, Tyre, Sidon, and so on).

Now, as for Question #2. Because we can clearly see that God does not oppose the wise and learned as a universal principle of salvation, that aspect can't be the sole reason why God hid his truth from these specific people. So why did he do that? Theologian Larry Richards offers this explanation:

The generation that rejected Jesus considered itself wise, yet the people did not recognize the significance of the miracles Jesus performed. In contrast the "babes," who were looked down on by the "mature," were eager to learn from Jesus.… God's activity in concealing "these things" from the wise and understanding was an act of judgment on those who had *already rejected* the divine message.

Source: ETJ 201–202

What does it mean to take on Jesus' yoke?

"Take my yoke upon you," Jesus taught the crowd. "Let me teach you, because I am humble and gentle at heart, and you will find rest for your souls. For my yoke is easy to bear, and the burden I give you is light" (Matthew 11:29–30).

A yoke in the literal sense was a device made of wood that fastened over the necks of two oxen and forced them to work as a team. Obviously, an allegorical instruction in Jesus' use, this beautiful promise has been surprisingly hard for theologians to parse down through the ages.

Some, such as Swiss theologian Eduard Schweizer, have interpreted this yoke as a symbol of complete surrender. As Dr. Robert Mounce describes it, "The yoke imposed by the victor on the vanquished." This view sees Christ's followers as those who've been spiritually defeated and humbled as "one who appears conquered" in battle. That militaristic interpretation seems lacking though, when placed within the gentle and restful context of Jesus' invitation.

The more reliable view appears to be that Jesus was showing a contrast between the hope of his grace and the hurtfulness of strident legalism. In this perspective, Jesus' symbolic wording called to mind the "yoke of the Torah." That was all about "work and duty" and was applied with exacting harshness by Israel's religious leaders (Matthew 23:4). Theologian Douglas R. A. Hare sees the contextual conversations about Sabbath obligations that immediately follow in Matthew 12 as insightful for interpretation as well. He explains "[Jesus'] invitation is issued neither to the work-burdened nor to the sin-burdened but to the law-burdened, upon whose shoulders 'the scribes and the Pharisees' have laid an intolerable load."

Christ's yoke, in comparison, called followers to be his partners in love, compassion, kindness, and forgiveness. The symbolism here carries two applications.

> First, taking on his yoke means following his teaching and wisdom of transforming grace that gives respite from the ruthlessness of legalism.

> Second, it means becoming God's "yoke-mate," one who works right beside Jesus, and who depends on Christ's strength and example to accomplish the work of holiness.

Sources: IMT 128–129; NIBC 108–109; ABC 975; BTC 167–168

A Discussion about the Sabbath
Matthew 12:1–8

What are the "sacred loaves of bread" mentioned in Matthew 12:4?

When Pharisees objected to his disciples plucking grain to eat on the Sabbath (a perceived violation of God's command to rest), Jesus plucked a truth from Jewish history as their defense: "Haven't you read in the Scriptures what David did when he and his companions were hungry?" he asked rhetorically. They "broke the law by eating the sacred loaves of bread that only the priests are allowed to eat" (Matthew 12:3–4). The event Jesus referred to here is found in 1 Samuel 21:1–6 and 22:11–20.

Before David was king, he and his men were fugitives pursued by King Saul. They had nothing to eat, so David went to a priest named Ahimelek, lied about his situation, and asked for food. The priest gave him loaves of "holy bread—the Bread of the Presence that was placed before the LORD in the Tabernacle" (1 Samuel 21:6). This sacred bread was part of a Sabbath worship ceremony and was reserved exclusively for those who were ritually clean according to Mosaic law. Basically, it had been consecrated for only priests to eat (Leviticus 24:5–9)—and David and his men were no priests!

According to 1 Samuel 22:10, Ahimelek "consulted the LORD" about whether to give the bread to David, probably by use of Urim and Thummim. These were small objects that today would be considered a "game of chance." Priests in David's time believed that God directed the Urim and Thummim to indicate his desired outcome.

God's response to Ahimelek was favorable, and so the priest violated the letter of the Mosaic law in order to obey God and feed David's men.

This is what Jesus referred to when he talked about the "sacred loaves" in Matthew 12:4.

Source: BKW2 161

What was the significance of Jesus claiming to be "Lord, even over the Sabbath"?

When Jesus asserted that he was Lord of the Sabbath, it likely shocked people into disbelief—and caused the Pharisees to grind their teeth in outrage. That's because, unless it was true, it was blasphemy.

There's only One who can be Lord of the Sabbath, only One with complete authority to enforce or suspend the command for Sabbath rest: that is, *God himself*. As pastor and theologian, David Platt, reveals in his commentary on Matthew 12:8, "Jesus is making clear that as Lord of the Sabbath, He **is God**. He is God in the flesh, and as God, He has the authority to determine Sabbath regulations for his disciples."

Imagine how you'd react if some itinerant preacher suddenly spouted of this phrase: "I am Commander in Chief of the United States military." Unless that person was actually the President of the US, you'd dismiss him or her as some kind of lunatic, or worse, a saboteur intent on overthrowing the government. It was that kind of absurd-unless-true statement that came out of Jesus' mouth when arguing with the Pharisees—except Christ's claim was more dangerous to them, because it was true.

Source: CEM 160

Jesus Heals on the Sabbath
Matthew 12:9–14

Exactly who were the Pharisees, and why were they so hostile about Jesus healing people on the Sabbath?

Of all the enemies of Jesus, the ones with the most sincere motives were Pharisees. This group of influential religious leaders honestly thought they were defending God's truth by opposing Christ.

Pharisees as a distinct political group have their roots in the Maccabean Revolt against Syrian rule in the second century BC. The Hasmonean dynasty of priest-kings that resulted from the revolt ruled Judea for about a century afterward. Through it all, these "separated ones" maintained deep devotion to God and to the law of Moses.

By the time of Christ, there were only about six thousand Pharisees left, but that was still enough to make them the largest sect of religious Jews in that era. They were instrumental in keeping faith and family as priorities in those ancient days. Bible historian Ronald Brownrigg reports, "[Pharisees] fostered synagogue life and worship, calling people back to a study of the Law and its application to their own time."

The faith-life of Pharisees boiled down to strict obedience to the 613 commands in the law of Moses. For help in that, they followed the oral teachings and traditions of history's Jewish elders. Their goal, says Bible scholar H. L. Ellison, was to "'make a hedge' about [the commandments] … so to interpret and supplement them that there would be no possibility of breaking them by accident or ignorance."

This is how it became a mark of spirituality to strictly observe all kinds of nonsensical commands on the Sabbath day of rest. The Jewish Mishnah (oral traditions applying Mosaic Law) prohibited thirty-nine kinds of work on the Sabbath, such as sewing more than one stitch or loosening a knot. Additionally, to avoid working on the Sabbath, the Pharisee wouldn't carry any load, or walk more than two thousand paces, or do any of the dozens of other arbitrary rules included in the Mishnah. The application of this type of legalistic holiness apparently also included a prohibition of Jesus healing the sick on the Sabbath day, because Pharisees saw that as "work."

So it appears that the core motivation for Pharisaical hostility about Jesus healing on the Sabbath was misplaced zeal for God.

Interestingly, off all the sects of Judaism at the time of Jesus, the Pharisees are the only ones who survived past the first century. By the year 200, they had become *the* principal spiritual leaders of Jewish communities. With some exceptions, the Pharisaic tradition continues in Judaism today, particularly in orthodox Judaism.

Sources: IBD3 1209–1210; WWB 357; BIB 868–869; LEB 133

Jesus, God's Chosen Servant
Matthew 12:15–21

I don't understand the connection Matthew makes to the prophecy from Isaiah. What's going on?

Matthew 12:18–21 quotes a messianic prophecy from Isaiah 42:1–4. This makes sense when we consider that Matthew wrote primarily for his fellow Israelites, with the aim of showing that Jesus was (and is) the Messiah that had been predicted in the Jewish Scriptures.

Although the Old Testament prophecies encompassed many aspects of the Messiah ("Anointed One") the most common view in first-century Israel was that God's Messiah would be exclusively a political and military figure. They expected a battle-hardened, miraculous, conquering hero who would liberate the Jews from their Roman oppressors. And that's understandable; if you were a Jew in the time of Jesus, wouldn't you want that too?

Matthew, however, challenges his readers' notions of what the Messiah must do and be. He highlights a passage from Isaiah about "the Servant of the Lord," a recognized messianic prophecy that revealed non-militaristic truth about their "Anointed One." By doing this, Matthew showed how Jesus fulfilled the ancient promise through his healing ministry, his humility and gentleness, and the hope he brought to both Jew and non-Jew alike. As seminary professor J. Knox Chamblin explains, "The quotation of Isaiah 42:1–4 … rejects false messianic notions and expounds true messiahship." That appears to be the point Matthew was making by connecting Jesus to this Old Testament verse.

Sources: EHB 474; HSB 154; BCB 736

Jesus and the Prince of Demons
Matthew 12:22–37

Why did Jesus' enemies keep saying his miracles were empowered by the "prince of demons"?

The sad truth is that many people in Jesus' time (and in the centuries to come) couldn't accept that Jesus could actually be the incarnate Son of God—but they still had to acknowledge his miraculous power. Rather than accept the evidence for what it was—and what it meant regarding the deity of Jesus—they searched for another, more plausible explanation for what Christ did and who he was. They chose the idea that he was a shaman in league with demons, and that his miracles were magic tricks akin to what Pharaoh's sorcerers did, as recorded in Exodus 7–8.

In ancient Jewish society, demons were credited as the cause of various ailments: blindness, deafness, muteness, and all sorts of illnesses. It's no surprise, then, that Matthew 12:22–24 combines the exorcising of demons with healing of blindness and muteness. None of Jesus' enemies could deny that these things had happened; the evidence was public and right before their eyes! So they accused Christ of demonic sorcery, which meant being a trickster doing magic from the devil (see also Matthew 9:34). This propagandistic accusation stuck around for centuries.

Later rabbinic literature tried to discredit Christ's healing miracles by saying, "Jesus the Nazarene practiced magic, and led astray and deceived Israel." A second-century critic named Celsus also preached that Jesus was a phony and a sorcerer, saying, "It was by magic that he [Jesus] was able to do the miracles that he appeared to have done.... He was brought up in secret and hired himself out as a workman in Egypt, and having tried his hand at certain magical powers he returned from these, and on account of those powers gave himself the title of God."

The historical evidence doesn't bear out any of these absurd claims. In fact, there's no evidence at all that Jesus practiced magic. He never used incantations or spells or called on any power other than himself to heal. This hearsay appears to be a case of Christ's enemies deliberately deceiving themselves in order to justify their predetermined disbelief. Very sad.

Source: BKB 200–201, 247

So what exactly is the "unpardonable sin"?

In Matthew 12:31, Jesus is recorded as saying, "Every sin and blasphemy can be forgiven—except blasphemy against the Holy Spirit, which will never be forgiven." This is a frightening truth, and one that's been parsed in so many ways over so many centuries as to make it seem indecipherable. What does it mean exactly to commit "blasphemy against the Holy Spirit"? Here are some of the theories that have been circulated over time.

> **THEORY #1:** *It was a sin specific to the Pharisees of Jesus' day, committed when they claimed Jesus' was empowered by Satan.* This was the view of early church fathers such as Jerome and John Chrysostom. According to them, this sin could only be committed when Christ lived on the earth, and so would not apply to anyone after that time.

> **THEORY #2:** *It is the stubborn unwillingness (the* impoenitentia finalis*) to repent, all the way until death.* St. Augustine and other historic theologians were proponents of this view. Basically, this is the idea that the unpardonable sin is a refusal to accept Jesus Christ by faith for the entirety of one's life.

> **THEORY #3:** *It is a "conscious, malicious, and willful rejection and slandering …* of the testimony of the Holy Spirit respecting the grace of God in Christ, attributing it out of hatred and enmity to the prince of darkness." This is the perspective articulated by influential Reformed scholar, Louis Berkhof. He adds that this sin is, "the audacious declaration that the Holy Spirit is the spirit of the abyss, that the truth is a lie, and that Christ is Satan."

> **THEORY #4:** *It is a hardened, irrational, irrevocable decision to reject Jesus.* The idea here is that of apostasy, of a deliberate and decisive rejection of Jesus as Lord. This is a popular view among evangelical theologians. Dr. Lawrence O. Richards sums up this thinking when he says, "Speaking against the source of Jesus' power was, first of all, a recognition of its supernatural origin, and second, a hardened rejection of Jesus Himself…. Their choice, made in the face of all the unique evidence which Jesus Himself had presented to them, was irrevocable; they had chosen to step beyond the possibility of repentance."

> **THEORY #5:** *It is deliberately honoring Satan for the work of the Holy Spirit.* This is also a common view, as articulated by Anglican Evangelical scholar, F. F. Bruce. He says the Pharisees were charged with blaspheming the Holy Spirit because "They deliberately ascribed the Holy Spirit's activity to demonic agency."

So what exactly is the unpardonable sin? I don't think anyone has yet come up with a complete definition—and I think that's OK. Bruce seems to speak for all opinions when he says, "The nature of this sin is such that one does not repent of it," and thus "The very fact of [one's] concern over having committed it proves that they have not committed it."

Sources: ST 252-253; TC 561; HSJ 89-90

The Sign of Jonah
Matthew 12:38-45

Jesus predicted his death and resurrection by saying he'd be "in the heart of the earth for three days and three nights"—but he wasn't. Was Jesus fudging the facts here?

Well, the math does seem suspect from a modern Western perspective. To our minds, "three days and three nights" should equal seventy-two hours, or three twenty-four-hour periods. So if Jesus died on a Friday afternoon, and then rose from the dead the following Sunday morning, by our count that would equal at best, two days and two nights "in the heart of the earth," or about thirty-nine to forty hours total.

However, this is a case of twenty-first-century bias being applied to first century culture. The error lies in our thinking, not in Jesus' math.

First, a "day" in that era and that place was typically considered to begin at dusk the night before, or roughly 6:00 p.m., and last until 6:00 p.m. the next. This is why the Sabbath began on Friday night and continued until sundown on Saturday.

Second, it was common in both biblical use (1 Samuel 30:12) and in the society of Jesus' time to refer to part of a day or night simply as a "day." The modern equivalent might be if you said to a friend, "I worked all day last Friday." None of your friends would assume you meant you'd worked a literal twenty-four-hour day; they'd know you meant you'd worked *part* of the day, typically eight hours or so—which is really only one-third of a literal day. Likewise, buying a three-day pass to Walt Disney World doesn't mean you get to spend seventy-two uninterrupted hours inside the park. We all know that means you get to spend time inside the park during the hours it's open, or for as many hours of each day as your travel schedules permit. Still, we speak of the parts of those vacation days as full days at Walt Disney World.

Likewise, when Jesus prophesied about "three days and three nights" in the grave, his hearers would've instantly understood that could reference parts of days or full days—or both.

Sources: EBD 328; EPB 299

When Jesus described a demon's journey after being cast out, was that a literal or figurative explanation?

The general thinking is that Jesus' description of the demon's journey is accurate in terms of events, but figurative in terms of details, meaning a demon does actually leave, does actually wander, and does actually return—but since we can't see into the spiritual realm there's no way of knowing what that literally looks like. So in that sense, Jesus' description is accurate in describing the events, but figurative in describing the way those events look (such as saying that a demon "goes into the desert").

Some theologians like Craig Evans consider these comments of Jesus to be one of his many parables. They see the structure of a parable in Christ's description of how an evil spirit travels through an indistinct "desert" searching for rest, and the return to a person that it now considers its "home." Additionally, the "seven other spirits" could be understood as symbolic phrasing in that, "the number seven often signifies severity, sometimes with the connotation of revenge" (see Genesis 4:15; 4:24; Psalm 79:12 and others). Real-life examples of what Jesus described are recorded in the accounts of the man with a "legion" of demons (Mark 5:1–20), and in Luke's comments about Mary Magdalene (Luke 8:2).

Regardless of whether it was a parable or not, the main idea seems to be that simply casting out a demon doesn't ensure the afflicted will avoid future suffering *unless* that act is accompanied by repentance and faith in Jesus. Taken in the context of Matthew 12, it appears Jesus was warning religious leaders that by opposing him their generation was inviting a more severe punishment from evil spirits hungry to return (Matthew 12:45).

Source: MAT 263–264

The True Family of Jesus
Matthew 12:46-50

When Jesus refuses to see his visiting family, that seems incredibly rude and out of character for him. What was going on there?

It does seem strange that Jesus would refuse even to see his mother and brothers after they had traveled to meet with him. This is particularly true in light of the cultural reverence for family at that time. Theologian Craig Keener points out that "to disavow literal family members was so repulsive that even using that image would have been culturally offensive."

So what was going on? The gospel of Mark sheds a little more light on the situation, revealing that Jesus' family had heard what he was doing—and was presumably aware of the danger he was stirring up for himself. They thought he'd lost his mind, so they'd decided to take him home and care for him. Pastor Chuck Swindoll explains their perspective: "From a distance, Jesus showed all the signs of a manic disorder. Unfortunately, His family was neither close enough to Jesus' intentions nor discerning enough to know better." So when they came to see Jesus, it wasn't a family reunion. It was to "take him away" and make him stop teaching, healing, and helping (Mark 3:21). This assumption of insanity seems reasonably consistent with Jesus' brothers (specifically James and Jude, who didn't believe in Christ until after he had returned from the dead), but unusual for his mother, Mary. She'd known who Jesus was from the moment of conception. Why would she have joined in this effort to end the work of God's Son? This is only speculation, but it's possible that, as a widow with adult sons who were in charge of her household, she was made to come with the rest of the family against her better judgment, and possibly against her will. Still, we don't know the exact nature of her participation in this event, except that she was there.

Regardless, Jesus refused to be manipulated by his family and declined to end his ministry. His work was more important than his family's feelings. As Keener says, "He is not rejecting his earthly family altogether but stating his priorities." Christ's actions at his execution bear out this observation. Even as Jesus was in agony on the cross, he still instructed John to care for his mother (John 19:25–27).

Sources: IBB 81, 144; IBD2 732; SMK 98

Parable of the Farmer Scattering Seed
Matthew 13:1-23

It seems a bit showy for Jesus to get into a boat to teach this crowd. Why would he do that?

As is often the case, geography seems to be the answer to this question.

Pastor Chuck Swindoll reveals that historians believe they know where it was that Jesus sat in the boat and taught the parables recorded in Matthew 13. It's a small cove beside the Sea of Galilee. Today it's called the Cove of the Sower, and also the Bay of Parables. Both names pay homage to this biblical event.

So why would Jesus sit in a boat to teach there? Most likely because of the acoustics.

Facing the inlet from the sea, the sloping hill of land would've formed a natural theater of sorts. According to an audio study conducted by B. Cobbey Crisler, the acoustics of that theater-cove would've allowed up to seven thousand people to hear a lone speaker positioned just off the shoreline.

Source: SSB 1158

Did Jesus invent the parable?

Matthew 13 marks a new phase in Jesus' ministry, which the gospel writer describes this way: "He told many stories in the form of parables." Mark and Matthew both affirm that Jesus "never taught without using parables" (Mark 4:34; Matthew 13:34).

A parable is a rhetorical device used to communicate a spiritual truth in figurative language.

> It can be a story, such as the parable of the prodigal son (Luke 15:11–32) or of the farmer scattering seed (Matthew 13:1–23).

> It can also be simply a figure of speech, such as "Don't throw your pearls to pigs" (Matthew 7:6)

> Or, it can be an extended simile or metaphor, such as when Jesus taught that "the kingdom of heaven is like …" a farmer, a mustard seed, yeast, and so on (here in Matthew 13)

The Greek word that Matthew used for "parables" means literally "laying by the side of." In a parable, something easily understood is compared—or laid beside—something more difficult to comprehend.

Greek philosophers Aristotle and Plato both used parables in their teachings over four hundred years before the birth of Christ. About a thousand years before Christ, Nathan the prophet famously used a parable to teach King David to repent over his sin with Bathsheba (2 Samuel 12:5–15). Some years later, a woman also corrected David by telling a parable of two sons fighting in a field (2 Samuel 14:5–7). In fact, the Old Testament is rife with parables, starting with Jotham's tale of trees choosing a king (Judges 9:7–21) and going all the way to Malachi's parable of judgment like a furnace (Malachi 4:1).

So while Christ was the master of parabolic teaching—and arguably the most famous in history—no, he didn't invent the parable. That rhetorical form had been around for centuries before he perfected its use.

Sources: NIB 851; RDC 318

Jesus was a carpenter, a skilled workman from a family of carpenters. So why did he teach parables about farming and scattering seed?

To answer this question, we have to do what Drs. Gordon Fee and Douglas Stuart call "the first task" of biblical interpretation. That is, to "discover the original, intended meaning ... to hear the Word as the original recipients were to have heard it." When we do that, it appears that Jesus' parables were often a product of his geography, unavoidably bound up with the Jewish society living in the region of Galilee during the first century. The parable of the farmer scattering seed is no exception.

For starters, Jesus grew up in the rural community of Nazareth, where my friend Dr. John A. Beck reports, "You ate what you grew and you wore clothing from local livestock." Second, most of Jesus' public ministry took place in and around Capernaum, a city about twenty miles from Nazareth. The two major economies of Capernaum were farming and fishing.

Fact is, Jesus spent most of his time ministering within a geographical radius of only about twenty miles or so in size, mostly in the Jewish villages along the western shore of the Sea of Galilee and in the hills of Lower Galilee. In that area, as well as in that society, farming (wheat and barley fields, olive groves, vineyards and more), would've been as normal and everyday to people as things like cars and the Internet are to us today. Recall, for instance, the conflict recorded in Matthew 12:1–2 that sparked when "Jesus was walking through some grainfields on the Sabbath. His disciples were hungry, so they began breaking off some heads of grain and eating them." The sight of grainfields and the knowledge of harvesting was so common that everyone involved—fishermen, tax collectors, carpenters, and religious elite—simply accepted and instantly understood what they were.

So when Jesus told a parable of a farmer scattering seed, to his hearers he was speaking their cultural language—and truthfully, the language of his own upbringing and geography as well.

Sources: HTR 27; ATR 40; RDA 179; DLJ 46

Parable of the Wheat and Weeds
Matthew 13:24-30

Why can't workers tell the difference between wheat and weeds in this parable?

Believe it or not, we actually know the kind of weed (called "tares" in some older translations) that Jesus was referring to in this parable. It was a toxic plant called darnel that was a common scourge to farmers in Jesus' day—and continues to be the same in our present time. In fact, one modern study of wheat harvests in Ethiopia showed that darnel made up nearly 10 percent of the crops. We also know, from ancient legal sources, that feuding farmers did sometimes seed a rival's fields with poisonous plants. So when Jesus told this parable, its details would've been common knowledge to his audience.

The cruelty of darnel is that, in its early stages, it looks exactly like wheat. One writer has even called it "wheat's evil twin." This is why the workers in this parable are unable to tell the difference between weeds and wheat. By the time wheat can be distinguished from its deadly doppelgänger, the roots of the weed have grown intertwined with the nearby wheat roots. There's no way to tear out the weed without destroying the good grain in the process.

Eventually darnel must be separated and eliminated, though, as Jesus indicated.

As it matures, darnel rots from the inside and is very dangerous for people to consume. In small doses, for instance, ground up and baked into bread, it's a mind-altering substance that causes dizziness and nausea similar to intoxication. In fact, the scientific name for it, *temulentum,* comes from the Latin word for "drunk." Ancient Greeks called it the "plant of frenzy" and used its hallucinogenic properties for ritual worship of Demeter and Persephone. In larger doses, darnel is actually a lethal poison, so it can't be allowed to mix with wheat forever.

Sources: CBS 1637; WET 1; NTE 27; ZP5 596

Parable of the Mustard Seed
Matthew 13:31–32

I'm not much of a gardener. What should I know about mustard seeds and this parable?

Let's see…

> A mustard seed was (and still is) so small it can be held, literally, on the tip of a finger—with plenty of room to spare.

> Jesus wasn't the first to use this seed as an example. In the first century, teachers and writers commonly referenced it to symbolize something that was very, very small.

> In ideal conditions, this tiny little seed can grow into a plant up to fifteen feet tall.

> The mustard seed is an annual plant. It grows, produces more seeds, dies, spreads, and grows again to be even larger as the new seeds take root.

> A fully mature mustard plant is large enough to attract birds that will nest within its branches. So Jesus wasn't kidding about that.

> In the symbolic context of Jesus' parable, the mustard seed represents the promise that, while the kingdom of heaven may seem so small as to be invisible, it is and always will be an unstoppable force that will dominate all of humanity in time.

> Renaissance scholar, Desiderius Erasmus paraphrased Christ's meaning for this prophetic parable this way: "The kingdom of God, precisely when it shall seem to be entirely extinct, that is when it shall extend itself most broadly."

Sources: SLU 358; VCEN 423; RCL 285

I get Jesus' main point of the mustard seed, but is there more symbolism in this parable?

For such a short text (only two sentences), the mustard seed parable contains a lot of food for thought. Here are a few to chew on:

Theologians like John Walvoord and Roy Zuck often connect this parable of Jesus with the parable of the cedar tree recorded in Ezekiel 17:22–24. That prophecy is messianic in nature, promising a coming kingdom from the descendants of David. Symbolically, it starts as a single, replanted branch and then grows to enormous size such that "birds of every sort will nest in it." Similarly, Jesus' mustard seed parable promises a messianic "kingdom of heaven" that starts small and grows to such a large size that "birds come and make nests in its branches." The reference to birds nesting in both the cedar and mustard plant are also significant, particularly in Ezekiel's description that they are "birds of every sort." The implication is that these birds symbolize the non-Jewish peoples—that God's messianic kingdom is intended to include all people groups, Jew and gentile alike.

Perhaps most important, the parable of the mustard seed reframes the work of the Messiah from one who arrives to impose an *established* kingdom to one who brings a *growing* kingdom. Dr. Leland Ryken and his colleagues explain, "Whereas [Jesus'] listeners probably expected God's kingdom to be inaugurated in a dramatic, earth-shattering manner, Jesus emphasizes that from the smallest of beginnings it will slowly grow to reach its full size."

This is an important distinction that's still misconstrued today, and a cause for people to dismiss faith in Jesus. Jewish author, Robert Schoen, speaks for many when he says, "When the Messiah comes, the world will no longer be a place of hunger, hatred, and injustice.... Jews do not believe, therefore, that the Messiah has come, and they do not recognize Jesus."

Interestingly enough, within forty years of Jesus' death and resurrection, the fledgling Christian faith—begun with a small group of ragtag disciples—had spread well into the Roman Empire. Just a hundred years or so later, by the end of the second century, the good news of Jesus had spread even farther into the known world of that time. A few thousand years after that, and Christ's Kingdom of Heaven is still growing in our day, every day.

Sources: BKO 1259; IMK 98; DBI 578; WIW 11; SLU 358

Parable of the Yeast
Matthew 13:33–35

Is this parable just a repeat of the parable of the mustard seed?

Well, if you look at the central theme of both the parable of the mustard seed and the parable of the yeast, then yes, they are pretty much the same. Both emphasize the idea of the unstoppable growth of the kingdom of God, starting with something small and expanding to something very large. However, there are nuances to this second parable that shouldn't go unnoticed.

First of all, yeast (or "leaven" in older Bible translations) is most often used biblically to illustrate negative consequences. For instance, Jesus warned his disciples to "Beware of the yeast [that is, the teachings and leadership] of the Pharisees and Sadducees" (Matthew 16:6). Similarly, the apostle Paul warned the people of Galatia against allowing legalism to infiltrate their religious practice because "false teaching is like a little yeast that spreads through the whole batch of dough" (Galatians 5:9). Jesus, on the other hand, rhetorically redeemed the symbol of yeast by having it stand-in for his own heavenly kingdom. This becomes more significant when we consider another nuance of the parable of the yeast.

In the ancient society of Jesus, gender roles were rigidly marked. Men worked in the fields, planting and harvesting—and we notice that, as recorded in Luke 13:19, Jesus specifically designated that it was a man who chose to plant the mustard seed. Women, by contrast, were rulers of the kitchen. It was in that domain where yeast was put into or excluded from a bread recipe—and we note that, according to both Matthew 13:33 and Luke 13:21, Jesus specifically says that it was a woman who chose to use yeast in making bread. The implication-by-example here seems to be that both women and men are equally welcome—and empowered—as workers invited to join with Jesus in helping his kingdom grow.

Source: DBI 498

Parable of the Wheat and Weeds Explained
Matthew 13:36–43

I'm a little unnerved by the idea that God refuses to separate "people of the Kingdom" and "people who belong to the evil one." What am I supposed to do with that truth?

It does take a certain amount of trust to accept that God has allowed us to live in this kind of dangerous circumstance—but that trust is not unwarranted. We can remember these things:

1. *God is faithful* to the end. He is not unaware of our difficulties, and he's already ordained the resolution to this problem (Matthew 13:40–43).

2. *God is gracious* to both "people of the Kingdom" and to "people who belong to the evil one." Remember, you once were also on the side of evil, destined for punishment until Christ redeemed you. He can, and will, do for those who are enemies what he did for you (1 Corinthians 6:9–11).

3. *God trusts you.* This "wheat and weeds" situation is not a one-sided affair. Just as we are trusting Christ to help us grow, he is trusting us to grow in him. After all, "God, who began the good work within you, will continue his work until it is finally finished" (Philippians 1:6).

So, what are you supposed to do with the truth of Matthew 13:36–43?

I like the wise advice that the late Bible teacher Dr. Warren W. Wiersbe gave in his commentary on this passage: "Our task is not to pull up the false, but to plant the true … We are not detectives but evangelists!… We must also sow the Word of God and bear fruit in the place where He has planted us." Amen!

Source: BEC 46

Parables of the Hidden Treasure and the Pearl
Matthew 13:44-46

What kind of treasure is Jesus talking about in this parable?

The Greek word for "treasure" in this parable is *thésauros*. Its usage and meaning in ancient times was fairly straightforward: it's a place where goods and precious items are collected.

In that era it was common to bury household valuables in order to hide them from thieves or invading armies. Archaeologists in Israel have uncovered "stashes" of this kind—buried, forgotten, and lost to their original owners. Stored in clay pots, or strongboxes, or other secure containers, inside they found valuables such as coins, precious gems, and fine pottery. So, the theory goes, perhaps a tenant farmer who was living and working on the property of a wealthy landowner, stumbled across a buried stash of coins, and sold everything to buy the property and gain the coins. Most think this kind of household *thésauros* was what Jesus was talking about—and that seems reasonably accurate.

There's one other remote speculation. For a treasure of such enormous value to be held in a container as small as a clay pot could seem odd. *Thésauros* in ancient contexts often referred to a room-sized storehouse of wealth. A number of classic writers, for instance, used that word to indicate riches on par with a royal treasury (Herodotus, Euripides, Plato, Aristotle, and more). So perhaps this treasure could have been some version of a large, underground storeroom of hidden wealth? Not likely, but possible. Still, that view is only speculation.

Sources: CWSN 49; TGE 290; ASB 1583; BIB 824; CBS 1638

What does the pearl represent in this parable?

Word-nerd alert! Sorry, but the language lover in me has to tell you this as the start of answering this question: There's an interesting difference between the parable of the pearl and the preceding parable of the treasure. In the parable of the treasure, Jesus says the kingdom of heaven is "like a treasure"—that is, an inanimate (albeit valuable) object. In the parable of the pearl, he says, the kingdom of heaven is "like a merchant" (or "merchant man" in some translations, as both words are there in the original Greek)—

that is, a living person who is searching for objects of value. This prompts the question: If the merchant represents the kingdom of heaven, what does the pearl represent? There are a few theories:

> The pearl represents the truth of the gospel as revealed to people (Matthew 7:6).

> The pearl represents the church, the collection of believers who will follow Christ. In this view, the "merchant man" represents Jesus, the literal embodiment of the kingdom of heaven.

> The pearl represents the faith legacy of the twelve patriarchs of Israel (Revelation 21:12, 21).

> Or it could be that I make too much of the linguistic distinction, and like the treasure parable, the pearl simply represents the precious greatness of God's kingdom found among people.

Sources: CWSN 49; DBT 312; NNI 1166

Parable of the Fishing Net
Matthew 13:47–52

What in the world is a "good fish" or a "bad fish"?

Biblical studies professor, Dr. Craig Keener, tells us that the Sea of Galilee in Jesus' time teemed with over twenty different kinds of fish. Laborers on the sea would cast a seine net (or dragnet) into the water to catch them. This was an enormous net about eight feet wide and up to hundreds of feet long. One side of it was weighted, to make that part sink to the bottom. Corks held afloat the other side, making something like a large tennis net or wall in the water.

Usually it took two boats to manage the seine net. Fishermen would position it in the water, then begin pulling it toward the shore, or pulling in the lower side with a rope to make a sort of "bag" that trapped fish inside. The good news was this caught a lot of fish. The bad news was it caught both good and bad fish.

According to Jewish dietary laws, good fish were clean, or kosher, meaning they had "both fins and scales, whether taken from salt water or from streams" (Leviticus 11:9). Bad fish were unclean: "Any marine animal that does not have both fins and scales is detestable to you" (Leviticus 11:12). Those bad fish were seen as disgusting, and good only for the rubbish heap.

With this parable, Jesus used his disciples' familiarity with the fishing trade and with Jewish dietary law to communicate that God's coming judgment would encompass people of all kinds.

Sources: CBS 1638; NMC 128–129; MAT 286

First in the parable of the wheat and weeds, and now in the parable of the fishing net, Jesus seems overly preoccupied with the concept of a literal, fiery hell. Is that really something to worry about?

Yes.

Source: Luke 16:19–31

Jesus Rejected at Nazareth
Matthew 13:53–58

What could Jesus have said while teaching in the synagogue that made people of Nazareth so offended by him?

Three of the gospel writers—Matthew, Mark, and Luke—include some version of this event in their history of Jesus. Mark 6:1–6 records pretty much the same information as Matthew, but Luke 4:14–30 fills in more detail.

According to Luke, Jesus went to the synagogue on the Sabbath, which was his known habit. Typically in a synagogue service, a selection of Scripture was read, followed by a Targum, or teaching/interpretation by one of the synagogue leaders. At this particular service, another leader handed Jesus a scroll containing the Old Testament text of Isaiah indicating it was expected that he'd teach the Targum. That's where things got a little dicey.

Jesus read from Isaiah 61:1–2, which was a prophecy of the Messiah. Then he had the audacity to declare, "The Scripture you've just heard has been fulfilled this very day" (Luke 4:21)—a claim that he himself was God's Messiah. Next, he insulted his hearers by saying they were unworthy of his miracles because "no prophet is accepted in his own hometown"

(Luke 4:24). This indicates that his hometown people had already rejected him before he even sat down to teach. To make things worse, for the reasoning behind his insults Christ cited Old Testament examples in which prophets performed wonderful miracles for hated, non-Jewish people—and left their fellow Jews to suffer.

The result was predictable: shock and outrage.

The people of Nazareth asked indignant questions of the "Who does this guy think he is?" sort and scoffed derisively at him and his family. Luke reveals that some formed a mob and even tried to kill him by pushing him off a cliff (Luke 4:29–30).

So, it was Jesus' as-yet-unproven, grandiose claim of being the Messiah, along with his insults of his audience in the synagogue that angered this hometown crowd so much.

Source: BKB 286-290

What does this mean: "He did only a few miracles there because of their unbelief"?

The connection between faith in Jesus and his miraculous outpouring is an interesting mystery. On the one hand, we know that Jesus often healed in direct response to a person's faith (see Matthew 9:20–22 and Mark 10:46–52, among others). At the same time, Jesus also worked miracles for people who had demonstrated little to zero faith in him.

For example, coming upon a funeral procession, Christ took the initiative and raised a widow's son, not because anyone asked for it, but because he wanted to do it (Luke 7:11–17). Likewise, he healed a lame man who had no idea who Jesus was—or what he could do (John 5:1–9). The demon-possessed men in Gadarenes screamed for Jesus to leave them alone, but Christ refused and healed them anyway (Matthew 8:28–34).

So when we read in Matthew 13:58, "And so he did only a few miracles there because of their unbelief," we have to ask the questions why, and what that means for us. There are two general theories.

> **THEORY #1:** *Jesus is prevented from performing miracles without the cooperation of our faith.* This "short-circuited" theory is a time-honored excuse whenever one has hoped for a miracle that doesn't come. The assumption is that we clearly didn't have enough faith or believe hard enough. This view, however popular, is inconsistent

with Scripture. Yes, Jesus does heal in response to faith—but just as obviously, he's not handicapped by any person's lack of faith.

> **THEORY #2:** *Jesus chooses not to reward intentional disbelief.* Notice that the people of Nazareth didn't struggle with timid faith or wavering belief. On the contrary, "they were deeply *offended* and *refused* to believe in him" (Matthew 13:57, italics mine). That's not a simple lack of faith, nor uncertainty of faith, nor even ignorance of faith. It's intentional disbelief that angrily, and foolishly, denies not only Christ's person, but also his power.

Though there are exceptions (the conversion of the apostle Paul comes to mind; Acts 9:1–19), it appears that in this situation Jesus chose not to force his miracles on those who were determined to despise him.

Sources: IB7 425; MAC 1454–1455

The Death of John the Baptist
Matthew 14:1-12

Was this Herod who killed John the Baptist the same Herod who tried to kill Jesus at his birth?

No, Herod the Great was the one who tried to kill Jesus at his birth. His son, Herod Antipas, is the one who killed John the Baptist.

When Herod the Great died, Rome installed Antipas as a "tetrarch" (which means literally "ruler of one-quarter") over the northern part of his father's kingdom. This made him king over Galilee in Israel, a position he held from roughly AD 4 to AD 39, and for most of Jesus' earthly life. History judges Antipas as a fairly competent ruler—after all, he did manage to stay in power for several decades—but also brands him as passive, indecisive, and weak. Jesus derisively called him a "fox" (Luke 13:32), and the gospel writers all paint him in unflattering terms. The tetrarch's first claim to infamy is reported in Matthew 14:1–12, where we learn he is to blame for the arrest and murder of John the Baptist. Antipas was also an enemy of Jesus (Luke 13:31), and responsible for cruel mockery and torture of Christ just before Jesus' execution (Luke 23:11). Herod Antipas's reign came to an inglorious end in AD 39. Browbeaten by his wife to demand the title of "king" from the Roman ruler, and betrayed by his nephew Agrippa, he was falsely accused of conspiracy against Emperor Gaius (better known as Caligula). This accusation was easily believed by the emperor that ancient historian, Seutonius, dubbed "the monster." Caligula imagined himself a god and was quick to torture and murder anyone he perceived as a threat to his supposedly divine rule. Antipas avoided execution at the hands of Caligula but was stripped of his kingdom and shamefully exiled to a remote part of Gaul (roughly present-day France), where he stayed until he died.

Sources: WOB 136-140; LEB 202; HER 313; EOR 62-63

I wonder why Herod Antipas at first was afraid to kill John because it might start a riot, but then not afraid at his birthday party. Would the crowds not be just as enraged at the senseless murder?

Antipas's actions at this point seem to be more about fear of political reprisals than fear of open rebellion. By the time of Matthew 14:1–12, John the Baptist had been imprisoned for about a year or so and, despite his obvious popularity, no crowd had assembled with violent demands for his release. That must have afforded some level of emotional security to Herod.

Meanwhile, Mark informs us that the people at Antipas's sleazy birthday party were, "high government officials, army officers, and the leading citizens of Galilee" (Mark 6:21). In other words, these were people who could actually overthrow Herod the tetrarch—and make it stick with the Roman overlords. The historian Josephus also reports that Antipas did believe John to be a seditious threat to power at some level. It's almost certain that view was shared by his army officers and government officials. When the young girl (who was probably only twelve to fourteen years old) did her dance and then asked for the head of John the Baptist on a platter, the partygoers looked to see what drunken Antipas would do. From their perspective, if he complied with her wish, he'd be keeping his word and also ridding them all of a known political and military threat. If he refused, then Antipas would've been viewed by them as weak and vulnerable, something that wouldn't sit well if messaged back to Rome.

So Herod Antipas was likely more afraid of political reprisals from the powerful insiders at his party than a possible rebellion from John's crowd of followers outside. That, it seems, is why he went through with the murder.

Source: ZB1 71, 90

Jesus Feeds Five Thousand
Matthew 14:13-21

Why did Jesus leave when he heard that John the Baptist had been executed?

Matthew tells us that "As soon as Jesus heard the news" of John the Baptist's execution, "he left in a boat to a remote area to be alone." The assumption is that by then, Jesus had returned to Capernaum, and then left Capernaum to sail across the northern tip of the Sea of Galilee. That short trip would've put him into a wilderness area somewhere outside of Bethsaida, on the northeast side of the sea. However, apparently Christ's destination wasn't a secret. Thousands of people in the surrounding area simply walked around the northern shoreline of the Sea of Galilee and were waiting for him by the time he arrived by boat.

Why did Jesus run away to hide in this place, or at least try to?

There are a few possible reasons. One, or all of them combined, may have prompted his movement.

> First, Christ may have wanted time alone to grieve the loss of John. We know he grieved with Mary and Martha over the death of Lazarus (John 11:32–36), so, grief over John would've been consistent with his character.

> Mark also indicates that Jesus took his disciples away just to give everyone a break from ministry. He emphasizes, "There were so many people coming and going that Jesus and his apostles didn't even have time to eat" (Mark 6:30–31).

> It's also possible that sneaking away was a security measure for both Jesus and the disciples. In the aftermath of John's beheading, it probably wasn't terribly safe for them to stay in the territory ruled by Herod Antipas. Would they be next on his list? Bethsaida was governed by Antipas's brother, Herod Philip. Antipas was unlikely to breach that border to arrest Jesus or his disciples.

Source: NIBC 142

How many people, including women and children, did Jesus feed that day?

According to all four gospel writers, there were at least five thousand men in the crowd that Jesus miraculously fed that day (Matthew 14:13–21; Mark 6:30–44; Luke 9:10–17; John 6:1–15)—but Matthew also points out that they didn't count women and children who were present.

Why count only men? In that era in Israel, women and children weren't allowed to eat with men in public, so they were almost certainly segregated into a different area of that remote setting. With the men all in one place, sitting in groups of fifty and one hundred (see Mark 6:40), they would've been easy to tally. Sadly, the others would've seemed unimportant to count—though Jesus still fed everyone, "unimportant" women and children included.

So how many people actually were there? We can only guess. If you assume that for every man present there was one woman and one child, that would've been an estimated fifteen thousand people who benefited from Christ's feeding miracle. Some experts in New Testament studies increase that number to around twenty thousand. But a more conservative estimate is that roughly ten thousand were miraculously fed bread and fish at this place.

Sources: ASB 1585–1586; ZB2 65

Jesus Walks on the Water
Matthew 14:22-36

This seems a little far-fetched, almost like a myth. Did Jesus really walk on water?

Aside from those who, as a presupposition, dismiss the entire Bible as myth, there aren't many who deny that this account in Matthew 14:22–35, or some version of it, was an actual historical event. The main question seems to be whether or not Matthew (and Mark and John) reported it accurately.

Most people fall into two camps on that question. Some believe that the disciples, including Matthew, Mark, and John, simply made a mistake when judging the distance. Others prefer the idea that Matthew, Mark, and John got it right when they reported this miracle over nature.

The argument of the first group is that it was late at night, the disciples were tired, and they were in the middle of a storm. When they saw Jesus walking, he was actually moving along the shoreline, but they mistakenly (superstitiously?) thought he was walking on the water. This view removes the need for a miracle, but it also has some inherent flaws:

> First, if Jesus were simply walking along the shoreline, that's not a terrifying event. Yet, even well after one would assume the disciples would've figured out the error, all gospel writers report being terrified by the sight, with no relief until Jesus steps into their boat … on the water.

> Second, this "made a mistake" view doesn't account for the report that Peter also walked on water—and then sank into water deep enough to make him call out for help. If he sank into water along the shoreline, there'd be no need to call for help because the water level would've been well below his head.

> Third, Matthew reports they were "far away from land" (verse 24). The Greek term used here is *stadious pollous*, which translates literally "many stadia." A single *stadion* is about six hundred feet—or the length of two football fields. "Many stadia" would be anywhere from one to three miles from land. That distance would've made it difficult for his disciples to even see Jesus on the shore, let alone hold a shouted conversation with him from the boat.

Finally, neither history nor scrutiny has judged Matthew a liar, which he would have to have been in order to fabricate a myth like this and present it as fact. To my mind, the most reasonable explanation is not that the disciples made a mistake, but that this event really happened, and it was a stunning miracle.

Sources: HAC 103-104; CWSN 53; NSC4 73, 83

Does the Bible teach that ghosts are real?

Matthew reports that when he and the other disciples saw Jesus walking on the water in the dark of night, they were terrified and assumed he was a ghost (Matthew 14:26).

Since the disciples clearly believed that ghosts were possible, some readers think this means that the Bible teaches ghosts do indeed exist in our world. Is that assumption biblically supported?

The Old Testament teaches that people have some kind of consciousness after death, but it doesn't teach that ghosts roam the earth. In those days people understood life after death as souls being held in a waiting area of sorts, a place called *Sheol* in Hebrew, which we typically translate as "the grave," "death" or occasionally "hell." *Sheol* in the Old Testament Hebrew is generally the same as the Greek word, *hades*, used in the New Testament.

According to biblical thinking, *Sheol/hades* was divided into two regions, one of which held righteous souls awaiting God's reward, and the other which held unrighteous souls awaiting judgment. This is the structure behind Jesus' story (which may or may not be a parable) of the rich man and Lazarus (Luke 16:19–31).

The Hebrew Scriptures record only one instance of a soul being called back from *Sheol*. That was when King Saul used a medium to try to communicate with the deceased prophet Samuel (1 Samuel 28:7–20). The results were predictably disastrous, and clearly an unnatural event. Other than that extreme exception, Dr. Lawrence O. Richards reports that "The Old Testament views the dead as powerless, unable to affect the world of the living for good or evil."

Despite that, by the time of the New Testament, pagan superstition had mixed in with Jewish belief and many people feared ghosts, believing that ghostly apparitions (*phantasma* in the Greek) could show up at any time to deceive and take vengeance on people. This *phantasma* superstition is what Jesus' disciples displayed when they saw him walking on the water.

Regardless of that, no *phantasma* ever shows up in the New Testament. In fact, the only time that word is used is in the telling of this water-walking event (Matthew 14:26; Mark 6:49). The closest thing is the moment of Jesus' heavenly transfiguration when Moses and Elijah appear and have a conversation with Jesus (Matthew 17:1–7). However, Scripture indicates that the two prophets were miraculously, physically present—not apparitions or ghostly appearances. This is attested to by the fact that Peter wanted to make physical shelters (tents) for each of them.

So, even though Matthew reports that Jesus' disciples superstitiously thought they might be seeing a ghost, it'd be error to translate that frightened response to mean that the Bible teaches ghosts exist. Scripture actually teaches otherwise. Jesus' story of the rich man and Lazarus indicates Christ himself didn't believe in ghosts that roam the earth. Paul taught that "to be absent from the body [is] to be present with the Lord" (2 Corinthians 5:8 KJV). And the writer of Hebrews taught us plainly, "Each person is destined to die once and after that comes judgment" (Hebrews 9:27).

Sources: RBD 430, 914; TGE 649

Jesus' Later Ministry

Jesus Teaches about Inner Purity
Matthew 15:1–20

So the disciples forgot to wash their hands before eating—why was that such a big deal?

These Pharisees weren't concerned with hygiene. They were upset that Jesus and his disciples weren't following their oral traditions, which they'd elevated to the point of holy law on par with the commands of Moses.

The code in question here was ritual hand washing, a symbolic act they believed made them more holy and pure. Neglecting this tradition, to them, was a terrible sin. In the Talmud, which collected their oral traditions into writing a century or so later, one rabbinic authority even taught that refusing to perform ritual hand washing was equal to having sex with a prostitute. So yeah, they took it seriously.

The Pharisees' expectation went like this: Before eating, men were supposed to get up and go to special jars filled with water that had been consecrated for holy hand washing. They were to pour a measure of the holy water over their hands as a ritual for purity. Only after they'd done that could they use those hands to eat.

You can imagine the logistical nightmares of this onerous obligation. First, great care had to be taken to make sure the water hadn't been used for any other purpose. Also, if something fell into the water, or perhaps something on a person's hands had discolored the water, it had to be replaced with more ritual water. The jars themselves had to be large enough to accommodate everyone at the meal. The amount of water for pouring had to be measured out to precisely, at least one and half eggshells full. (Anything less than that simply wasn't enough to purify.) After washing, the hand had to be raised to avoid letting any polluted water drip back into the jar. And so on and so forth.

Exodus 30:17–21 had specified that ritual hand washing was to be done by priests only, and only one time before each offering was made at the altar of the temple. Yet the Pharisees and their oral tradition had extended this ritual to the home and expanded it to be required multiple times during every meal. These tedious purifications were so frequent as to border on obsessive-compulsive behavior. Despite that, Pharisees insisted this was a true test of whether anyone loved God.

Jesus took great issue with this flawed opinion: "Listen," he said, "and try to understand. It's not what goes into your mouth that defiles you; you are defiled by the words that come out of your mouth" (Matthew 15:10–11).

Sources: SLU 307–308; RHW 1

Earlier in Matthew, Jesus said, "If you love your father or mother more than you love me, you are not worthy of being mine" (Matthew 10:37). Why is he changing his tune here?

In Matthew 10:37–39, Jesus advocates the primacy of God over all areas of life, including family relationships. Here in Matthew 15:1–9, Jesus again advocates the primacy of God over all areas of life—including God's command to care for family. The practice of the Pharisees that Christ railed against in this passage was something called *corban*. In the Old Testament, it referred to various kinds of offerings that were dedicated to God. For instance, cattle or sheep (Leviticus 1:2), silver, gold, grain, incense, and so on (Numbers 7). By the first century, *corban* had been corrupted by greedy tradition. Its meaning had changed to be something along the lines of property held in trust for God *someday*, but still available for any use by its original owner. Theologian Daniel Doriani explains how this scheme worked:

> The ploy said that if a parent asked a[n adult] child for material or financial help, and the child did not want to help, the child need only say "Corban" over the goods in question. That made the child's possession a gift, dedicated to God (cf. Mark 7:11–12). Since it was dedicated to God, it could not be given to or used by anyone else. Yet the child was free to deliver the gift to God many years later, so he could use it until then, even while his parents could not.

The Pharisees fully accepted the warped tradition of *corban*. By giving primacy to their selfish practices over God's command and intent for families, they did exactly what Jesus accused them of doing: "You cancel the word of God for the sake of your own tradition" (Matthew 15:6). The primacy of God in all areas was Christ's desire, both in this instance, and in his teaching recorded in Matthew 10.

Interestingly, the Mishnah (a collection of Jewish oral traditions written down years after the gospels were produced) appears to include an update to *corban* practice. According to the revised tradition, if the vow of *corban* left a person unable to support parents, that person was to go ahead and break that vow in favor of mom and dad.

Sources: RBD 248; REC2 40; HBD 181

The Faith of a Gentile Woman
Matthew 15:21-28

I know almost nothing about Tyre and Sidon. Can you fill me in a little bit?

Tyre (pronounced TIRE) and Sidon (pronounced SIGH-done) were two non-Jewish cities in ancient Lebanon, inhabited mostly by descendants of Phoenician peoples. These sister-cities were part of the Roman province of Syria in Jesus' time. In the Old Testament, Phoenicians were skilled sailors and well-known merchants/traders throughout the Mediterranean. They traveled as far as modern-day Spain and the southwest regions of Britain. Solomon hired Phoenicians to create his navy, and also used Phoenician labor and timber from Lebanon to build the Jerusalem temple.

Tyre was situated profitably beside the Mediterranean Sea, which was the primary source of its economy. The community lived both along the coast and on an island less than half a mile offshore. Tyre's claim to infamy was that Israel's wicked queen, Jezebel, came from there. In Jesus' day it was a busy seaport and commercial center. Today it's called Sur, in Lebanon, and sits about fifteen miles north of Israel's border.

Sidon, in our time, is called Sayda and it's located north of Tyre, about halfway between Israel's northern border and Beirut in Lebanon. Also a coastal city, in ancient days it was famous for its fine cedar wood, for its wine, and luxurious purple dyes. One of Solomon's many wives was from Sidon (maybe more), and it was a city outside of Judea that Herod the Great improved with beautifications.

Jesus called both Tyre and Sidon "wicked," but he also indicated that the gentiles there would've turned from their sins if they'd seen the miracles he did for Israel (Matthew 11:21–22).

Sources: WWA 347–348, 370; WWB 427–428; RDA 237, 240

Why was Jesus so cruel to the gentile woman?

Of all the questions in this book, I think this is one of the harder ones for me to answer, for two reasons. First, the whole episode just seems so out of character for Christ. Second, I am a descendant of the Arab world; my great-grandfather earned American citizenship for our family over a century ago by fighting for the US in the trenches of World War I. He, and my entire family since, are from Lebanon by heritage—the same area where this gentile (or Canaanite, in the original Greek) woman lived. When I read about this event, I hear the cries of a distant mother, someone to whom I could honestly be related. It breaks my heart when Jesus ignores her and infuriates me when he compares Jews to children and my people to dogs. Yet I also know personally of his kindness and love and cannot judge him wrong who had no sin (2 Corinthians 5:21; Hebrews 4:15). Why was Christ so cruel? I don't have a firm answer, so I'll just tell you what the teachers tell me:

> ❯ Some say this woman was part of an aristocratic class that made a habit of "appropriating" (stealing) much-needed grain from poor Jews living in Tyre and Sidon. They suggest that Jesus' off-putting behavior and mention of "bread" was to raise the issue of social injustice, and to challenge her to prove that she was sincere.

> ❯ Others believe Jesus was simply testing the woman's faith. As Reformed theologian Dr. Daniel Doriani explains it, "Real faith does not falter at the first obstacle, it perseveres."

> ❯ Some accuse Jesus of sharing Jewish prejudice, which was later broken down by the woman's persistence. Or possibly, he was not yet ready to have his earthly ministry encompass gentiles, as he said, "I was sent only to help God's lost sheep—the people of Israel."

> A repeated theme is that Jesus did this to mirror the awfulness of prejudice in the attitudes of his disciples. Always the master teacher, the thinking goes, his behavior was an object lesson to his disciples to teach that their prejudice against gentiles was contrary to his ultimate plan, which included the great commission: "Go and make disciples of all the nations" (Matthew 28:19).

> Dr. Charles Swindoll also believes that Jesus intended to "provoke the woman to demonstrate her persistence, not to crush her spirit." He points to the Greek word for dog used by Matthew to suggest the recorded conversation was more playful banter and less direct insult, which could explain why she felt comfortable enough to respond with a quick wit. The Greek language has two words for dog. *Kyōn* referred to filthy, scavenging, wild dogs. *Kynarion* was a term of endearment that referred to a little house pet, or a puppy. *Kynarion* is the word used in Matthew 15:26.

Regardless of Jesus' motivation, the fact still remains that in the end he complimented her publicly as a woman of great faith, and he did indeed heal her daughter. So which of these explanations above is the most likely? I have no idea. I guess we'll both have to choose for ourselves.

Sources: CSB 1159; REC2 50-51, 55; ILJ 128-130; SMA 331-332; WWB 427-428

Jesus Heals Many People
Matthew 15:29-31

According to Matthew, Jesus healed everybody back then. Why doesn't Jesus heal everybody now?

"They laid them before Jesus, and he healed them all." I've heard these words from Matthew 15:30 preached many times as proof that God *always* wants to heal the sick. You've probably heard that a time or two as well. And yet, our churches overflow with sick people, despite our prayers of faith and fervent teachings. Jesus does still heal people in this day and age. I've seen it happen, and even experienced a miraculous healing myself once (carpal tunnel syndrome anyone?). Jesus also *declines* to heal many people today—something else I've seen and experienced. Why?

The discomfort we feel when we compare Christ's ancient healing ministry to our experience today could be a problem of misdirected application. We read Bible verses like Matthew 10:30 and assume that what Jesus did in a *specific situation* should apply in *any situation* for us now. That leap of logic seems unwise.

Jesus pointed to his miraculous healings *then* as physical evidence that he, in the flesh, was divine in nature—proof that he is the Son of God and the Messiah that he claimed to be (Matthew 11:2–6; John 10:36–38). He also indicated that when he was no longer among us in the flesh, this kind of miraculous physical evidence wouldn't be so readily available. Recall that after his resurrection he said to doubtful Thomas: "You believe because you have seen me. Blessed are those who believe without seeing me" (John 20:29).

John's gospel immediately follows that statement of Christ with this commentary: "The disciples saw Jesus do many other miraculous signs in addition to the ones recorded in this book. But *these are written* so that you may continue to believe that Jesus is the Messiah, the Son of God" (John 20:30–31, italics mine). John's point here seems to be that we can take faith in Jesus because of the testimony of his past miracles, not because we are entitled to future miracles.

We also know that there were times Jesus simply didn't heal everyone. For instance, John 5:1–15 tells of a scene at the pool of Bethesda where "crowds of sick people—blind, lame, or paralyzed—lay on the porches" waiting for miraculous healing (John 5:3). Jesus healed only one man out of that crowd. Apparently, he left all the others untouched in their suffering.

The late Vineyard pastor, John Wimber, wrote of specific times in Scripture when God simply refused to heal his followers (2 Corinthians 12:7–10; Galatians 4:13–14; Philippians 2:25–27; 1 Timothy 5:23; 2 Timothy 4:20). "These exceptions," Wimber wrote, "indicate that one does not control God: prayer is answered by faith, not magic or human reward.... We have no right to presume that unless God heals in every instance there is something wrong with our faith or his faithfulness."

So why did Jesus heal everybody then and not everybody now? The answer, it seems, is because he wanted to then, and doesn't want to now. Healing was, and always is, in his hands alone—not in our presumptive demands.

Sources: EDB 330–331; KS 26–28

Jesus Feeds Four Thousand
Matthew 15:32-39

This sounds very similar to when Jesus fed five thousand people in Matthew 14. Are they just the same story, told in different ways?

This is one of those questions that gets asked a lot. From what I can see, very few question the historicity of Jesus feeding the five thousand, or Matthew's account of it, but some think that two miraculous feedings seems a bit far-fetched. They assume that with the feeding of four thousand, Mathew was just trying to puff up Jesus' reputation with an extra miracle, so they prefer to believe only one feeding occurred. But there are a few reasons why I believe both miraculous feeding accounts should be taken at face value.

First, if Matthew's intent were to deceive, he did what would appear to be a deliberately bad job of it. He placed the second feeding shortly after the first in his text. He included similar details, such as a few loaves of bread, a large crowd, and baskets for collecting scraps. And if his motivation was to bolster Jesus' reputation, there was no real need to invent a lesser feeding miracle when the first feeding was already such a stunning event. Reason suggests the second fictional event would've been something grander like, "The feeding of the six thousand!"

Second, there are several key differences between the two events. The location of the four thousand (discussed in more detail next), the number of people, the number of loaves of bread, the number of baskets of scraps, and so on. All of those details are consistent with the geography, population, and culture of that time, and the differences between them and the feeding of five thousand are distinct, but not unrealistic. Certainly not enough to brand them as intentional lies.

Third, it's significant that Mark's gospel places this feeding of four thousand people near the Decapolis (or the "Ten Towns"), on the east side of the Sea of Galilee (Mark 8:1–10). Bible historian John A. Beck reports that was "home to pigs and pagan excesses that were shunned by orthodox Jews." Matthew wrote for a Jewish audience, and had just quoted Jesus as saying, "I was sent only to help God's lost sheep—the people of Israel" (Matthew 15:24). A feeding miracle for the detestable gentiles immediately following that pronouncement would seem to discredit Matthew's writing among Jewish readers—unless it really happened.

Fourth, Mark reports that this crowd had been with Jesus for three days (Mark 8:2) and Matthew gives the reason why: Jesus was healing anybody and everybody who came to him (Matthew 15:30). That would certainly be enough incentive for a crowd of four thousand to gather around him. To borrow from the lingo of police investigations, Jesus had means, motive, and opportunity: he was likely guilty of the miracle.

Fifth, I find no record anywhere indicating that this account of feeding four thousand was ever disputed in Matthew's lifetime—nor that Mark's account was suspect. Given the intense opposition to Jesus and his fledgling church, a massive lie like this, if the event were fictional, would've been a prime target for exposure. Why did no one attempt that? Probably because there were literally thousands of witnesses to its happening. Children in the crowd were likely still living at the time of Matthew's writing, and some of the adults too—and most of their extended families would've heard about the event as well. Why attempt to dispute something thousands could testify about?

So, were the two miraculous feedings in Matthew really just one and the same thing? You know my opinion on that question. I guess now it's up to you to decide what your view is.

Sources: AST 1432, 1482; BKB 311–312; DHB 258–259

Leaders Demand a Miraculous Sign
Matthew 16:1-4

How bad was it to have the Pharisees team up with the Sadducees against Jesus?

Well, it wasn't good. The Pharisees were very influential in the homes and synagogues of Israel and could sway popular opinion with their edicts (see the commentary on Matthew 12:9–14). The Sadducees were Jewish aristocrats, and rivals to the Pharisees. When they uncharacteristically joined forces with the Pharisees, they added money and political power—backed by the Romans—to their opposition of Jesus.

In Christ's time, Sadducees (also called "chief priests") controlled the two most important institutions of Jewish society: the Jerusalem temple (known as Herod's Temple) and the Sanhedrin. The Sanhedrin was the governing political body for both the religious and legal issues of the Jews. The high priest of the Sanhedrin was given king-like authority—and was almost always a Sadducee.

These enemies of Jesus were known as much for their wealth and corruption as for their religious devotion. In fact, wealth seems to have been the number one "belief" of the Sadducees. They ran the temple for their own financial gain, scamming worshipers with bogus inspections and trumped-up money-changing fees. Those crimes, among others, had been established by Annas, a Sadducee high priest just before the time of Jesus' ministry, and were enforced by what Dr. Charles R. Swindoll describes as "an extensive organized crime network in the temple, not unlike a quasi-religious mafia."

Corruption in the temple was so brazen, it was commonly known as the "Annas Bazaar"—a system through which Sadducee leaders stole fortunes from their helpless countrymen. It's no surprise that of all the ruins of ancient homes discovered in Jerusalem, the Sadducee homes have been the most opulent.

Ancient chroniclers tell us the Sadducee high priest at this time, Caiaphas (Annas's son-in-law), was known for his many bribes, for sending thugs to steal "tithes" from farmers at harvest time, and for having people beaten who refused his shakedowns. Josephus, a first-century historian, sums up Caiaphas this way: "He knew how to get money." The tithes that his goons stole were supposed to go to poor priests working at the temple, but the high priest and his cronies kept those for themselves. The result was that some priests—literally—starved to death.

So why did Sadducees oppose Jesus so fiercely? Well, first of all, Jesus threatened their erroneous belief system; if Christ's teaching was right then most of what they lived and taught was wrong. Second, Jesus threatened their cozy relationship with Rome and the political and societal benefits that the arrangement provided. Probably most important, though, was this: *Jesus attacked them first*, in both his teaching and his actions.

Ray Stedman, a prominent Bible teacher in the latter part of the twentieth century, points out what many tend to overlook today:

If Matthew and John are correct regarding the timelines recorded in their gospels (and I believe they are) Jesus single-handedly drove the Annas Bazaar out of the temple *twice*—once at the beginning of his ministry, and once near the end (John 2:13–22 and Matthew 21:12–17). This violent act of Christ was a premeditated, direct attack on Annas, Caiaphas, and the whole corrupt Sadducee system. It shut down their crooked operations for at least a short time. One can see why that'd make enemies out of religious mobsters.

Interestingly, Sadducees disappeared from history within a lifetime after the execution of Jesus. Their wealth and power were inextricably tied to the Jerusalem temple. When it was destroyed by the Roman General Titus in AD 70, the Sadducees simply couldn't survive.

Sources: SLU 451; NIB 210, 1007; BIG 222-223; JOB 278-280; WOE 20; JHE 118-119, 137

What was the protocol behind the demand for a new sign? Was that an Old Testament thing or did they make it up?

First, we must understand that the demand for a sign by the Pharisees and Sadducees was not sincere. Yes, prophets in the Old Testament did occasionally offer signs as proof that God was using them, most notably Moses, Elijah, and Isaiah (Exodus 7:8–13; 1 Kings 18:16–39; Isaiah 7:10–12), so the Pharisees and Sadducees, didn't make that up. But Jesus had already performed numerous fantastic miracles. Those should have been all the signs they needed, but they chose to blind themselves to that.

Matthew tells us that the "Pharisees and Sadducees came to test Jesus" by asking for a sign. The intent was to provoke a response they could use to discredit Christ. It's possible they wanted to publicly accuse him of being a false prophet, tricking him into failing to perform a sign that he claimed he could do. Or they may have wanted to showily accuse him, again, of being in league with Satan. Or maybe they had something more violent in mind. For instance, in AD 45 (not long after Jesus' death and resurrection), a Messianic-style leader named Theudas promised to miraculously part the Jordan River, and he led a crowd out there. Rome responded quickly, unleashing soldiers to brutally quell what they perceived as a threat of rebellion. Similarly, in AD 56, another would-be Messiah from Egypt promised to miraculously bring down the walls of Jerusalem. Again, Roman legionnaires crushed that movement with extreme violence and speed. Maybe the Pharisees and Sadducees were asking for a sign like that, one that would bring the Roman forces down on Jesus the Messiah.

Sources: MFE2 2-3; MAT 261-262

Yeast of the Pharisees and Sadducees
Matthew 16:5-12

What is the "yeast" of the Pharisees and Sadducees?

In the literal, cultural context, "yeast" (better rendered as "leaven" in other translations) was a small lump of fermented bread dough that was kept to put into new bread dough to make it rise before baking. (Interestingly, this is still the method used today by many bakers around the world.) As we discussed with Jesus' parable of the yeast, its primary characteristic was unstoppable growth (Matthew 13:33–35).

However, Jesus used "yeast" in this teaching in Matthew 16 to represent corrupt moral influence, the kind that could easily spread unchecked if allowed to do so. Specifically, Jesus was warning his disciples to carefully guard against the untruths that the Pharisees and Sadducees spread through their teachings and practices. A little of that deceptive teaching was like poison that would multiply relentlessly through all of a person's life and community.

Sources: DOB 440; ABC 1010

Jesus seems really angry at his disciples for not understanding the symbolism of yeast. Does he feel that way about me too?

Well, the text does communicate that Jesus was frustrated during this encounter with his disciples, and we do have evidence that he occasionally expressed anger at others (Matthew 11:20–24 and 21:12–17, for example). It's risky, though, to assume this specific response in a unique situation applies to everyone, everywhere today. It's virtually impossible to duplicate that moment in your life today, simply because you're not one of Jesus' original twelve disciples who has spent years walking beside Christ physically and hearing him teach this in person, face to face, for the very first time.

And consider the context. Jesus' real anger as seen here, was toward the Pharisees and Sadducees and the deceptive danger they posed. In that situation, Christ's frustration expressed toward his disciples comes across more as parental correction than a wrathful outburst.

Even though Christ was obviously upset with his disciples in this moment, notice that his response to them was not punishment, but *patience*.

Instead of pronouncing judgment, he used a series of rhetorical questions to help them understand for themselves the truth of the situation. Then, after leading them in the right direction, as Dr. Daniel Doriani notes, "Jesus does something surprising, yet very wise. He does not explain his teaching at all, he simply repeats it. The disciples' ignorance is culpable but not incorrigible." With Jesus' help, the disciples quickly come to full understanding of what Jesus was saying.

If we're going to universalize anything from this Scripture passage, that's probably what it should be—that Jesus will be patient enough to help us understand his truth, even when we just don't get it at first.

Sources: SMB 17; REC2 72

Peter's Declaration about Jesus
Matthew 16:13–20

What did it mean for Peter to call Jesus the "Christ"?

Both history and geography are important in this moment that Matthew recorded. Let's start with the geography.

Caesarea Philippi was located roughly twenty-five miles north of the Sea of Galilee, near the base of Mount Hermon. It was a hotbed of pagan worship. Early Canaanites used this area in bloody service to Baal, a detestable god whose ritual worship included child sacrifice and group sex. When Greece took control, that area was rededicated with a shrine to Pan, a nature god whose worship ritual was dramatic for its drunkenness and orgies. During the Roman era, Herod the Great added to the area a temple in which people were expected to worship as a god his patron emperor, Caesar Augustus. It's notable that it was in this bastion of idol worship where Jesus asked his disciples, "Who do you say I am?" (Matthew 16:15).

Now, regarding history. When Peter spoke for the group and said, "You are the Christ, the Son of the living God" (Matthew 16:16 NKJV), he made a stark contrast to the polytheism of the pagan worship center where they stood, placing Jesus firmly within the monotheistic history of Israel that proclaimed only one God: "Hear, O Israel: The LORD our God, the LORD is one!" (Deuteronomy 6:4 NKJV). Theologian Robert Mounce explains why this is important:

Christos is the Greek translation of the Hebrew word for Messiah ("the anointed one"). Used with the article ["the"] it refers to the central figure of Old Testament expectation. By his confession Peter is saying that Jesus is the One who comes in fulfillment of Israel's hopes and dreams. He is the Son of the Living God.... Peter's use of the title was deeply rooted in a Hebraic background. When Jesus accepts Peter's ascription, Son of God, he reveals his own consciousness of a unique and intimate relationship with his heavenly Father.

It's unclear at this point how much Peter actually understood about his declaration. Matthew reports that a few minutes later he tried to reprimand Jesus for even talking about his upcoming death and resurrection (Matthew 16:21–23). Still, at this moment, Peter got it right.

Sources: NIBC 159-161; DOB 68; JHT 306; FCC 1

Gates of Hades? What's that about?

Jesus renamed Simon to Peter (meaning "rock") in Matthew 16:18, and continued by saying, "On this rock I will build my church, and the gates of Hades will not overcome it" (NIV). Some Bible versions translate "gates of Hades" as "gates of the underworld" or "powers of hell," although this phrase could also refer to a Jewish saying that more closely communicates, "powers of death." Still, these phrasings are close enough to be almost the same in meaning.

However, there's another interesting aspect to Jesus' words here that's more literal in the way it addresses pagan superstition about the spiritual realm. Standing where they were in Caesarea Philippi, Jesus and his disciples would've been in view of a famous cave cut into the rock of Mount Hermon. Bible geography expert, Dr. John A. Beck, tells us that the Romans believed this ominous opening was a demonic portal, a literal gateway to Hades, the underworld where dead souls were held captive.

So when Jesus told Peter, "The gates of Hades will not overcome," he may have motioned toward that superstitious cave opening to emphasize his divine power over all things, the living, the dead, and everything in between.

Sources: CEM 217; ATR 87

Was the binding and loosing thing that Jesus promised just for Peter, or for everyone?

There are different opinions about the scope of Jesus' meaning when he told Peter, "I will give you the keys of the kingdom of heaven; whatever you bind on earth will be bound in heaven, and whatever you loose on earth will be loosed in heaven" (Matthew 16:19 NIV). Still, read within the context of this Scripture itself and rabbinic cultural tradition, most agree that Jesus was talking about "permitting" or "prohibiting" access to news of God's kingdom in some fashion.

Dr. Craig Keener sees in these verses the idea that Jesus was speaking physically to Peter at this moment, but also speaking metaphorically of Peter representing the church that would come after him (verse 18). From this perspective, Jesus is declaring that the church will have the authority to proclaim the message of Christ's redemptive work. In that way, the secrets of the gospel are bound or loosed, depending on the faithfulness of Christians to share about Jesus.

Still others see this verse as a prophetic utterance that foretold Peter's role in preaching of the resurrected Christ. Thus, binding and loosing would refer to the way that Peter historically opened the gospel to the world at key moments of the early church. Michael Wilkins, professor of the New Testament at Talbot Theological Seminary, explains this view:

> Peter, as the representative disciple who gives the first personal declaration of the Messiah's identity, is the one in the book of Acts who opens the door of the kingdom to all peoples (Acts 1:8). On each of three occasions [in Acts], it is Peter's authoritative preaching and presence that opens the door to the kingdom—first to Jews (ch. 2), then to Samaritans (ch. 8), and finally to Gentiles (ch. 10).

So was the binding and loosing thing that Jesus promised just for Peter, or for everyone? I lean toward Professor Wilkins's view. What do you think?

Sources: AST 1433; IBB 90; CEM 218; ZB1 103

After all that they'd seen and done, why did Jesus forbid his disciples from telling people he was the Messiah?

You're not the first to ask this question! In fact, it's a theological conundrum called "The Messianic Secret." No one can say for sure why

Jesus wanted to keep his identity hidden, but here's the speculation:

> The messianic secret is a literary style of dramatic irony the Gospels use to increase the interest and awe about who Jesus really is.

> It was a practical consideration because it was a time when the authorities distrusted charismatic leaders. So, keeping a low profile would've been the wise move.

> It was intended to prevent confusion among the people, because Jesus' role as the suffering Messiah couldn't be fully understood until after his death on the cross and his resurrection from the dead.

> It was just the gospel writer's way of trying to explain why Jesus was not accepted as Messiah until after the resurrection.

> Messiah was a kingly title, and Jesus was not "coronated" as the Davidic king until after his death on the cross.

> It was part of the tradition of Old Testament prophets who accomplished their missions by working in stealth, not in loud showy ways for their own glory.

> Jesus' role as Messiah was vastly different from any of the political views about messiahs in his day, and thus calling himself Messiah in that context would've been an inadequate definition for him until after his resurrection.

Sources: JAN 68; IBB 133–134

Jesus Predicts His Death
Matthew 16:21–28

Does the Greek word for "cross" in "take up your cross" only literally mean a death-torture device, or could it mean something else?

I'm sorry to report that the Greek word Matthew used here was *stauros*, which was only literally the death-torture device used by the Romans (and before them, by Phoenicians and Greeks).

It would've been shocking for any of Jesus' disciples to hear that he must "take up your cross, and follow me" (Matthew 16:24). Christ was referring to the cruel practice that required the condemned person to carry the heavy crossbeam (the *patibulum*) to the place where it would be used to murder him. Nineteenth-century Greek linguist, Dr. Joseph H. Thayer reported that, with rare exceptions, the cross was used to execute only the worst criminals, slaves, and insurrectionists. All of Jesus' disciples would've known these things and, in fact, some were indeed crucified in later years, including Andrew and Peter.

At the same time, Jesus was also clearly delivering a metaphor of the great sacrifice symbolized by the cross. Luke, when reporting on this scene, includes a fuller quote by Jesus saying, "Take up your cross *daily*, and follow me" (Luke 9:23, italics mine). The apostle Paul expanded on this metaphor when he said, "My old self has been crucified with Christ. It is no longer I who live, but Christ lives in me" (Galatians 2:20).

The message seems to be clear. Although physical death at the hands of Christ's enemies is always a possibility, we must also live each day prepared to sacrifice ourselves in service to Jesus, enduring suffering with the same determination he did.

Easier said than done, I think—and impossible without the power of his Holy Spirit to help.

Sources: CWSN 60; TGE 586; HSJ 150-151; NAS 1277-1280

The people standing around Jesus all died before he came back "in his kingdom." Was Jesus mistaken, or is there an explanation for this?

Matthew 16:28 does record Jesus as saying, "Some standing here right now will not die before they see the Son of Man coming in his Kingdom."

The first reference, "some standing here" obviously indicates at least one of his disciples. The second reference, "coming in his Kingdom" is less clear. That phrase in Greek translates literally as, "coming with his reign." It could mean his physical second coming as described in 1 Thessalonians 4:16, or it could mean something different that has similar attributes.

None of Jesus' disciples saw Christ's physical second coming, simply because it hasn't happened yet, and they are all now dead. Some conclude that's reason enough to dismiss this passage, or Jesus, or Christian faith, or the Bible, or all of the above. But that's an extreme position that doesn't take into account at least four other legitimate conclusions about Jesus' prophetic statement about himself.

First, at least one disciple, John, did in fact "see" Christ physically "coming with his reign." He wrote about that dramatic vision extensively in what we call Revelation, the last book in our New Testament.

Second, all of Jesus' disciples (except Judas Iscariot) saw Jesus after his death and resurrection. That absurdly impossible return to life could easily be interpreted as Christ "coming with his reign," as it demonstrated forcibly his deity and power over life and death.

Third, Matthew reports that only six days after Jesus made this statement, Peter, James, and John all witnessed firsthand a miraculous transfiguration in which "Jesus' appearance was transformed so that his face shone like the sun, and his clothes became as white as light" (Matthew 17:2). Peter wrote about that moment when he testified that "We saw his majestic splendor with our own eyes" (2 Peter 1:16). The transfiguration of Christ was a stunning preview of glory which can also legitimately be a description of Jesus "coming with his reign."

Fourth, at the day of Pentecost, Christ's Holy Spirit came upon his disciples in an extraordinary display, ushering in our modern era where God's kingdom rules over the hearts and lives of believers. Again, all the disciples (except Judas) saw and experienced firsthand this fantastic event of Jesus "coming with his reign."

These four historical events took place within the lifetimes of Jesus' disciples, and any one of them could have been what Christ prophesied—or all of them together, or even something else entirely. All that to say: No, Jesus wasn't mistaken. If there are doubts about this prophecy, it's more likely error (or bias) on our part rather than his.

Sources: BAH 291-292; HSJ 153-155

The Transfiguration
Matthew 17:1-13

Why was it significant that Moses and Elijah were the ones who met with Jesus when he was transformed?

Well, the appearance of Moses and Elijah with Jesus was certainly not an accidental pairing. The question is whether it was meant as a symbol for us or was simply a practical meeting for Jesus. But before we get into that, it's worth noting a few key things about this incredible meeting on a mountaintop.

First, every account of this transfiguration in the Gospels presents it as a literal, physical event (Matthew 17:1–13; Mark 9:2–13; Luke 9:28–36). Although we know that Moses and Elijah are deceased, not one of the gospel writers even hints at the idea that they appeared before Jesus as ghosts or disembodied spirits. Simon Peter's offer to build shelters for each of them also attests to that fact (ghosts wouldn't need a roof over their heads!). Nor was this just a vision or a dream. In fact, Luke records that this visitation woke up all three disciples from sleep. In some miraculous way, perhaps in the way angels appear and disappear, Moses and Elijah were physically present in this moment.

Second, the appearance of the long-dead Moses and Elijah vividly demonstrates the eternal nature of the human soul. It also indicates that each soul is unique to itself, not reincarnated or recycled into multiple lives or beings. There was one Moses and one Elijah, and those unique individual people retained their own selves, even after death.

As for the significance that Jesus was visited specifically by these two Old Testament heroes, there are a few theories. Dr. Tony Evans sees Moses and Elijah, along with Peter, James, and John, as symbols of the unifying work of Christ. In that view, Moses represents the Old Testament Law, Elijah represents the Prophets, and the disciples represent the New Testament. "Thus, the Old and New Testaments are both centered on Jesus."

Similarly, Craig Keener teaches that, "This passage includes so many allusions to God revealing his glory to Moses on Mount Sinai that most ancient Jewish readers would certainly have caught them." Jewish belief in that time expected that both Elijah and Moses would return as a sign of God's coming kingdom, so the sight of those two with Jesus would have confirmed that Jesus was the Messiah.

And, of course, there was one other significant participant to this conversation: God the Father spoke from the cloud (again, reminiscent of God speaking to Moses at Sinai), affirming that Jesus was (and is) indeed the Son of God.

Sources: IBB 91, 158; TEB 979

What did Moses and Elijah say to Jesus at his transfiguration?

We don't have a record of the actual conversation that took place at the time of Christ's transfiguration. However, we do have the benefit of multiple author viewpoints reporting on the same event.

Matthew and Mark give roughly the same summary, writing simply that Moses and Elijah "appeared and began talking with Jesus" (Matthew 17:3; Mark 9:4). Luke, though, was able to give a little more insight as a result of his "having carefully investigated everything" (Luke 1:3). According to Luke's report, Jesus, Moses, and Elijah "spoke about his [Jesus'] departure, which he was about to bring to fulfillment at Jerusalem" (Luke 9:31 NIV). The Greek word translated as "departure" in Luke 9:31 is familiar to us because it's also used to describe the departure of the Israelites from slavery in Egypt: *exodus.*

Acknowledging *exodus* and Luke's reference to Jesus' coming execution in Jerusalem, New Testament professor N. T. Wright believes that the conversation at the transfiguration was saying that, "In other words, Jesus' death will be the new, true, 'exodus,' consequent upon Israel's God 'visiting' his people at last."

Sources: NTI 621

Jesus Heals a Demon-Possessed Boy
Matthew 17:14-21

Jesus was pretty harsh on his disciples for not being able to cast out a difficult demon. Was that warranted?

First, it's important to distinguish that Jesus' outburst about a "faithless and corrupt people" (verse 17) was not directed at his disciples, but toward the watching crowd and, by extension, to Israel as a whole. Still, you're right, it was a harsh condemnation of those people, even if it was deserved.

We can reasonably assume that the crowd's disbelief and fickle self-interest were what prompted his frustration. It was a stubborn "unfaith" that persisted despite all Jesus had done and shown to them. In that sense, some see Jesus here as making himself a symbol of, and successor to, Moses.

Remember when Moses went up on Mount Sinai and received the law from God (Exodus 32:1–29)? As he came down the mountain, he found the people had grown faithless and corrupt. While Moses was gone, they'd created an idol, a large golden calf. Moses's response was fury and violence. The similarities are there in Matthew 17:14–21 as well. Jesus, like Moses, went up a mountain where God's glory was revealed. Then upon returning from that peak, he found that faithlessness had bloomed while he was gone. So yes, Jesus' outburst is understandable.

However, this still doesn't answer what I think is the deeper, more personal question we really want to know: *Is our Christ allowed to act emotionally toward us?*

The gospel accounts make it clear that Jesus is emotional, whether we want him to be or not. In the pagan world of that time, an emotional god meant scandalous displays of capricious and abusive behavior. Jesus, however, doesn't fit that mold. Unlike us (and the false gods we create), he alone is able to express emotion without making it sinful (Hebrews 4:15; 1 John 3:5). As Daniel Doriani describes it, "Jesus had the power to become angry without becoming enraged, the power to love a woman without lusting after her."

It's also the emotionality of Jesus that gives us the courage to approach him honestly with our feelings, knowing he understands and will respond with empathy. As the writer of Hebrews told us, "This High Priest of ours understands our weaknesses, for he faced all of the same testings we do, yet he did not sin. So let us come boldly to the throne of our gracious God. There we will receive his mercy, and we will find grace to help us when we need it most" (Hebrews 4:15–16).

Sources: IMT 201-202; BTC 216; REC2 119

Since no one has ever moved a mountain, does that mean that hope for "faith even as small as a mustard seed" is unrealistic?

If we interpret Jesus as speaking literally here, then yes, it's apparently unrealistic. However, most would agree that he was speaking with hyperbole, using intentional exaggeration to make a point. Matthew records that Jesus commonly did that, for instance, when he spoke of people who had logs in their eyes (Matthew 7:3) or when he accused the Pharisees of swallowing a camel while straining out gnats (Matthew 23:24). The point of Jesus' hyperbole about moving mountains seems not to be that faith should be small or large, but that just the presence of faith in him is enough to accomplish seemingly impossible things.

Mark's account of this story can be helpful in understanding Jesus' teaching because it gives a few more details (Mark 9:14–29). Let's recap: A father begs Jesus to free his son from a demon that causes something akin to epileptic seizures. The father is unsure, saying to Jesus, "If you can do anything, take pity on us." Jesus regards the father curiously, answering, "'If you can? Everything is possible for one who believes." The father cries out, "I do believe; help me overcome my unbelief!" It's worth acknowledging that Jesus didn't immediately respond to the father's request for healing—but he did respond without delay to the man's request for faith. And what did he do then? He cast out the previously impossible-to-exorcise evil spirit, and quite possibly raised that man's son from the dead.

Can you imagine the faith that swelled in that helpless father when he saw his son healed, restored, and safe? In that act of healing, Christ bolstered faith, answering the man's plea for Jesus to "help me overcome my unbelief!" Then, only moments later, while debriefing his disciples about that specific exorcism, Jesus announced "faith even as small as a mustard seed" was all that was needed for impossible miracles such as mountain moving—something that's equivalent, perhaps, to the casting out of unmovable demons (Matthew 17:20). As Daniel Doriani puts it, "Even a little faith is enough if it relies upon the great God. Faith can move a mountain, not because of the strength of our faith but because of the strength of our Lord. That is why a little faith is enough."

So the context of verses 14–21 seems to indicate strongly that Christ was pointing his disciples to that father's doubt-filled, tiny faith (that they'd just witnessed firsthand) as an object lesson expressed through hyperbole. That was the truth to be taken from this teaching, not necessarily that a *literal* mountain had to be moved in order to prove Christ's point.

Given their history after his resurrection, it appears the disciples got the message.

Sources: ZB1 109; SLU 407–408; REC2 122

Jesus Again Predicts His Death
Matthew 17:22-23

Did Jesus have a death wish?

Well, I don't know that "death wish" is the right choice of words, but it'd be difficult to say that a sacrificial death was not Christ's intention. Perhaps, "purposeful life wish" that must end in death?

Matthew 20:28 records Jesus telling his disciples that his purpose was "to give his life as a ransom for many." John 12:23–32 also documents Jesus speaking to a crowd about his impending death, alluding that he would be "lifted up" on a cross, and saying "*this is the very reason I came*" (italics mine).

Additionally, some of Jesus' actions seem calculated to facilitate his march toward crucifixion. For instance, his violent attacks on the corrupt Sadducee money-making system at the temple appear to be intentionally provocative (Matthew 21:12–17; John 2:13–17). "No one could make a commotion in the temple," says one Dr. Craig Keener, "and challenge the priestly elite, as Jesus did, and *not* expect to be executed … Jesus intended to die."

Mark 14:53–65 also reports that during the trial before the Sanhedrin, Jesus said nothing in his defense while his accusers floundered. Finally, only once, he spoke up. In just two short sentences, he basically pled guilty to the "blasphemy" charges leveled against him, announcing that he was "the Messiah, the Son of the Blessed One." Without that deliberate confession, there wouldn't have been enough evidence to convict and execute Jesus. One has to expect Christ knew how his judges would react to his defiant confession; one might also reasonably assume he intended to provoke that reaction.

So, no matter what we decide to call it, the basic fact is that Jesus did exactly what he set out to do: "The Son of Man came not to be served but to serve others and to give his life as a ransom for many" (Matthew 20:28).

Sources: CBS 1644-1645

Payment of the Temple Tax
Matthew 17:24-27

Does Jesus' example suggest it's OK to cheat on your taxes?

The short answer to that question is: No. For the longer answer, maybe a little cultural context will help us better understand Christ's actions.

The temple tax wasn't a governmental tax in the same way we understand taxes today. It was an offering to God, instituted by Moses, that covered expenses associated with maintaining the "tent of meeting" (Exodus 30:11–16). The importance of this offering, though, was significant—so much so that it was originally called *kôpher* in Hebrew, which translates figuratively as "ransom" or "redemption price." In this context, it makes much more sense that Jesus equated the temple tax with conquered peoples paying ransom to kings.

Eventually, this "ransom" was simply regarded as an annual, religious "tax" to be paid by every Jewish man aged twenty or older. In Jesus' time, this tax funded the upkeep and daily operations of the revered Jerusalem temple.

This is where things got a little dicey for Peter. When the tax collectors asked him, "Doesn't your teacher pay the Temple tax?" (verse 24), it was a challenge as much as a question. If Jesus didn't pay the tax, it would've been construed as tantamount to disowning Israel's God and history, and the sacred religious authority of the temple. Peter told the collectors that yes, Jesus did pay the tax, but the subtext here suggests that *maybe* Jesus didn't, and *maybe* Peter was just covering for his master out of fear.

In the end, Jesus complied, miraculously paying the tax for both he and Peter. The miracle—finding a coin in a fish's mouth? *What?!*—is absurd on the surface. What's often overlooked is that this miracle was evidence of the implicit claim Jesus had made to Peter just moments before: By demonstrating complete control over the randomness of nature, Christ proved that he was the divine authority for *everything*—the Spirit-embodied King over creation, over the Jerusalem temple, and the entire Jewish religious system as well.

Sources: VGG 56–57; CWSO 231; NSC3 66

The Greatest in the Kingdom
Matthew 18:1-9

When discussing greatness, what did Jesus want his disciples to see in this small child?

Many sermons have been preached on this passage, and much has been made about the character of a child and how we are to imitate a child's innocence. We must become teachable, or guileless, or responsive, or obedient, or trusting, or … fill in the blank with some positive adjective. There's a place for that kind of teaching, to be sure—but I don't see that meaning at all here.

In this gospel account, Jesus appears to be using an object lesson to demonstrate *position*, not character. The disciples had asked about hierarchies in heaven, no doubt trying to figure out how they could hold the greatest places in eternity (Mark 9:33–36; Luke 9:46–48). His response was to spotlight the lowest position in the culture of that time: *the child*.

In that context, to "become like little children" (Matthew 18:3) would've meant to voluntarily forego the significant rights and privileges associated with being an adult man in an intensely patriarchal community. That would've been a bitter pill for Christ's disciples to accept. The child in ancient Israel was effectively powerless, and therefore insignificant or unimportant in the social strata of that day. In fact, when Jesus tells his disciples to become "humble as this little child" (verse 4), the Greek verb for "humble" is from the root, *tapeinos*, which in Greek culture referred to the shamefully powerless ones of society.

So what did Jesus want his disciples to see in the example of the small child? In order to be truly great in the kingdom of heaven, they must abandon any ambition for greatness. Instead, Christ's followers must deliberately choose to make themselves powerless like a child—completely dependent on God for help and favor.

Sources: PHS 204-207; NTL 69

Is hell a literal, fiery place?

This is one of those questions I dislike answering, just because I hate my conclusion. I can make no claim for understanding God's "why" behind hell, nor the specifics of the experience of it. But I can't ignore that Jesus spoke frequently about hell—and that he seemed to view it as a literal, fiery place.

The Greek word used for "hell" in Matthew and the New Testament is *gehenna*. It was a symbolic reference to a literal place: the Valley of Hinnom, located just south of Jerusalem. In times of ancient kings, this valley was where some Israelites detestably murdered their children in sacrifice to idols. In Jesus' day, this *gehenna* was basically a large garbage dump that was always smoldering, where "the maggots never die and the fire never goes out" (Mark 9:48). Here the city's refuse mixed with corpses of condemned criminals, burning to ash and completely abandoned. This is the hell that Jesus described.

C. S. Lewis said of hell, "There is no doctrine which I would more willingly remove from Christianity than this, if it lay in my power. But it has the full support of Scripture and, specifically, of Our Lord's own words." As to whether that hell is "purely mental existence" or "a world or reality," Lewis refused to speculate except to say, "It will be as actual as—as—well, as a coffin is actual to a man buried alive."

My friend and scholar, Len Woods, also offers this sobering insight which seems a fitting way to end this section of commentary:

> Hell—not simply the word but the terrible truth it represents—ought to cause us sleepless nights. The biblical descriptions of a place of unquenchable fire (Matthew 5:22), utter darkness (Matthew 22:13), and ceaseless, restless torment (Revelation 14:10-11) are horrible beyond words. Even if one regards these images as symbolic or metaphorical, the reality of hell is infinitely worse than we can grasp for this one reason: Hell is the logical destination for those who want nothing to do with God.

Sources: CSLB 821, 1072; IWB 168-169

Cut off your hand or foot, and pluck out your eye? This seems extreme. What does your hand or foot have to do with the temptation to sin?

This is another example of Jesus using hyperbole to emphasize a point for his hearers. That's a rhetorical strategy that uses obvious exaggeration to evoke an emotional response—something Christ did on several occasions (see Matthew 6:3 and Luke 14:26–27, among others).

The teaching here was never intended to be taken literally, not even by Jesus, as is evidenced by the ensuing lives and leadership of his apostles. For example, Paul called himself the worst of sinners (1 Timothy 1:15) yet slicing off appendages was never prescribed for his sins—nor for the sins of any other of Christ's followers.

Still, it's worth noting that this is the second time Jesus used this particular hyperbolic statement. Matthew records him saying it previously during the famed Sermon on the Mount (Matthew 5:29–30), so the point was clearly important to him. What was this extreme exaggeration supposed to teach his disciples?

"Jesus wasn't advocating literal self-mutilation as a solution for removing stumbling blocks in our lives," says Pastor Chuck Swindoll. "Rather, He wanted His followers to have uncompromising standards when it came to temptation and sin."

Sources: QST 1359; SMB 73

Parable of the Lost Sheep
Matthew 18:10-14

Does Matthew 18:10 support the idea that all children have guardian angels?

This passing statement by Jesus has been used as the primary proof-text for belief in guardian angels, along with Acts 12:15.

Theologians like Dr. Louis Berkhof, however, say these verses are flimsy evidence on which to base the larger doctrine. Others, like the sixteenth-century Reformer John Calvin, are skeptical of the idea but unwilling to rule out guardian angels completely. Calvin wrote, "When Christ says that the angels of children always behold the face of his Father, he insinuates that there are certain angels to whom their safety has been entrusted. But I know not if it can be inferred from this, that each believer has his own angel."

Calvin does acknowledge, however that early church fathers held "a common belief that every believer has a single angel assigned to him." This was consistent with the Hebrew culture of Jesus' time that also affirmed a belief in at least one guardian angel for every Jewish person.

As for me, I'm inclined to believe that guardian angels do exist and work in concert with the greater angelic host to fulfill God's intentions toward his people. I see that as an easy logical assumption from Matthew 18:10 and other Scriptures (for instance, 2 Kings 6:15–18; Psalm 91:9–11; Luke 16:22; Acts 12:15, among others). The existence of guardian angels is also something that's consistent with Christ's character and care as revealed in Scripture.

Ron Rhodes, expert in angelology, sums it up well, I think:

> Whether each of us has just one angel watching over us or many, we cannot say for sure. Yet one thing is certain: If we as Christians were more fully aware of God's provision of angelic protection ... we would most certainly be less fearful.

Sources: ST 147; ICR 94; AAU 167-168, 170; IBB 93

If God is all-powerful, and his will is that no one should perish, then why do people perish?

Ah, now we must finally enter the age-old debate of predestination versus free will in regard to the human soul. Yours is a question that's been asked for centuries, hotly debated yet without any obviously definitive consensus.

With that in mind, I won't try to give you anything more than prominent opinions, then my uncertain opinion, and then you can decide for yourself what you think is best.

The crux of this debate goes as follows: Scripture teaches that whatever God wants to do, he does (Job 23:13, among others). Scripture also teaches that God wants no one to perish, but desires *all* to return to him (Matthew 18:14; 2 Peter 3:10). Yet the reality is that billions upon billions have "perished" in the spiritual sense. Why is that?

There are two general schools of thought:

1. *Free will rules over God's will.*
   This belief is widely held, particularly in the Western world, and has been for centuries. In this view, the blame for unrescued souls rests squarely on the idea that every person has complete free will to choose or not choose God's way. This is not because God can't overrule free will, but because he won't. Nineteenth-century theologian A. Lukyn Williams summed up the "free will rules" view

of Matthew 18 like this: "It is inconceivable that anyone can hold the doctrine of the eternal reprobation of certain souls. The whole passage is opposed to the theory of irrespective predestination."

2. *God's will rules over free will.*

Historically, this is the other popular perspective. It takes the view that all people are so depraved by sin that no one can choose God unless God first regenerates the soul to make that choice possible. They point to verses like John 6:44 and Romans 9:16 to conclude, "God predestined particular individuals to salvation on the basis of his own glory, not on the basis of any human choice or work."

My opinion falls more in line with option #2 above—though I can see why others reasonably disagree with me on that.

As for Jesus' pronouncement that "it is not my heavenly Father's will that even one of these little ones should perish," I think Luke's gospel sheds some light on that. It's informative to me that both Luke 15:3–7 and Matthew 18:12–14 tell a parable of a lost sheep—but the sheep symbolizes a different group in each telling (which also indicates that Jesus probably told this parable more than once).

In Luke, Jesus makes it clear that the wayward sheep represents a "lost sinner." The statement of the Father's will is conspicuously absent. In Matthew's record, though, Jesus presents the wandering animal as an obvious representation of a believer—specifically one of the "little ones" he has just been using as an object lesson of faith for his disciples (Matthew 18:1–10). Only in Matthew's context is the statement included that "it is not my heavenly Father's will that even one of these *little ones* should perish" (italics mine).

This suggests to me that God has different expectations (and thus outcomes) for "lost sinners" and his "little ones." While both may stray, God won't allow any "little one" to perish because that would violate his sovereign will. Peter's second epistle seems to support this view as well. His stated audience for this letter is believers. He says at the opening: "I am writing to you who share the same precious faith we have…" (2 Peter 1:1). Then in 2 Peter 3:9 he emphasizes that God "is being patient *for your sake.* He does not want anyone to be destroyed" (italics mine). Like the Matthew 18:14 pronouncement, God's will here seems to be clearly applied exclusively to believers, not to "lost sinners."

Of course, I have friends who disagree with me on this point, and maybe you do too. So now I leave you to your own "free will," to decide for yourself which perspective you prefer.

Sources: PCXV 211; PRO 166; ESB 1858

Correcting Another Believer
Matthew 18:15-20

Is the church today still supposed to practice discipline as outlined in Matthew 18? And if so, does that mean the church decides the salvation of the person being disciplined?

In broad strokes, the answer to the first part of your question is yes. Both this passage and Paul's instruction in 1 Corinthians 5:1–13 indicate that this process applies to the church at large, not just to a specific time and circumstance. Matthew outlines the proper procedure, while 1 Corinthians shows a real-life example. In both cases, it's a method for Christian people to enact judicial solutions among themselves—with love, faith, family, and forgiveness in mind. Otherwise, they'd be dependent on the harsh and faithless municipal courts to make judgments among them (see also 1 Corinthians 6:1–8).

However, we must pay attention to the context and reason for Jesus' guidance in Matthew 18 as a whole, not simply in these three verses. This teaching of Jesus is primarily about *reconciliation*—not what some are quick to label as "church discipline." Note the one-to-one, personal and familial nature of Jesus' statement in verse 15: "If *another believer* sins against *you*..." (italics mine). It's about relationships between Christians and about how to restore them, and how to forgive one another.

There are, of course, cultural and generational differences that impact how this process plays out today. Remember, that in the time of Jesus and Paul, the synagogue assembly was the norm, and that assembly was much more a part of everyday life than religious institutions are in most people's lives today. Still, the process in Matthew 18 is valid, and it works. When wronged, first take your grievance directly to your brother or sister. Failing to reconcile, bring two or three witnesses and try again (Deuteronomy 19:15).

Again failing to reconcile, bring it to the church for resolution. In Jesus' day, this was the synagogue, so for us today it would probably be something like the church leadership team or a small group within the larger church body.

And if the offending believer rejects the efforts to reconcile? Well, at that point the person has refused to live at peace within the church family, and it's time to disassociate. N. T. Wright says, "We don't like the sound of this, but we need to ask what the alternatives are. If there is real evil involved, refusal to face it means a necessary break of fellowship."

This brings us to the second part of your question: Does this process mean the church is judging the salvation of the person being disciplined? No, that interpretation of this Scripture would be a stretch. Remember, Jesus called this person a "believer" (Matthew 18:15). But it does mean that the offending person is excluded from the benefits of church family until, it's hoped, he or she is finally willing to reconcile.

Sources: MFE2 34–36; MAT 334

My experience of prayer tells me the promise of Jesus in Matthew 18:19–20 is not true. What am I to do with that?

The problem here is not in the promise, but in the misapplication of it to prayer. "If two of you agree here on earth concerning anything you ask," Jesus said, "my Father in heaven will do it for you. For where two or three gather together as my followers, I am there among them." This is a wonderful promise—but it refers to Christ's instructions for justice and reconciliation among Christians, as just discussed. It's not a blanket statement about prayer. In fact, biblical scholar Larry Richards pointedly says, "These verses almost certainly do not deal with prayer at all."

The language about forbidding and permitting in verse 18 (or binding and loosing in some translations) is a lead-in to the promise of verses 19–20; it's about convicting or acquitting in the case at hand. Along those same lines, Richards points out that *aiteisthai*, the Greek verb we translate as "ask" in verse 19, when used in a judicial context as this is, means "pursuing a claim," or seeking a judgment in a civil conflict. He concludes, "What Jesus promises is that wherever two or three (appointed as judges to suggest a solution to the conflict) gather in Christ's name, Jesus will be present with the judges to provide the wisdom needed to reach an appropriate solution."

Sources: ETJ 191; MAT 334

Parable of the Unforgiving Debtor
Matthew 18:21–35

Forgiveness seemed to be a high-value topic to Jesus. How was that concept understood in his time?

Forgiveness is definitely a crucial element of Jesus' teaching, and it always carries both vertical and horizontal applications. "Forgive us our debts" Jesus said in Matthew 6:12—a vertical, us-to-God appeal. That was followed immediately by, "as we have also forgiven our debtors," which was a horizontal, us-to-others commitment.

Jesus emphasized this dual application again at the end of his parable of the unforgiving debtor, telling of great punishment for unforgiveness and saying, "That's what my heavenly Father will do to you if you refuse to forgive your brothers and sisters" (Matthew 18:35). That seems to be a lot riding on an attitude of forgiveness! So how was that concept understood in Jesus' time?

The root Greek word translated "forgive" in both Matthew 6:12 and Matthew 18:35 is *aphiēmi*. Its literal meaning is, "to send away." And, according to the symbolism of the parable of the unforgiving debtor, we experience it first from God and then pay it forward to others.

The image of *aphiēmi*, then, is that of God picking up all the wrongs we've done and flinging them forcefully into nonexistence—something the Old Testament refers to as God sending our sins "as far from us as the east is from the west" (Psalm 103:12). It's as if, when we pray for forgiveness, we're asking God to perform a miracle, hurling our sins like a cosmic baseball so far away that they cease to exist, therefore absolving us of the required punishment for those sins. And that's what he does in response to our prayer.

What's even more amazing about this miracle of forgiving is its ability to transform everything and everyone it touches. When God pours his forgiveness over the life of a man or woman, he not only answers the "Forgive me..." plea, but he also empowers that man or woman to enact forgiveness toward others. Mother Teresa explained it this way, "When we realize that we are all sinners needing forgiveness, it will be easy for us to forgive others. We have to be forgiven in order to be able to forgive." In other words, *we are transformed* by the experience of God's selfless forgiveness, which in turn opens the door for us to be changed again through the act of forgiving others. Here's what this means for us today: The shackles of our hurtful experiences aren't ones we have to wear. We can "send away" that pain by seeking God's forgiveness first—and then gratefully choosing to forgive others in turn.

Sources: VCEN 250; NGL 110

Discussion about Divorce and Marriage
Matthew 19:1-12

Did the Pharisees teach no-fault divorce?

Divorce in Jewish society was generally frowned upon, but yes, as far as men were concerned, "no-fault divorce" was firmly in place—and had been for thousands of years.

The accepted reasoning in ancient Israel was that a man could divorce his wife for being "displeasing to him because he finds something indecent about her" (Deuteronomy 24:1). Of course, that left the definition of "something indecent" up for broad interpretation.

Rabbinical teaching by Jesus' time offered wide-ranging justifications for a husband to divorce his wife. If she claimed to be a virgin before betrothal and marriage and was later found to not be virginal (either during betrothal or after the wedding), that was cause for divorce. If a wife overcooked her husband's food, that was cause for divorce. If a husband decided his wife was "less beautiful" than another woman, that was cause for divorce. Basically, as long as a man could point to any reason why his wife was "displeasing to him," that was counted as "something indecent" and a legitimate cause for divorce. The wife, though, was not afforded any justification for divorcing her husband.

It was in the context of these lax social mores that Jesus made this radical statement: "Whoever divorces his wife and marries someone else commits adultery—unless his wife has been unfaithful" (Matthew 19:9).

That opinion would've been appalling to most of Jesus' audience—perhaps labeled extreme, intolerant, and unrealistic, as it is today. Even Christ's own disciples were taken aback, saying, "If this is the case, it is better not to marry" (verse 10).

For some reason, though, Jesus was unconcerned about how people would react to this hard teaching of his.

Source: HSJ 56–57, 59

Does Matthew 19:4–6 allow for homosexual marriage?

Ah, now you're just trying to get me into trouble because no matter how I answer this, someone will be angry. But you asked a fair question, so I'll try to give you a fair answer.

Dr. Gregory Coles is a good friend of mine and a prominent gay Christian. He wrestled with this question, not in the abstract, but as an issue that impacts his personal life every single day. "If we truly love Scripture," he says, "we have to love it enough to let it prove us wrong. And, at the same time, we have to love it enough to let it tell us what we don't want to hear.... When I pursued it, I got the answer I feared, not the answer I wanted."

His conclusion was this:

Not only does Jesus speak against sexual immorality as Jews would have understood it, but he also reaffirms the sanctity of the marriage bond between male and female. In Matthew 19 (paralleled in Mark 10), when Pharisees come to question him about Moses' divorce laws, Jesus explains that the marital mystery in which "the two become one flesh" is rooted in the creation story. "Haven't you read," he says, "that at the beginning the Creator 'made them male and female?'" (Matthew 19:4). Given the opportunity to define the basis and purpose of Christian marriage, Jesus points to the sexual beauty of men and women, as distinct expressions of the divine image, being united to reflect the fullness of God.

I tend to agree with that view. So to answer your question, I'd say no, Matthew 19:4–6 doesn't allow for homosexual marriage.

That said, I strongly do *not* agree with the idea that Christians are justified in discriminating against, or otherwise treating unkindly, anyone with same-sex attraction. Scripture teaches respect and kindness for all (Matthew 7:12; 1 Peter 2:17). I take that to mean everyone, regardless of whether that person agrees with my theology of sexuality, prefers to be called he, she, or they, is straight or part of the LGBTQ community.

Source: SGC 35, 37, 41

What are eunuchs?

Well, it's not pretty, but eunuchs were men (typically slaves) who had been castrated to qualify them for service in some kind of official capacity.

Men like this were frequently put in charge of royal harems—the assumption being that since they were sexually incapable, they could be trusted not to molest a king's lover. They also served as court officers and advisors to kings and queens. For instance, an Ethiopian eunuch was an early convert to Christianity, and the Bible tells us that he was both the treasurer for his queen and a man with "great authority" in his country (Acts 8:26–39). Because this kind of situation was common, eunuchs were often influential people—though Jewish law forbade them from being "admitted to the assembly of the LORD" (Deuteronomy 23:1).

In Matthew 19:10–12, Jesus expanded the idea of eunuchry to include those who had been born with some kind of genital defect that rendered them incapable of sex, and more importantly, as symbolic of those who chose to abstain from sex (and marriage) out of devotion to God. Both Jesus and the apostle Paul were part of that last category of "eunuch."

Sources: IBD1 485; SMA 105

Jesus Blesses the Children
Matthew 19:13–15

Why did Jesus' disciples hate kids?

It's probably unfair to say that Peter, James, John, and the others "hated" children.

The more likely explanation for their unfortunate attitudes and actions in this passage is that they were simply a product of their time.

In the ancient world in which they lived, children—especially other people's children—were largely viewed with contempt as irrelevant, annoying, and worthless. Jewish families gave somewhat greater value to their *own* kids, but not so much to children in the community as a whole. Dr. Roy B. Zuck and other Bible historians don't exaggerate when they say that children in the ancient Jewish world were insignificant, and adults thought it a waste to spend time with children. In fact, until age twelve, young ones were not even allowed to attend religious meetings (girls were excluded longer—but that was a different problem).

The situation was even worse among non-Jewish peoples. Archaeologists have uncovered a letter from around the first century in which a husband directs his pregnant wife not to allow their newborn child to live if it turns out to be a girl. Tragically, that was the norm rather than the exception. In pagan cultures, unwanted infants were abandoned along roadsides or, worse, discarded in garbage dumps! One Roman custom was that when a child was born, it was laid at the father's feet. If he picked up the baby, it could live. If he didn't, the child was abandoned to die.

Most abandoned infants perished from exposure. Some were scavenged to be used as future slaves, gladiators, prostitutes, or even human pets. In one obscene perversion, there's evidence that professional beggars would at times pick up an abandoned infant, break its bones or otherwise mutilate it, and then publicly display the infant's agony to gain sympathy and get more alms from passersby.

Within this cruel world, the attitude of the apostles was certainly not excusable—but it was understandable. What they did was socially acceptable, much milder than their contemporaries, and mistakenly intended for Jesus' best interests. Regardless, Christ would have nothing to do with it. He rebuked his men sternly and, in the process, elevated *other people's children* to hallowed status (verse 14).

Jesus' example made a huge difference that changed lives long afterward. In fact, his followers in the Roman Empire gained a reputation for this absurd, counter-cultural adoption practice: When early Christians found abandoned infants, they picked them up and took them into their homes, raising them as their own treasured children.

Sources: PHS 207, 213; BTC 240; IB7 468–469; ARF 22, 160; NNI 1176; SOC 60

What did it mean for Jesus to "bless" the children?

When "parents brought their children to Jesus so he could lay his hands on them and pray for them" (Matthew 19:13), it was a practice rooted in centuries of Jewish history.

At the Day of Atonement each year, the tradition was for children to be brought to scribes who would then pray blessings over them. It was also fairly common anytime of the year for an elder or someone else in authority to place a hand on a person (child or adult) as part of a pronouncement and prayer of blessing. So when these children were brought to Jesus, it was consistent with those kinds of customs.

What did that request for blessing mean?

In the simplest sense, it was a prayer that asked for God to show his favor and kindness to a person. In over four hundred references within the Old Testament, blessing carries a legitimate hope for God to grant things like success, health, prosperity, longevity, and a full, satisfying life. The New Testament carries on that meaning of well-being, but also imbues into it the aspect of "a spiritual inheritance reserved in heaven for the believer."

Most likely, those faithful parents saw in Jesus a wonderful, new hope that life for their children could be better than the hardships they themselves were enduring. That was a blessing they longed for their kids to receive—and one that Jesus was eager to give.

Sources: PHS 212; SLU 424; EDB 130-131; DBI 99

The Rich Man
Matthew 19:16–30

Who was this rich man that came to Jesus?

We don't actually know much about the unnamed man who approached Jesus and asked, "What good deed must I do to have eternal life?" (Matthew 19:16). The few facts we have are gleaned from this passage and parallel accounts in Mark 10:17–31 and Luke 18:18–30.

Matthew observes that this man was young, indicating he was at least younger than that disciple—perhaps in his late teens or early twenties. The young man also had many possessions, which in that society likely meant substantial holdings in land and other property. Because of his young-ish age, it's realistic to assume that he inherited that wealth rather than earned it himself.

Luke tells us the man was "very rich" (Luke 18:23), which would convey the impression that, in addition to his lands, he'd probably inherited a large store of money that was now at his disposal. Luke 18:18 also reveals that he was "a religious leader," (or "a ruler" in other translations). So perhaps he was now stepping into his predetermined role as a leader in the community and provider for his family. Maybe he saw Jesus as some kind of wise father figure who could give good advice to help him succeed in these new responsibilities.

Mark reinforces the characterizations of Matthew and Luke, adding the detail that the rich young man "knelt down" in front of Jesus (Mark 10:17). This showed he was well trained in the protocols of religious hierarchy.

All these things taken together suggest that this rich young ruler was possibly an up-and-coming leader among the Sadducees, an influential aristocratic group in Jesus' day. They were the religious and social elite, holding significant wealth and power in Israel. Still, the gospel writers never specifically call this young man a Sadducee, so that's only speculation.

Source: SMB 112

Is Jesus teaching that salvation comes through good works?

Scholars agree that Jesus' demand to sell everything and give to the poor, as recorded in Matthew 19:16–30, was mostly to make a point—a challenge that forced the rich man to confront his mistaken view that heaven could be earned through his good deeds. "These verses do not teach salvation by works," says theologian H. Wayne House in summing up the consensus. He adds, "Jesus was proving the error of the man's claim to have fulfilled God's law."

But I'm getting ahead of myself, so let's back up a moment.

It's significant that, when rattling off a sampling of God's commandments, Jesus included Leviticus 19:18, "Love your neighbor as yourself"—which was *not* one of the famous Ten Commandments. The Hebrew term for "love" here is *wĕʾhaḇātâ*, which emphasizes "the need for direct action toward one's neighbor. It stands in direct contrast to … showing apathy toward someone in need." Immediately following this verse, God makes it clear that "You must obey *all* my decrees," which the rich man, given his legalistic background, would have known (Leviticus 19:19, italics mine).

And how were God's people expected to keep the command to love their neighbors? Here are just a few examples from the Old Testament:

> ❯ "If there are any poor Israelites in your towns when you arrive in the land the Lord your God is giving you, do not be hard-hearted or tightfisted toward them … I am commanding you to share freely with the poor and with other Israelites in need" (Deuteronomy 15:7, 11).

> "Those who oppress the poor insult their Maker, but helping the poor honors him" (Proverbs 14:31).

> "If you help the poor, you are lending to the Lord—and he will repay you!" (Proverbs 19:17).

> "[Josiah] gave justice and help to the poor and needy, and everything went well for him. Isn't that what it means to know me?" says the Lord" (Jeremiah 22:16).

When presented with righteousness through keeping the law, the rich man proudly proclaimed, "I've obeyed *all* these commandments" (Matthew 19:20, italics mine). However, it was simply impossible that this man had kept *all* of the law, and in particular all the commands about loving neighbors and helping the poor. Jesus knew he hadn't done that; the rich man's hoarding of expansive wealth testified against that claim.

And so this is what happened next: "Jesus called his bluff," says Dr. Michael Vanlaningham, a professor at Moody Bible Institute, "and proved that he had not and would not do what he claimed to have done." Dr. House adds, "If the young man loved his neighbor to the extent required by the Law of Moses ... he would have had no difficulty giving away his wealth to needy people."

The rich man went away sad. Christ's disciples were astounded. They asked, "Who in the world can be saved?" (Matthew 19:25) And here in verse 26, Jesus makes the same point with his disciples that he'd just made for the rich man:

"Humanly speaking, it is impossible."

"But with God everything is possible."

The message here is clear, and one that will be articulated again and again throughout the rest of the New Testament: "It is by grace you have been saved, through faith—and this is not from yourselves, *it is the gift of God—not by works,* so that no one can boast" (Ephesians 2:8–9 NIV, italics mine).

Sources: BKW1 324; MBC 1488–1489; NNI 1176

Does Jesus want me to give away all I have to the poor?

Here's exactly what Jesus wants of you: "'You must love the Lord your God with all your heart, all your soul, and all your mind.' This is the first and greatest commandment. A second is equally important: 'Love your neighbor as yourself.' The entire law and all the demands of the prophets are based on these two commandments" (Matthew 22:37–40).

For the rich man in this passage, this meant selling all he had and giving the proceeds to the poor. In Scripture, he's the only one of whom that total financial sacrifice was asked, and that request appears to have been mostly to make a point rather than a real demand (see previous commentary above). For others in the Bible, giving is a natural part of the Christian faith— particularly giving to the poor—but the amount given is a matter to be determined between the giver and God: "You must each decide in your heart how much to give," the apostle Paul instructed in 2 Corinthians 9:7. "And don't give reluctantly or in response to pressure. 'For God loves a person who gives cheerfully.'"

That was also the standard for the early church. Around AD 150, Justin Martyr reported that the weekly Christian practice was this: "They that are prosperous and wish to do so give what they will, each after his choice. What is collected … gives aid to the orphans and widows and such as are in want."

Generosity is a hallmark of Christian people, an expression of gratitude in response to what God has given us, and a means through which God increases joy in his children. Giving is also intended to be more than simply money: time, talent, encouragement, effort, advocacy—all these things and more are included in the act of giving.

As to what that means in your particular economic and social situation, that's something you're going to have to discuss with God and then "decide in your heart."

Sources: DCC 71; Proverbs 3:27; 11:25; Luke 6:38; Acts 20:35; 1 Timothy 6:18-19; Hebrews 13:16; James 1:27

Parable of the Vineyard Workers
Matthew 20:1-16

What's the main point of this parable of vineyard workers?

The parable of the vineyard workers is rich with meaning and symbolism. As such, some teach that the unconditional generosity of God (represented by the landowner) is the main takeaway. Others emphasize the perils of discontent (represented by the complaining workers) or highlight the rewarding power of grace as the key theme (represented by everyone receiving the same wage).

All of those meanings are easily seen in this parable—but Jesus' *main* point appears to be something different. Notice that Jesus taught this story in response to the question asked moments earlier. While debriefing the encounter with the rich man (Matthew 19:16–30), Peter asks Jesus, "We've given up everything to follow you. What will we get?" (Matthew 19:27).

Christ answers by speaking of God's future kingdom and saying, "Many who are the greatest now will be least important then, and those who seem least important now will be the greatest then" (Matthew 19:30). That statement becomes the launching point for the parable of the vineyard workers. Jesus then ends that parable with this summary: "So those who are last now will be first then, and those who are first will be last" (Matthew 20:16).

In other words, the hierarchy of heaven is not what we'd assume it to be from our experience with the hierarchies that rule us here in this life. As James 4:6 teaches, "God opposes the proud but gives grace to the humble." Since Jesus emphasized that truth both before and immediately after telling this parable, it seems clear that his main point of this story is: *The first will be last and the last will be first.*

Sources: ETJ 70; ATP 20-221; ILJ 196

Who are the last and the first in Matthew 20:16?

Jesus said, "Those who are last now will be first then, and those who are first will be last." So whom, exactly, was he talking about?

This question is even more intriguing because Jesus made this kind of pronouncement several times—it was obviously a core truth he wanted his followers to understand. Matthew 19:30; 20:26–27; Mark 9:35; 10:31; and Luke 13:30 all say essentially the same thing as Matthew 20:16. Other Scriptures imply this message as well, including Matthew 8:11–12; 18:2–5; and 25:31–46. Although we don't have space to explore every instance here, let's at least look at a few for comparison.

> Matthew 19:30 and 20:16 are paired with the parable of the vineyard workers. We'll explore this parable more in a moment, but for now let's note that in this context, the "last," represented by the poor laborers, appears to be a reference to Jesus' disciples. The "first" appears to refer to the rich and powerful in the world at large as well as in Jewish society (such as the rich man from Matthew 19:16–30).

> The Mark 9:35 pronouncement followed a discussion about which of Jesus' disciples was "the greatest." In that setting, those disciples (who viewed themselves as great) appear to be the "first." Lowly servants and a powerless child are the "last."

> Luke 13:30 was part of a discussion about entry into heaven. Here the "last" are represented by gentiles: "people … from all over the world" (Luke 13:29). The "first" appears to be Jews who considered themselves superior to, and therefore "first" over, non-Jews.

Now, let's go back to the parable of the vineyard workers in Matthew 20. The imagery of the day laborer that Jesus used in this context is striking. In that time there were three main classes of servants: Bondsmen (slaves in honored standing within a family), servants (subordinates to a family's slaves), and hirelings (not associated with a family, but simply hired out for specific tasks).

All slaves and servants were in the lower strata of the social order—and hirelings like the ones in Jesus' parable were the lowest of that lower class. They lived hand-to-mouth, scrabbling each day for enough food to eat, never guaranteed income or even a fair wage.

Mosaic law was supposed to guard basic rights for these workers, but biblical sources reveal they were often mistreated (Jeremiah 22:13; Malachi 3:5). Pointing to Job 7:1–3, Dr. Leland Ryken and his colleagues comment, "The image of a hireling [is] a spectacle of misery." If this was Jesus' literal representation of "the last," you can image how it must have felt for his disciples to see themselves in that light—they, who thought themselves great, were really the hirelings!

In modern society, the roles and names have changed somewhat, but the "first" would still be those with power and affluence—celebrities, businesspeople, famous religious and political leaders, and so on. And the "last" would be those without power and affluence—the homeless, the ill and impaired, prisoners, the vulnerable and poor, and so on.

Now that you know this, what will you do with Jesus' words in Matthew 20:16?

Sources: GNM 394–395; DBI 385

Jesus Again Predicts His Death
Matthew 20:17–19

Who were "leading priests and the teachers of religious law," and why were they so powerful in Jewish society?

"Leading priests" ("chief priests" in some translations) were the ruling party of Sadducees. "Teachers of religious law" were scribes, and they held an important place in ancient Jewish society. Since we've talked about Sadducees in more detail previously (see the commentary on Matthew 16:1–4), let's focus on the scribes here.

In the ancient world, literacy was fairly rare. Boys in Jewish family culture were typically taught to read and write enough to participate in Scripture study, but generally speaking the norm was illiteracy except among certain professions like merchant, tax collector, or politician. Dr. John A. Beck estimates that, in that era, as many as 90 percent of the people living in the land of ancient Israel (both Jew and gentile) were functionally unable to read or write.

In that world, highly literate, professional scribes were needed for recording agreements, bills of sale, historical records, political decrees and so on. They were experts in language, composition, and interpretation. In Israel, especially as old copies of the Hebrew Scriptures were lost or destroyed, scribes were charged with copying again and again the *Tanakh* (the Law, Prophets, and Writings). This naturally meant that scribes became very knowledgeable about what Scripture said.

Following the example of Ezra (who was a prominent scribe in Israel's history; see the Old Testament book of Ezra), these men became influential scholars credited with preserving and teaching the Hebrew Bible to their countrymen. By the time of the New Testament, they were a distinct class of learned men that was closely associated with the ruling party of Sadducees, and sometimes with the Pharisees. Scribes were also recognized as unquestioned experts in all matters of biblical interpretation and application, hence they're called "teachers of religious law."

These scribes were among the highest accepted authorities over how Scripture was to be understood and lived out. As such, they served not only as teachers, but also as magistrates in legal matters concerning the Mosaic law. Nineteenth-century biblical scholar Samuel Bagster informs us that scribes "were immediate judges in important cases, and the ultimate judges in all."

Given that role, and such an honored place in that society, it's easy to see why their opposition to Jesus was a powerful force in the push toward having him executed.

Sources: BIG 228-230; HBD 914; BBH 93

Jesus Teaches about Serving Others
Matthew 20:20-28

How is it that greatness is measured in service?

As it's recorded in Matthew 20:26, Jesus told his disciples, "Whoever wants to be a leader among you must be your servant." So how is greatness measured in service?

Since the true nature of greatness in service is something of a mystery, I'm going to speculate a little bit here. After looking at both this passage and John 13:1–17, here's what I've been thinking lately ...

First, we must deal with the mistaken, common assumption that we *earn* greatness through service. To my mind, this is a backward view of the facts. When Jesus washed his disciples' feet (John 13:1–17), that added nothing to the greatness already inherent within him. He didn't earn greatness by that act; he was already great.

Second, we need to acknowledge that what Jesus taught in Matthew 20:24–27 was a radical break from all of human history. Two thousand years later, we use the term "servant leadership" with such ease that we forget *it did not exist* until Jesus taught it to his disciples. Christ literally invented that concept, and now it's actually part of MBA leadership textbooks. For example, Dr. Peter Northouse of Western Michigan University describes Christ's invention when he teaches: "Leaders who serve are altruistic, they place their followers' welfare foremost in their plans ... and make decisions pertaining to them that are beneficial and not harmful to their welfare."

Third, when we look to Jesus as the firm and foremost example of this teaching, we see that service is not the same as subservience. As Dr. Northouse said, servant leaders like Jesus "place their followers' welfare foremost in their plans." Sometimes that requires refusing to cooperate when a follower wants a servant leader to act against that follower's best interests. This is why, during the act of serving Peter, Christ actually denied Peter's commands (John 13:6–12), and it's why, today, a servant leader would, for example, refuse a request for tequila from someone known to be a recovering alcoholic.

Finally, John 13:3–5 tells us that just before washing his disciples' feet, "*Jesus knew* that the Father had given him authority over everything.... *So* he got up from the table" (italics mine). Or as Dr. H. Wayne House commented on that passage, "Jesus did what he did because he knew what he knew."

With all that taken into consideration, I'm going to suggest that greatness is *not measured* in service. Rather, like Jesus, our inherent greatness through Christ's Holy Spirit *expresses itself* in service instead. I think that's the point Jesus was making in Matthew 20:26.

My two cents.

Sources: LEA 351-352; NNI 1344

Why did Jesus refer to his death as a ransom? Did he have to pay Satan to release our souls?

Matthew 20:28 records Jesus prophesying about his death by saying, "The Son of Man came not to be served but to serve others and to give his life as a ransom for many."

That word *ransom* feels strange to our American ears because it suggests that Satan has taken us hostage and God is paying off the devil for us. That in turn makes God seem weak and ineffectual, as though Satan somehow gained an upper hand against our all-powerful Father. The problem here is not the word, but our cultural understanding of it (which has, no doubt, been influenced by portrayals we've all seen in suspense movies and TV shows!).

The Greek word used in verse 28 is *lútron*, and yes, it's translated correctly as "ransom." However, in Jesus' day it wasn't seen as a hostage payment. Its literal meaning is "to loose," and it was the common term for the price of freeing a slave. This is important because *we are not slaves to Satan*; therefore he receives nothing from Christ's ransom.

Jesus instead taught that *we are all slaves to sin* (John 8:34–36). This is a reference to the sin nature within each of us that pulls us in hurtful directions away from God. The apostle Paul later explained that because of Christ's sacrificial death and resurrection, "Now you are free from your slavery to sin, and you have become slaves to righteous living" (Romans 6:18).

So no, Jesus didn't pay any ransom to Satan for your soul. Instead Christ paid the cost to set you loose from the corruption of sin that once completely enslaved your own human nature.

Sources: CWSN 74; CWDN 930

Jesus Heals Two Blind Men
Matthew 20:29-34

Why is this passage in Matthew different from the same story told in Mark and Luke?

It is interesting to note the minor differences in the telling of this event within the gospels of Matthew, Mark, and Luke. For instance, both Matthew and Mark indicate that Jesus was *leaving* Jericho (Matthew 20:29; Mark 10:46). At the same time, Luke 18:35 reports that Christ was *approaching* Jericho. Additionally, Mark and Luke record only one beggar on the road (Mark 10:46 and Luke 18:35), while Matthew 20:30 indicates there were two. Finally, Mark gives a name to the beggar, Bartimaeus—but neither Matthew nor Luke provides a name (Matthew 10:29–34; Mark 10:46; Luke 18:35–43).

Some see nefarious intent in these discrepancies. They assume that all three gospel writers were either lying or simply unreliable. Others, like church father, Origen, tried to explain divergences like these as some kind of benign, divine dishonesty. Writing in the early third century, he theorized that God intentionally put "a few phrases which are not true" into Scripture to "challenge the more skillful and inquisitive to devote themselves to a painstaking examination of the text." (Insert eye roll here...) I'll admit I'm not among the "more skillful and inquisitive," but neither of these accusations strikes me as in any way plausible.

Most agree that the reason for the differences is simply that three different people wrote three accounts of the same event, each emphasizing what seemed important to him. It reminds me of the time I took my son to see a Denver Nuggets basketball game. Afterward, he reported to his mother all the exciting parts of the halftime show, what snacks he ate, and how cheerleaders cannoned t-shirts into the stands. He completely left out the fact that basketball was played or who won—it was up to me to include those facts in my account of the night. My son and I noticed different details, but we both saw the same NBA game. As Dr. Larry Richards observes, "It's not at all uncommon for three people reporting on the same event to mention different details."

Irenaeus, bishop of Rome at the end of the second century, tells us that "Mark, the disciple and interpreter of Peter, himself handed down to us in writing the substance of Peter's preaching." Peter probably knew and remembered Bartimaeus, and since Bartimaeus was the main "shouter" in this event, Mark included his name and opted not to mention the second beggar. Irenaeus also reports that, "Luke, the follower of Paul, set down in a book the gospel of his teacher." As such, Luke gives a just-the-facts account that focuses only on unnamed Bartimaeus, the primary beggar in that moment. And Matthew was an eyewitness to this miracle; he likely remembered both blind beggars and chose to mention them together. Same event, three viewpoints.

But what about that "leaving Jericho" and "approaching Jericho" discrepancy? Turns out that the city of Jericho in Jesus' time wasn't just a single dot on the map, but a larger city divided in two.

First, there was old Jericho, the ancient part of the city that was in decline and some ruin. Then, nearly two miles south of the old part of the city was the new Jericho, a renovation project spearheaded by King Herod the Great where he'd built "an elegant winter palace" to escape the cold of Jerusalem. Old and new Jericho had different entrances, but both were still called Jericho.

So if we can assume that Jesus was walking within the one to two mile stretch between the old and new sections of Jericho when he encountered the blind men, he could literally have been "leaving" Jericho and "entering" Jericho at the same time—just as the gospel writers said.

Sources: BIE 62–63; BAH 296; DCC 29–30; WWA 190; ASB 1647; ZP3 455

Do we know any background about the blind men who were healed at Jericho?

Well, we know nothing about one of them except that he was blind, impoverished, and Jesus healed him. The other, Mark 10:46 tells us, was a man named Bartimaeus. Like his companion he was blind and impoverished, and like all blind men, they both would've been banished from the temple, forbidden to worship God there with the rest of their countrymen. Mark also reports that after receiving his sight, Bartimaeus "followed Jesus down the road" (Mark 10:52), which is corroborated by both Matthew and Luke. Scholars like Steven Barabas of Princeton Theological Seminary hypothesize that the formerly blind man probably didn't stop there.

It's likely Bartimaeus followed Jesus from Jericho into Jerusalem, witnessing the triumphal entry. It's probable that he was also one of the extended group of "all the believers" mentioned in Acts 2:1. That means it's very possible the former blind man saw the cross, saw the resurrected Jesus, saw the arrival of the Holy Spirit at Pentecost, and more. In fact, Dr. Barabas suggests that Mark mentions Bartimaeus by name because Mark and/or Peter knew him personally—because the old beggar actually went on to become a recognized disciple of Christ in his lifetime.

How cool is that?

Sources: ZB1 266; IBB 164; ZP1 481

Jesus' Last Week

Jesus' Triumphal Entry
Matthew 21:1–11

Was Jesus' triumphal entry into Jerusalem a spontaneous event or a planned processional?

All indications are that Jesus' impressive parade into Jerusalem was planned, a carefully orchestrated processional with one main objective: to publicly announce, at last, that Jesus was indeed God's promised Messiah.

Twentieth-century Bible scholar S. MacLean Gilmour argued that the way Jesus had his disciples go and acquire the donkey was "no doubt … evidence of Jesus' omniscience," but to my mind a less supernatural explanation is more probable. Jesus, who was already in nearby Bethany, may have simply made prior arrangements with someone in Jerusalem to borrow a few donkeys for use in the processional. It's possible that Christ rented the donkeys, or that the owner was a follower who loaned them freely. Either way, the owner knew that when someone said, "The Lord needs them," it meant Jesus had sent his people to get the donkeys.

Christ riding a donkey into the city was important because it was part of a well-known messianic prophecy:

> Rejoice, O people of Zion! Shout in triumph, O people of Jerusalem! Look, your king is coming to you. He is righteous and victorious, yet he is humble, riding on a donkey—riding on a donkey's colt. (Zechariah 9:9)

This is the Scripture that Matthew paraphrased in his account. In this context, the donkey symbolized at least three things for the people:

> ❯ Royalty—reminiscent of kingly visits in that time, and Solomon's coronation (1 Kings 1:38)

> Peace (Zechariah 9:9–10)

> Victory—Romans had invented this kind of triumphal procession to celebrate a general returning from a major victory in battle.

Additionally, the direction of Jesus' entry into Jerusalem was thick with messianic significance. Zechariah prophesied, "On that day his feet will stand on the Mount of Olives, east of Jerusalem … and the LORD will be king over all the earth" (Zechariah 14:4, 9). Jesus' pathway into Jerusalem was exactly what had been prophesied—except instead of bringing war, Christ came in victorious peace.

Jesus' disciples also primed the crowd's response. Luke 19:37 reports that with Jesus on the road was a "whole multitude of the disciples" (KJV). This multitude probably included the twelve disciples, plus women who had traveled with that group from Galilee, as well as a those from the outskirts of Jerusalem, among them Lazarus, Martha, Mary, and others (see John 12:1–3). That group alone could have numbered a hundred or more. They then attracted even more people from the city of Jerusalem, including those who were not necessarily disciples of Jesus but who had followed this miracle-worker as he traveled—curiosity-seekers, and even religious leaders like the Pharisees.

When this already-large-and-growing-by-the-minute mob on the road neared the entrance to Jerusalem, Luke 19:37–38 records that Christ's "multitude of disciples" were the ones first to start joyfully shouting praise about Jesus. Once they sparked that kind of excitement, the rest of the crowd soon followed suit, shouting and singing along the road and through the gates of the city.

All of these things lead to the conclusion that Jesus' triumphal entry into Jerusalem was clearly a pre-planned, detailed, well-executed event. "Fully aware of other prophecies about the Messiah's coming," says Stephen M. Miller, "Jesus arranged to bring them to life."

Sources: IB8 336; ILJ 205, 207; JOB 296–298; DBI 897; HAC 136

Hosanna, palm leaves, chanting, and garments on the road? Was there special meaning behind all this?

Each of these things had symbolic meaning at the time of Jesus' royal entry into Jerusalem. Here's a quick summary:

> **Hosanna.** This is a transliteration into Greek (and then English) of a Hebrew word with the literal meaning, "save us" or "save now." This is how it was used in Psalm 118:25. As time went on, it also came to be known as a "shout of welcome" and an utterance of praise to God (Jeremiah 31:7). Comparing the gospel accounts, it appears that both meanings might've been present during Jesus' final entry into Jerusalem (Matthew 21:9, 15; Mark 11:9–10; John 12:13).

> **Spreading Coats on the Road.** When people in the crowd spread their outer garments onto the road for Jesus to cross over, that was a declaration of submission to him as royalty. It was a statement of political support for one they viewed as their coming king.

> **Palm Leaves.** These "symbolized Jewish nationalism and victory, such as when Judas Maccabeus and his followers recovered Jerusalem and the temple desecrated by Antiochus." (That was the height of the Maccabean Revolt against the Greek, Seleucid dynasty, about a hundred and fifty years before Christ.) It was a symbolic statement that the people perceived Jesus as their messiah and national liberator, presumably from the occupation by the Romans.

> **Chanting and Singing.** The chanting and singing that accompanied Jesus' entry was clearly a messianic declaration, particularly the linking of the terms "Hosanna" (typically reserved for God) and "Son of David," which refer to a messianic promise. However, the revelers that day apparently misunderstood Jesus to be a military messiah who would deliver them from Rome rather than the spiritual messiah who would redeem from sin.

Sources: ZP3 206; HAC 136-137

Jesus Clears the Temple
Matthew 21:12-17

Why did Jesus take such dramatic action against the merchants in the temple?

Jesus' stated reason for clearing the temple was, "The Scriptures declare, 'My Temple will be called a house of prayer,' but you have turned it into a den of thieves" (Matthew 21:13). Still, a little background on that might be helpful.

Mark's gospel tells us that Jesus had gone into the temple the night before, and "After looking around carefully at everything, he left because it was late in the afternoon" (Mark 11:11). He returned the next day and immediately flew into a controlled rage: "He knocked over the tables of the money changers and the chairs of those selling doves, and he stopped everyone from using the Temple as a marketplace" (Mark 11:15–16).

So Jesus' dramatic actions were premeditated and deliberate, intended to stop, at least briefly, criminal activity in the name of God. That appears to be one reason for clearing the temple. We've already talked previously about the criminally corrupt Annas Bazaar which the Sadducees were operating in the temple at that time (see the commentary on Matthew 16:1–4), so I won't repeat that here. But suffice it to say that Jesus was justified when he "stopped everyone from using the Temple as a marketplace." But that also suggests a possible second reason why Jesus cleared the temple: *to force the Sadducees to respond.*

Jesus' tirade would've been a huge disruption in the temple economics that fattened the purses of the Sadducees, and the chief priest himself. In addition to the normal population of Jerusalem, there were thousands of pilgrims who had also come to the city to observe Passover that week. Ancient historian, Josephus, reported that during one Passover week alone, more than 250,000 lambs were bought, sold, and sacrificed! So there was big money changing hands that day and, as they say, if you really want to hurt somebody the best place to hit them is in the wallet. That's exactly what Jesus did when he cut off the fast flow of money.

Mark 11:18 reports that, "When the leading priests and teachers of religious law heard what Jesus had done, *they began planning how to kill him*" (italics mine). Anyone in that time and place had to know that would be the response. This leads me to believe that Christ deliberately intended to provoke a deadly reaction from his enemies with this premeditated attack (see the commentary on Matthew 17:22–23). The case can be made that he was intentionally pushing circumstances that would lead to his crucifixion—the ultimate reason that he came: "to give his life as a ransom for many" (Matthew 20:28).

Also, notice how Mark mentions that Jesus said, "My Temple will be called a house of prayer *for all nations* (Mark 11:17, italics mine). The part of the temple that Jesus cleared was the outer section, called the court of the gentiles. A stone (known as the Soreg inscription), recovered from the ruins of this temple in modern times, served as a threatening sign declaring in Greek that any foreigner who was caught entering a part of the temple off limits to gentiles would be executed—and have only himself to blame.

Why was it significant that Jesus cleansed the court of the gentiles? Dr. Timothy Keller explains:

> This was the only part where non-Jews were allowed. It was the biggest section of the temple, and you had to go through it to get to the rest. All the business operations of the temple were set up there … It was popularly believed that when the Messiah showed up he would purge the temple of foreigners. Instead, here is Jesus clearing the temple *for* the Gentiles—acting as their advocate.… Jesus was challenging the sacrificial system altogether and saying that the Gentiles—the pagan, unwashed Gentiles—could now go directly to God in prayer. This was amazing." (italics his)

Sources: KC 156–157; JOB 284

Does Jesus' violent act in clearing the temple justify other Christians to act violently against authorities?

The short answer to this question is: unequivocally, no.

When we look at the New Testament as a whole and at the testimony of the early church, violence toward authorities is never practiced nor justified. We must remember that Jesus himself, as God incarnate, was the final authority over the temple. In that specific situation, only he had the authority to do what he did. Christ did not extend that authority to us. In fact, his command to his followers after his resurrection was simply to "make disciples," not to overthrow human authorities.

What's more, Christ modeled this nonviolent perspective himself. Never once during his trial and execution did he raise a fist, nor did he command his many followers to rise up against his enemies. When Simon Peter tried to defend Jesus by slashing off a man's ear, Christ put a stop to it immediately, even healing the ear that had just been cut off (Luke 22:49–51; John 18:10–11). Additionally, Jesus held back thousands of angels from attacking on his behalf (Matthew 26:53).

After Jesus' resurrection and ascension into heaven (Acts 1:9), exactly zero of Christ's followers became revolutionaries. Instead they went around preaching, teaching, healing, helping the poor, and living lives of peace— even when they were tortured and executed for faith. The New Testament letters of Paul and Peter reinforced that choice, telling Christ followers to "live in harmony and peace" (2 Corinthians 13:11) and "search for peace, and work to maintain it" (1 Peter 3:11).

The early church after the apostles continued this pursuit for peace, even to the point of pacifism. Under fierce persecution from Roman emperors and other authorities, our ancient brothers and sisters went willingly to cruel and brutal deaths, refusing to take up arms against their oppressors.

So the long answer to this question is the same as the short one: No, Jesus' act of clearing the temple does not justify other Christians to act violently against authorities.

Source: SOC 63, 67

Jesus Curses the Fig Tree
Matthew 21:18-22

It seems kind of petty for Jesus to curse a fig tree when he was hungry. What's really going on here?

This is one of the more curious episodes in the life of Jesus. Why would he care whether a random fig tree was producing fruit? Besides, it was too early in the season for ripe figs, so why did Jesus expect to find any?

Let's deal first with why Jesus even cared about this. The general consensus is that this was, as noted Bible teacher Herschel Hobbs called it, "an acted parable," or what we might say today is an object lesson. It was likely a continuation of a spoken parable Christ told earlier in his ministry. Luke 13:6–8 records that earlier story.

In that Luke parable, a man plants a fig tree that bears no fruit for three years, so he orders it to be cut down. Common interpretations view the man as representing God, the three years as representing Christ's years of ministry, and the fig tree as representing Israel as a political nation. Did Jesus' disciples remember that parable when he cursed a real fig tree? No one knows for sure, but it had been part of his previous teaching.

Fast-forward to Matthew 21:18–20, and again scholars typically agree that, as Dr. Walter Wilson explained it, the fig tree represented the nation of Israel. With that in mind, we can explore why Jesus expected to find fruit and how that applied to Israel at that time.

The normal fruit-bearing seasons for fig trees in Israel were June and September, so it was too early for ripened figs. However, a healthy tree could at times bear partially ripened fruit ahead of season. The sign of that would be branches full of leaves. This was because figs start growing before the leaves bloom, so a fig tree full of leaves should've had some pre-season figs on it—but Jesus found none.

"The point in this incident," says Hobbs, "is that the tree gave evidence of fruit, yet produced none. It was promise without performance." This symbolized the gross hypocrisy of the nation of Israel, he says, and unless Israel's leaders repented and turned to Christ, it too would suffer the same fate as the withered fig tree.

So, first, Jesus told a parable about a barren fig tree, giving a warning to Israel. Next, he gave that warning a second time, prophetically acting it out by cursing a literal fig tree as a stand-in for Israel. And then, tragically, the prophetic warning came to pass when the nation of Israel itself was finally uprooted by the Roman army less than a generation later.

That appears to be the meaning of Jesus' actions recorded in Matthew 21:18–20.

Sources: DBT 154-155; ILJ 215-216

Jesus' statement, "You can pray for anything, and if you have faith, you will receive it," seems to contradict his own prayer in the garden of Gethsemane, and also so much of human experience. Why?

This is a confusing aspect of Jesus' teaching, one that's often misrepresented (sometimes in hurtful ways). Still, you ask a fair question, so I'll do my best to give a helpful answer.

Generally speaking, we have to assume that when Jesus spoke of faith that could move mountains, he was speaking symbolically and not literally (see commentary on Matthew 17:14–21). After all, in all of recorded history, no one has ever moved a mountain by faith. Bishop Tom (N. T.) Wright, when exploring this scripture, points to the importance of the phrase *"this mountain"* in verse 21, which indicates Christ was speaking specifically about the Temple Mount in this moment. Some think that he was perhaps prophesying about its coming destruction at the hands of the Romans in AD 70.

Still, even if this particular statement was limited to that specific circumstance and spoken as a metaphor rather than a literal truth, we have to acknowledge that Jesus made broad statements about faith like this on several occasions (Matthew 17:20; Luke 8:50; John 14:12, and others). So, if Jesus speaks true (and I believe he does), then in some mysterious way, faith really can accomplish things previously considered impossible.

I think you've also hit on another important aspect of understanding Christ's Matthew 21:22 statement when you reference Jesus' prayer in Gethsemane (Matthew 26:36–46). Faith, by Jesus' example, is not making a wish or simply hoping fervently for a miracle—or even getting your heart's desire. It appears, instead, to be clearly understanding and then acting upon, the certainty of God's intention. In that sense, Jesus did receive what his prayer of faith asked for at Gethsemane. He made it clear that his overriding request was: "Yet not as I will, but as you will" (Matthew 26:39 NIV). That was overwhelmingly accomplished in Christ's death and resurrection.

One other thing to think about: Mark reports that, according to Jesus, forgiving others is a critical aspect of accessing God's intention in the prayer of faith: "If you believe that you've received it, it will be yours," Jesus said, "But when you are praying, first forgive anyone you are holding a grudge against, so that your Father in heaven will forgive your sins, too" (Mark 11:24–25). I think perhaps we often forget this important faith practice when we pray.

Finally, Pastor Chuck Swindoll reminds us:

> The apostle John—who himself had been present when Jesus cursed the fig tree and uttered His promise about prayer—provides a clarifying perspective on the confidence we have in God answering our requests. Some sixty years after this event, John would write, "This is the confidence which we have before Him, that, if we ask anything according to His will, He hears us" (1 John. 5:14).

All this teaches me two things:

> ❯ Faith that can move mountains is actually possible, and

> ❯ If I honestly want to produce that kind of faith in my life, I need to deliberately forgive others and wholeheartedly pursue the miracle-maker himself so I will better understand what miracles he actually intends to perform through me.

Sources: MFE2 72-73; SMB 154

The Authority of Jesus Challenged
Matthew 21:23-27

Why it was a big problem for the leading priests to ask Jesus where he got his authority?

First, let's put this in context of the events of Jesus' Passion Week so far. Remember, just the day before Jesus had visited the temple and made a violent mess, driving out merchants and moneychangers (Matthew 21:12–17).

In doing that, he'd aroused the fury of the Sadducees who were the "leading priests." They made a ton of money from their corrupt marketplace in the temple (see the commentary on Matthew 16:1–4). When Jesus threw out the merchants and moneychangers, it was a direct attack on their illicit livelihood.

Matthew 21:23 picks up the very next morning. Jesus is back at the temple, teaching people as if nothing had happened. The Sadducees are still enraged about yesterday's attack, so they come out to confront him. When they say, "By what authority are you doing all these things? Who gave you the right?" they're not referring to Jesus' teaching ministry. They're heatedly demanding an explanation for Christ's violent outburst the day before.

Second, they weren't just asking for explanations, these men were actually threatening Jesus with retribution (a threat they'd fulfill in only a few days). The Sadducees were priestly aristocracy that ran the temple and its functions. They felt that only Roman government officials had the authority to overrule their money-making schemes, so they were trying to corner Jesus into admitting his actions were unsanctioned crimes against Rome. That came with an understood threat that Rome would take up their cause and arrest or kill Christ.

Third, these leading priests knew—and rejected—the idea that Jesus was acting under God's authority. They saw themselves as God's sole incarnate authority in the temple. In their view, to oppose them was to oppose God. So they tried to redefine the debate into one where Jesus would look to be both an enemy of God and a traitor to Rome. If they could succeed in that, then even the followers whom Christ was teaching that day in the temple would've abandoned him. That was the big problem with this confrontational question they asked about Jesus' authority.

Source: IBB 166, 243

Why was Jesus so tight-lipped about where his authority came from?

The Bible doesn't state any specific reason why Jesus refused to answer, but it's not hard to read between the lines and see what's really going on. Consider the following: The leading priests (Sadducees) weren't simply asking a rhetorical question about Jesus' authority. They were actually challenging his credibility as a religious leader and threatening him with criminal retribution from the Roman military government. If Jesus said his authority was from God, they could successfully argue the case that they were God's appointed authority over the temple and they hadn't authorized his actions. If he claimed Roman authority, they could prove that was a lie. So it wasn't a legitimate question in need of an answer, but a challenge designed to discredit Jesus no matter which answer he gave. (It's like someone from the IRS asking you, "Do you still cheat on your taxes?" There's no way to answer that question yes or no and not get yourself in trouble.) There was no acceptable answer to give, not even the truth.

The other aspect of this is found in Jesus' skillful reaction to the Sadducees. According to the general rules of debate in that time, counter-questioning was a respected debating practice. It's no accident that Jesus made John the Baptist the centerpiece of his counter-question. John was widely regarded by the people as a holy man of God—and John had unequivocally endorsed Jesus, saying he was "one who is more powerful than I, whose sandals I am not worthy to carry" (Matthew 3:11 NIV).

This turned the tables on the Sadducee priests. Now, suddenly, whatever response they gave would condemn them. If they said John was from God, they'd be admitting that Jesus (the "more powerful" one) was also acting as God's agent, which would supersede their authority in the temple. If they said John was not from God, they'd be discrediting themselves in front of the multitudes that held John in high regard.

The result was that the Sadducees wisely decided to back down, at least for the moment. Because they withdrew from accepted debate practices, they also had to release Jesus from any obligation to answer their threatening question.

Sources: IBB 166–167; OPB 1274

Parable of the Two Sons
Matthew 21:28-32

In the Parable of the Two Sons, is Jesus saying works are required for salvation?

The point of the Parable of the Two Sons was to rebuke the leading priests (who were Sadducees) and elders for their hypocrisy of belief. "The chief priests and Pharisees gave lip-service to obeying God," says Dr. Larry Richards, "but when put to the test they rejected His messenger [John the Baptist] and thus rejected Him."

In fact, as Jesus pointed out in Matthew 21:32, their rejection was twofold. First, they refused to believe the message that God sent through John. Then, even after seeing the powerful, positive change that message made in the lives of "sinners," they still refused to believe it was God's work.

So, does this mean that Jesus advocated salvation based on works of righteousness? No.

Christ's teaching here echoes the theology of James 2:14–26 and the idea that "faith is dead without good works" (James 2:26). As Jesus had said earlier, "A tree is identified by its fruit. If a tree is good, its fruit will be good. If a tree is bad, its fruit will be bad" (Matthew 12:33). Even rabbinic teaching testified to this way of thinking, as in this Jewish parable given in commentary on Deuteronomy 28:

> If one learns the words of the Torah and does not fulfill them, his punishment is more severe than that of him who has not learned at all. It is like the case of a king who had a garden, which he let out to two tenants, one of whom planted trees and cut them down, while the other neither planted any [trees] nor cut any down. With whom is the king angry? Surely with him who planted [trees] and cut them down. Likewise, whosoever learns the words of the Torah and does not fulfill them, his punishment is more severe than that of him who has never learned at all.

So, it is not good works that create faith, nor salvation. But *sincere faith naturally expresses itself in good works.* The Sadducees and other religious leaders had proven the dishonesty of their supposed religious fervor by their sinful actions. Likewise, the newly formed faith of tax collectors and sex workers showed itself to be genuine by their repentance and changed lives.

Sources: ETJ 237; MBC 1492; MAT 368

Why didn't the leading priests and elders believe in John the Baptist's preaching?

John the Baptist came preaching for people to repent from their wrongdoing and baptized them as a public symbol of that change of heart. People who knew they were "sinners" flocked to the opportunity to renew a relationship with God. That included crooked, traitorous tax collectors and sex workers. But the religious elite—people who should've come running to John—scorned the Baptist and his preaching.

Why was that the case? Factors such as money, power, and politics probably played a role, but the main reason seems to be pride. See, the chief priests (who were Sadducees), and elders, and other religious leaders were caught by a problem that continues to plague us church folk today: *They thought they were good people.*

Why repent if you don't think you're a sinner?

The Sadducees and religious leaders were, as theologian Robert Mounce stated it, "confident in their own spiritual superiority." These people knew and studied Scripture, and they followed religious laws. They were wealthy, intelligent, admired, and influential professionals in their religion. As such, they justified their wicked hypocrisy with hair-splitting theological arguments and arrogantly assumed John's preaching was meant for someone else, for people lesser than they.

It was a tragic mistake of pride that Jesus exposed with his parable of the two sons. And, sadly, it's a mistake that multitudes of us today are still guilty of making.

Source: NIBC 199

Parable of the Evil Farmers
Matthew 21:33–46

I understand that God is represented by the landowner in this parable, but I'm a little confused about all the other characters. Can you help?

This parable is an allegorical indictment against the corrupt religious and political leaders of Israel at that time, particularly the chief priests (Sadducees) and Pharisees. This is why, immediately after hearing the parable, Matthew says those groups "realized he was telling the story against them" and "wanted to arrest him" (Matthew 21:45–46).

So, in the parable of the evil farmers, the symbols are as follows:

> The *vineyard* is Israel and is actually described using imagery reminiscent of prophecy found in Isaiah 5:1–2.

> The *landowner* is God, who built Israel and invited its people to partner with him.

> The *tenant farmers* are the people of Israel, specifically the religious leaders (Sadducees and Pharisees) who, by their actions, demonstrate opposition to God.

> The *servants* sent by the landowner represent all the prophets of the Old Testament, such as Moses, Elijah, Isaiah, and the others.

> The *landowner's beloved son* is none other than Jesus himself.

> The *other tenants* mentioned at the end of the parable are gentiles. This is a reference to non-Jews (*ethnos* in the Greek) who will be allowed to inherit coequally the promise first made to Abraham and his descendants.

Sources: TYM 204; BIB 840

Why are Pharisees identified separately from the leading priests? Weren't they the same?

Because of their shared opposition to Jesus, it'd be easy to assume Pharisees and leading priests were all from the same group. But there were actually several prominent political and religious factions that were active during that time.

Pharisees grew out of the Jewish Maccabean Revolt against Syrian rule in the second century BC. By Jesus' time, they were well-respected and influential rule-makers in Jewish life (see the commentary on Matthew 12:9–14).

The leading priests were from the party of the Sadducees. They were the wealthy chief priests and political leaders of the Jews. These men were in charge of the temple—and its crooked moneymaking schemes (see the commentary on Matthew 16:1–4).

Pharisees and Sadducees didn't often agree, but when it came to Jesus they were (mostly) united in opposition to him.

Other influential groups in Jewish society at that time included scribes (see commentary segment on Matthew 20:17–19), as well as Essenes, Zealots, and Herodians. Essenes were the group that created the Dead Sea Scrolls. They mostly separated themselves from society because, for them, even the Pharisees weren't religiously pure enough. Zealots were a group that advocated an armed revolt against Rome, even committing acts that we'd consider terrorism today. And Herodians were wealthy aristocrats who supported Rome and, by extension, the various Judean kings in the line of Herod the Great.

So even though most of these groups were united in opposition against Jesus (except possibly the Zealots and Essenes), they were still distinct enough from each other for the gospel writers to identify some of them by name.

Sources: IBD3 1209, 1210; SLU 451; JOB 282

What is the stone that the builders rejected?

When Jesus spoke of a cornerstone that had been rejected, he was referencing several Old Testament messianic prophesies about himself.

> The first was Psalm 118:22–23, which is quoted in Matthew 21:42.

> The second was Isaiah 28:16, which reads in part, "Look! I am placing a foundation stone in Jerusalem, a firm and tested stone. It is a precious cornerstone that is safe to build on."

> Another was Isaiah 8:14–15, which declares, "to Israel and Judah he will be a stone that makes people stumble, a rock that makes them fall. And for the people of Jerusalem he will be a trap and a snare. Many will stumble and fall, never to rise again."

> And finally, Christ's words brought to mind the image of a dream recorded in Daniel 2:34–35: "A rock was cut from a mountain, but not by human hands. It struck the feet of iron and clay, smashing them to bits. The whole statue was crushed into small pieces of iron, clay, bronze, silver, and gold.... But the rock that knocked the statue down became a great mountain that covered the whole earth."

A cornerstone was a carefully chosen, very important stone in a building. It could be either the top stone of an arch that indicated the builder's approval of the finished structure, or the weight-bearing foundation stone that kept a building from crumbling down.

Christ's messianic claim here was clear—so much so that the leading priests and Pharisees wanted to arrest Jesus over it. Additionally, Peter later preached this same "cornerstone" message again before the Sanhedrin (Acts 4:8–12) and included a variation of it in his letter to Christians living outside of Israel (1 Peter 2:4–8). "These references were linked by the first

Christians," reports the *Dictionary of Biblical Imagery*, "because they point to Jesus as the Messiah foretold in Scriptures … though their Messiah had caused division and was rejected by many, this had been predicted."

So in this context, the stone the builders rejected symbolized Jesus himself—the living cornerstone (1 Peter 2:4) that would one day crush those wicked religious leaders in judgment.

Sources: IBD3 1488–1489; DBI 816

Parable of the Great Feast
Matthew 22:1–14

What does the imagery of the wedding feast represent in this parable?

Here's the run-down:

> The *king* represents God the Father.

> The *king's son*, in whose honor the feast is held, is Jesus.

> The *wedding feast* itself seems to represent the victorious "wedding feast of the Lamb" (Revelation 19:6–9) at the culmination of Christ's second coming (though some would disagree with me on that).

> The *original invited guests* (who refuse to come) would include the Jewish leaders of Jesus' time specifically, and the faithless people of Israel throughout history.

> The *servants* who keep inviting guests certainly include the ancient prophets and teachers in Israel. They could also include God's angels, the Old Testament Scriptures, and even the Holy Spirit himself.

> The *"good and bad" guests* who filled the banquet hall in the end represent people like you and me, and people from all ends of the earth who accept the gospel message—Jew and gentile alike.

> The identity of the *man* without proper wedding clothes is ambiguous, but at the core he represents those who would expect to be included in heaven but will be judged as people who do not belong (see Matthew 7:21–23, and 25:31–46).

Sources: TYM 206-207; ATP 228-231; ETJ 238

Several rounds of invitations are sent and received, messengers are insulted and killed, and an army razes a town in response! Are we really supposed to believe all these things could happen on the day of a wedding feast?

From a twenty-first century Western-world perspective, your question makes complete sense. From an ancient Middle Eastern point of view ... not so much. It's a problem of cultural disconnect that leads to mistaken assumptions. For many people, a wedding is an afternoon affair, often with a reception dinner in the evening—and then everyone goes home.

Not so in Jesus' time.

Back then a wedding celebration and accompanying feast could last for up to a week! This was particularly true among aristocrats and royalty. There would be days of wine and revelry (remember Jesus' first miracle at the Cana wedding; John 2:1–11?), delicious food, ongoing festivities, toasts, music and dancing, random amusements—all part of the celebration. In that culture, a weeklong wedding feast could easily accommodate all the events of Jesus' narration.

If that still sounds unrealistic to you, then I'll tell you this: I am of Middle Eastern descent, and even as late as the twentieth century this kind of days-long wedding celebration was still going on. I remember, as a child, being regaled by my grandmother with tales of her wedding to my grandfather back in "the old country" of Lebanon. According to her (and my sainted Nanaw would never lie!), their raucous celebration and feasting lasted one full week, with the highlight being a semi-drunken "strength test" of her new husband by her protective big brothers.

Makes you wonder what we've been missing with our tame wedding ceremonies today, doesn't it?

Source: ASB 1599

Why did the king punish the man for not wearing a wedding garment? What point is Jesus making?

This is a curious twist to the end of Jesus' parable. The king fills his (apparently massive) banquet hall so that it's teeming with guests. Then he comes down to join the party and the first thing he sees is "a man who wasn't wearing the proper clothes for a wedding" (verse 11). A minor *faux pas*, right? Well, actually, no. In this king's home, entry without proper wedding clothes is a severe crime punishable by banishment to "outer darkness, where there will be weeping and gnashing of teeth" (verse 13).

The symbolism of "outer darkness" as hell is pretty clear. What isn't clear is why the man's subpar fashion sense is deserving of hell. There are no definitive answers, so I'll just tell you a few theories.

> **THEORY #1:** R. V. G. Tasker informs us that Protestant theologians often find allegorical equivalence of the wedding clothes to the idea of heavenly "robes of righteousness," seen in scriptures like Isaiah 61:10 and Zechariah 3. In those passages, righteousness is bestowed by God himself, and symbolized with an exchange of filthy rags for finest clothing. With that in mind, St. Augustine's assumption that "the garment was provided by the royal host" has come to be widely accepted (though Tasker himself disagreed with that line of thinking). Applied to this parable, then, the wedding robe would be the righteousness of Christ, freely given by him to all the guests at the celebration. Thus, to be found without a robe would mean that the person had rejected the offer to be covered by the righteousness of Christ, and he was a trespasser rather than a friend or invited guest of the groom.

> **THEORY #2:** Other theologians, like Stanley Hauerwas, prefer the idea that, instead of Christ's righteousness, the wedding clothes represent a person's own righteousness earned through virtuous acts such as baptism and being people who "live lives worthy of the Lamb." Although I admire much about Dr. Hauerwas, I disagree pretty strongly with this view, as it's at cross-purposes with the overall New Testament message that salvation is by faith in Jesus alone, not by works (John 5:24; Ephesians 2:8–9; Romans 9:16, among others). But this view is taught, so I thought you'd want to know about it.

> **THEORY #3:** One final position is that the guest at the wedding represents Judas Iscariot, the disciple who betrayed Jesus. Those who hold this view are intrigued by the salutation, "Friend" (Matthew 22:12), which was unique to Matthew in the New Testament. It's used only three places: (1) in a similarly themed parable recorded in Matthew 20; (2) here in Matthew 22; and (3) finally spoken by Jesus to Judas at the moment of betrayal (Matthew 26:50). "Perhaps," Professor R. V. G. Tasker speculated, "in the context in which verses 11–14 were originally uttered, Jesus had Judas directly in view as the disciple who was in the kingdom of God under false pretenses."

I lean toward the first theory above, but as always, you'll have to make your own choices as to the symbolism of the wrongly dressed man.

Sources: TYM 207–208; BTCM 189

Taxes for Caesar
Matthew 22:15-22

I don't get all the dynamics in this confrontation over taxes—can you help?

OK, picture the scene in this passage as a game of strategy, like a chess match. On one side was Jesus, and on the other side were his enemies, the Pharisees. They wanted to find a way to maneuver Jesus into losing his following and/or his status—that was the game they were playing. So they made the following strategic moves.

First, the Pharisees came up with a doozy of a trick question and armed their own disciples with it. After their past humiliating experiences with Christ, it seems, they didn't want to risk confronting him themselves, so decided to send their lesser proxy instead.

Next, they paired those disciples with supporters of King Herod, that is, members of a political party called "Herodians." It's worth noting here that Pharisees and Herodians were not common allies; in fact, they were often enemies. But they were unified in their opposition to Jesus, so apparently that was enough to bring them together.

Finally, they sent this group of Pharisee wannabes and Herodians to try to flatter Jesus into complacency and then corner him with their checkmate-style trick question: "Is it right to pay taxes to Caesar or not?" (Matthew 22:17).

Why was this such a loaded question? A few reasons:

> Most Jews passionately hated the Roman government that was occupying their land. If Jesus supported paying taxes to Caesar, a good many of his followers would think him to be a traitor to Israel.

> The coins required to pay taxes were minted by Emperor Tiberius—who Romans worshiped as a god—and imprinted with his image on them. Thus, many Jews considered them to be idolatrous and a violation of both the first and second of Moses's Ten Commandments (Exodus 20:2-4). If Jesus approved the tax, he'd be accused of idolatry, which would likewise discredit him among his followers.

> If Jesus spoke out against the tax … well, that's where the Herodians came in. Those influential aristocrats were ardent supporters of the Roman occupation because that kept Herod Antipas in power as the de-facto king of Judea. If Jesus spoke out against the tax, they would've had him arrested as a traitor to Rome.

The problem for the Pharisees was that Jesus was simply smarter than they were. He saw through their subterfuge instantly and, with one quip— "Give to Caesar what belongs to Caesar, and give to God what belongs to God" (Matthew 22:21-22)—he demolished their strategy and beat them at their own game.

Sources: CEM 292-293; OPB 1275

Discussion about Resurrection
Matthew 22:23-33

Seven brothers have to marry the same woman? How is that part of Moses's law?

The Sadducees, in their exaggerated challenge to Jesus about resurrection, were referring to a centuries-old practice called "levirate marriage" which means literally "husband's brother marriage." This custom had been formalized by Moses (Deuteronomy 25:5–10) but predated him to the days of the Patriarchs (see for example, Genesis 38:6–11).

In an ancient patriarchal society where war was common and early death was frequent, levirate marriage appears to have been a practical solution to care for widows left behind. It was a means for continuing a family name and protecting family inheritance.

The basic provisions went something like this: "When an Israelite died without leaving a male heir, his nearest relative should marry the widow in order to continue the family name of the deceased brother ... The firstborn son by her took the name of the deceased brother, continuing his name in the family register." Importantly, this kind of marriage was not a legal requirement, but viewed as an act of loving devotion to the deceased by both the brother and the widow.

The most famous example of leviratic marriage in Scripture is the Old Testament book of Ruth, where Boaz steps in as the nearest willing relative (though not a brother-in-law per se) to marry Elimelech's widow, Ruth.

Source: OPB 358

How does Old Testament grammar prove the concept of resurrection?

In Matthew 22:31–32, Jesus demonstrates mastery of inductive reasoning to show the Sadducees that "there will be a resurrection of the dead." So before we go on, here's a quick primer on logical argumentation. Basically, it boils down to two forms: deductive or inductive reasoning. A deductive argument uses general information to reason out specific facts. For instance, the classic syllogism that goes, "All men are mortal. Socrates is a man. Therefore, Socrates is mortal." Inductive reasoning is just the opposite. It takes specific information to reason out general facts. For instance, "Serena ate a walnut. Serena broke out in a rash. Serena is allergic to nuts."

Bible scholar, Larry Richards, explains Jesus' inductive argument this way (italics his):

Jesus' argument hinges on the tense of the Hebrew verb. He points out that the Old Testament does not quote God as saying "I *was* the God" of these patriarchs. Instead the Lord said, "I *am*." This clearly implies that Abraham, Isaac, and Jacob still live, even though they died long before God spoke these words to Moses.

Christ's argument rested upon two beliefs that both he and the Sadducees would've already agreed upon. First was the accepted reliability of Scripture. It's important that Jesus chose to quote from Exodus 3:6, because Sadducees only accepted the Torah (the first five books of the Old Testament, which includes Exodus) as Scripture. Thus, logically speaking, by choosing a verse from Exodus Jesus met the Sadducees on common ground.

The second thing the Sadducees would've agreed with is the fact that God is not prone to misspeaking. If God had meant to say, "I am the Person who *was* the God of Abraham, Isaac, and Jacob," or "I *was* the God of Abraham, Isaac, and Jacob," then that's what he would've said. But God said, "I *am* the God of Abraham, the God of Isaac, and the God of Jacob" (emphasis mine). God didn't get the verb tense wrong; he meant what he said.

Sources: BAH 297; WWC 289

The Most Important Commandment
Matthew 22:34–40

What does it really mean to "love the Lord your God"?

If we're going to dig into this "most important commandment," we need to take a look at three things: (1) the immediate context of the command, (2) word definitions in the original languages, and (3) usage of terms elsewhere in the Bible.

1. Context

When Jesus said, "You must love the Lord our God with all your heart, all your soul, and all your mind" (Matthew 22:37), he was both quoting and offering commentary on Deuteronomy 6:5, which states, "And you must love the LORD your God with all your heart, all your soul, and all your strength." That Scripture, then, is the context for this command.

It's worth noting that Jesus changed the last word of Deuteronomy 6:5 from "strength" to "mind." This was not an error, nor an attempt to rewrite the Old Testament passage, but an exposition or commentary to provide added understanding of the Deuteronomy command. The Pharisees to whom Christ was talking at that moment would've long-ago memorized Deuteronomy 6:5, and would've understood Christ's variation was a teaching, not a replacement. This is evidenced by the fact that none of his enemies objected to his modified quote.

With that in mind, both the Deuteronomy 6:5 and Jesus' modified version of it indicate that loving God is first an act of will. It's a choice we make which involves the heart (the core of our desire), the soul (the eternal self which defines our unique being), and strength of mind (unwavering determination to continue to love).

2. Definitions

The Greek word for "love" in Matthew 22:37 is a command form of the root, *agapaō*, "to love." Similarly, in the Hebrew text of Deuteronomy 6:5 the word for love is from the root, *'āhaḇ*, "to have affection for." Entire books could be written about the depths and shades of meanings of these two tiny words, but for our purposes here we'll just say this: Both terms certainly carry an emotional attachment toward the person who is loved, but they encompass oceans more as well. Generally speaking, "love" in these definitions includes elements such as joyful devotion, prizing (or prioritizing) one above others, liking, gratitude toward, concern for the wellbeing of, to be full of goodwill toward, desire for, respect for, and generally seeking only the best for the person who is loved—even if it means enduring the worst for oneself.

3. Usage

In the Old Testament, *'āhaḇ* is first used by God himself to describe Abraham's relationship with his son, Isaac (Genesis 22:2). From there, that word or some variant of it is used to characterize a number of close relationships, including Isaac and his wife Rebekah (Genesis 24:7), a bond servant and master (Exodus 21:5), Ruth and her mother-in-law Naomi (Ruth 4:15), David and his close friend Jonathan (1 Samuel 18:1), God and the people of Israel (Jeremiah 31:3), and so on.

In the New Testament, *agapaō* or some variation of it is used over a hundred and forty times, showing up in twenty-two of the twenty-seven books, including all four gospels and in the letters of Paul, Peter, John, James, and Jude. Most famously, it appears in 1 Corinthians 13, where Paul describes with poetic beauty the attributes and impact of love. Needless to say, love was a core driver of the message of the New Testament. It was used to describe pretty much any healthy relationship possible between God and people and between people and others.

So, what does it really mean to "love the Lord your God"? If I had to sum it up into one sentence, I'd say: *Each day, every moment, I choose to pursue God, with joy, determination, and honest affection.*

And now I'm curious: How would you sum up what it really means to "love the Lord your God"?

Sources: CWSN 82; NSC4 1; CWDN 64; CWSO 491; NSC3 3; TGE 5-6; CWDO 20; VCEO 141-142

And how do I love my neighbor as myself?

As we did in the previous commentary segment above, we need to examine: (1) the immediate context of this command, (2) word definitions in the original languages, and (3) usage of terms elsewhere in the Bible.

1. Context

When Jesus said, "Love your neighbor as yourself" (Matthew 22:39) he was quoting part of Leviticus 19:18 which says in full, "Do not seek revenge or bear a grudge against a fellow Israelite, but love your neighbor as yourself. I am the LORD." In the immediate context of the Matthew and Leviticus Scriptures, a few things pop out.

First, Jesus gives equal standing to loving neighbors as to loving God (Matthew 22:39). That's a little bit unexpected, as we would assume that loving God would always be a higher priority. Jesus, though, intertwines loving him with loving neighbors, both here and elsewhere (see Matthew 25:31–46, for example). Swiss New Testament scholar Eduard Schweizer taught:

> By fusing those two [commands] he also prescribes how to perform the first: only the first commandment is called "great," but the second is equal to it, for one can love God only by loving one's neighbor.

Second, Leviticus 19:18 similarly gives a practical suggestion for how to fulfill the command to love your neighbor as yourself. Right before the command to love your neighbor, it reads, "Do not seek revenge or bear a grudge against a fellow Israelite." The first step toward loving others is, apparently, the refusal to retaliate for a wrong endured and a steadfast determination to forgive. Matthew highlights these principles in Jesus' teachings elsewhere as well (Matthew 5:38–48; 18:21–35).

2. Definitions

The Greek and Hebrew words for love in both these Old and New Testament passages are, respectively, *agapaō* and *'āhab*. Since we just discussed them in the previous commentary segment above, I won't rehash their definitions here. I will say, though, that the meanings described for these words are not passive; one doesn't simply sit back complacently and accumulate *agapaō* or *'āhab*. This kind of love is *active*, a motivation for movement that's not dependent on the perceived worthiness of the one loved but on the goodwill aspirations of the one doing the loving. It actively seeks out opportunities to do good, to build up others with kindness, to express generosity, and to plant joy (see Galatians 6:10; Romans 15:2; Hebrews 13:16; 1 Thessalonians 5:16).

3. Usage

Again, please look at the previous commentary segment just above for an overview of how *agapaō* and *'āhab* are used elsewhere in the Bible. For this discussion, though, I'd like us to focus on one particular usage found in 1 John.

This, I think gets to the heart of the answer to your question, "How do I love my neighbor as myself?" "We love each other because he loved us first" (1 John 4:19). From my point of view, loving our neighbors—all of the Christian life, really—is, at its core, an expression of gratitude. Church father, Augustine, put it this way: "God shows compassion to us because of his own kindness, and we in turn show it to one another because of his kindness."

We who experience God's great love each day (if we are paying attention) will instinctively feel gratitude for his undeserved kindness—which naturally will express itself in generous love toward others. That's how to love a neighbor as yourself.

Sources: GNM 426; CWSN 82; CWSO 491; VCEN 381-382; OCT 24

Whose Son Is the Messiah?
Matthew 22:41–46

What was the point of Jesus asking the Pharisees whose son the Messiah is?

Up to this point in Matthew 21–22 the religious and political leaders (Pharisees, Sadducees, Herodians) have been asking Jesus question after question in vain attempts to either discredit him before the people or to criminalize him in the eyes of the Roman government. Their concerns stem largely from the fact that the common people in Jerusalem are viewing Jesus as Israel's promised Messiah, even calling him by the messianic title, "Son of David" (Matthew 21:9, 15).

Now, after answering their last question about the greatest commandment (Matthew 22:34–40), Jesus goes on the offensive. He asks a question that forces the religious leaders to admit their preconceived notions of God's promised deliverer are wrong. As N. T. Wright observes, "The answer the opponents couldn't question was followed by the question they couldn't answer."

Christ's query was based on an accepted messianic prophecy from Psalm 110:1, which he abbreviates. The full text reads, "The LORD said to my Lord, 'Sit in the place of honor at my right hand until I humble your enemies, making them a footstool under your feet.'" The Hebrew translated as "Lord" in this sentence is actually two different words. The first is *Yhwh* (Yahweh), which is God. The second is *dōnî*, which would typically indicate a king. The literary construction here is fascinating because Israel's supreme ruler, King David, is the one speaking this Psalm—yet he refers to another as king over him. Thus his reference to *dōnî* means "Lord" in the divine sense—a Lord over lords, or a King over kings. Additionally, the declarations of that *dōnî* sitting at the right hand of *Yhwh* and having complete dominion over his enemies indicates "the most exalted position imaginable."

It's the King over kings aspect that the religious leaders of Jesus' time couldn't see. New Testament scholar Mike Wilkins reveals, "The Jews did not generally believe that the Messiah would be divine, but here Jesus confounded them by showing that ... he sustains a divine relationship to Yahweh."

So the point was this: Jesus had already been proclaimed Son of David, the human Messiah. Now he was claiming to also be the *divine* Messiah, the King over kings about whom David himself had prophesied.

This was a *radical* change of understanding. Theologian Robert Mounce explains, "The Pharisees expected the Messiah to come as the Son of David to carry out a military mission ... [but] the implication is that the Messiah is to play a more exalted role than the Pharisees expected." In that view, N. T. Wright sees Matthew hinting that Jesus has come not to eliminate the "nationalist enemies" of Israel (such as Rome), but to conquer "the ultimate enemies of the whole human race ... sin itself, and death, which it brings."

Matthew reports that Christ's brief, radical enlightenment of Psalm 110:1 so stunned his enemies that, "No one could answer him. And after that, no one dared to ask him any more questions" (Matthew 22:46).

Sources: MFE2 93, 95; UBP 414; HAC 149; NIBC 211

Jesus Criticizes the Religious Leaders
Matthew 23:1-36

What is "Moses's seat" in verse 2?

There are two main theories about what Jesus meant when he referred to Moses's seat—or in some Bible translations, the "chair of Moses." According to Dr. Craig Keener, they're as follows:

1. Many scholars point to the discovery of "a prominent seat" in some ancient synagogues that archaeologists have uncovered, and so interpret Christ literally here. Their thinking is that this unnamed seat was obviously an important place in synagogue services. Additionally, since Moses's writings from the Torah were taught in synagogues, and since rabbis sat down to teach, this prominent chair was possibly called "Moses's seat," where rabbis and teachers would sit while teaching.

2. Another, and more plausible, interpretation is that Jesus was using the phrase "Moses's seat" figuratively. The Pharisees and teachers of the law were standing in (well, sitting in) as successors to Moses

and his authority as a representative of God. That's why some Bible versions translate the Greek phrase less literally. Instead of "the Pharisees sit in Moses's seat," your Bible might say they "are the official interpreters of the law of Moses."

The tragedy of this situation in Matthew 23—however you translate the phrase—is that even though the Pharisees and teachers of the law had been given authority to teach truth about God, they didn't effectively live out the truth that they taught. That prompted Jesus to give his hearers the heartbreaking advice, "So practice and obey whatever they tell you, but don't follow their example" (Matthew 23:3).

Source: CBS 1657, 1659

What was so showy about prayer boxes and tassels? Didn't Jesus wear tassels?

Yes, Jesus wore tassels on his robe as was the custom among Jews of that time (see Numbers 15:38–39). In fact, those tassels are what the woman in Matthew 9 reached for when she wanted secret healing from Jesus.

Additionally, prayer boxes—translated as "phylacteries" in many Bible versions—were also common. Exodus 13:9 and Deuteronomy 6:8 say to tie the Lord's commands to your hands and wear them on your forehead—an instruction most likely meant to be figurative, but some Jews took this very literally. People would take little leather boxes, insert short scriptures written on fragments of parchment, and then strap them onto an arm, hand, or forehead.

Jesus' problem in Matthew 23 was not that tassels and/or phylacteries were being worn. It was that these religious leaders had co-opted those sincere expressions of faith to use them as opportunities for aggrandizement. They made their phylacteries clunky and wide and their robe tassels extra long, with the intention of drawing attention to, and admiration for, their pious demonstrations.

Today we'd probably call that practice a "humblebrag." (If you don't know what that means, just Google "funniest humblebrags" and you'll catch on pretty quickly.) Those Pharisees and religious leaders took something that was supposed to be personal and unobtrusive and turned it into a way to show off their supposed religious devotion.

Source: OPB 1276

Wait—I'm not supposed to call anyone father or teacher?

Matthew 23:8–10 records Jesus explicitly commanding that we should not call anyone rabbi, father, and teacher—yet we still use those terms freely, even in Christian circles. So what gives? Notice that Jesus gives this command within the context of rebuking the Pharisees and religious leaders, and as such, most agree that Christ's instructions here are cultural in application rather than universal.

In the first century, *rabbi* as a title didn't refer to a formally trained and ordained member of the clergy. Terms such as rabbi, father, and teacher signified one's high status within their society. Those who demanded to be called these kinds of titles considered themselves superior to others and insisted on being recognized as such. It reminds me of a time I worked in retail while in college. I got a new boss who ordered me to call him "Mr. Uhlman"—but freely called me "Mike" whenever he felt like it. When I asked to be called "Mr. Nappa" as a sign of mutual respect, he was deeply offended and harshly refused. In his view, I was beneath him and to prove my subservience he demanded to be "Mr." to me. (No, I didn't work there long after that!)

This was the attitude of those religious leaders who demanded self-important, sacred-sounding titles for themselves. They wanted to feel important at the expense of others. One Bible scholar explains: "The Pharisees saw the community of faith as a hierarchy and scrambled desperately to reach the top." But they'd missed the point, which Jesus restated forcefully for them: "All of you are equal as brothers and sisters" (Matthew 23:8).

Interestingly, the rabbinical tradition of those selfsame Pharisees echoed Jesus' reprimand. Craig Evans reports:

The Rabbis agree with Jesus views here, criticizing those who wish to show off their learning: "One should not say, 'I will read Scripture that I may be called a sage; I will study, that I may be called a Rabbi; I will study, to be an elder and sit in the assembly'; but learn out of love, and honor will come in the end."

Sources: MAT 390; ETJ 244

My Bible translation titles verses 13 and following as "Seven Woes." Did that mean something special in Jesus' time?

The "Seven Woes" of Matthew 23 are heartbreaking and depressingly realistic. They're also a form of literary expression similar to the Beatitudes that Jesus spoke during his Sermon on the Mount. For example, Matthew 5:1–12 records Jesus talking through a series of "Blessed are…" statements; now in Matthew 23 he employs the same form of address, this time using "Woe to you…" statements directed at the hypocritical religious leaders. (Some Bible versions translate this expression as "What sorrow…" or "How terrible….")

In the Old Testament, this literary style was used in "cursing" proclamations found in the Law and in prophetic utterances. For instance, in Deuteronomy 27:15–26 we find a series of recitations condemning specific sins that all begin with "cursed is anyone who…" (NIV). Isaiah 5:11–30 and Amos 5:18–24 are both passages of "woes" directed to the people of Israel for persistent disobedience.

So, Jesus' series of "woe to you…" statements recorded in Matthew 23 utilized a familiar and historically powerful literary style to declare judgment on the disbelieving Pharisees and religious leaders. (The fact that Christ was able to incorporate that style on the spur of the moment is actually kind of impressive to a word nerd like me.)

Jesus' condemnations in Matthew 23 all center on sins of religious arrogance and hypocrisy (see the commentary on Matthew 6:5–18 for more on that). The "woes" are pretty self-explanatory, but I do want to point out Jesus' reference to "blind guides" and "blind fools" in verses 16 and 17—just because I think it's funny. Jesus might have been alluding to an oral tradition among rabbinical sources about "The Bruised Pharisee." This was an allegory about a Pharisee so obsessed with self-righteousness that he kept his eyes closed to avoid seeing (and lusting after) any women—and thus kept bumping into things everywhere he went. Hence, he was always a "bruised Pharisee."

Of course, Jesus might not have had that story in mind, but if he did … well, that possibility kind of cracks me up.

Sources: IBB 108; BTCM 197

Who was "Zechariah son of Berekiah" in Matthew 23:35?

This is an interesting question, mainly because the identity of Zechariah here is contested among Bible scholars and historians.

For instance, as my good friend Dr. Timothy Paul Jones explains it, a number of theologians see Jesus making a sweeping "A to Z" type of statement here—not because the people he identifies have names that begin with A and Z, but because of the arrangement of the Hebrew canon of Scripture. The Tanakh (our Old Testament) was a collection of twenty-four scrolls that began with Genesis and ended with 2 Chronicles. Genesis 4:1–16 records Abel as the first person murdered in the Bible. Similarly, 2 Chronicles 24:20–22 recorded the killing of a righteous priest named Zechariah as the last murder in the Tanakh. So, the thinking goes, Jesus was emphasizing that his hearers would "be held responsible for the murder of all godly people of all time" (Matthew 23:35).

The problem with this theory is that the Zechariah mentioned in 2 Chronicles 24 was not the son of Berekiah as verse 35 declares. That man was a son of Jehoiada, a priest who served in the court of Israel's King Joash (see 2 Chronicles 23 and 24). Zechariah son of Berekiah was a prophet who lived long after Jehoiada, and who is author of the Old Testament book that bears his name (Zechariah 1:1). So even though there is nice symmetry to the "A to Z" theory, it seems unjustifiable given the text of Matthew 23.

Some have also argued that in Matthew 23:35 Jesus was prophesying about the future murder of another man named Zechariah. He was a wealthy Jew killed in much the same way as the son of Jehoiada, murdered by rebels in the temple area in AD 69, some thirty-plus years after Jesus' death and resurrection. Obviously, this is possible, but again, seems unlikely according to the context of Matthew 23.

I tend to be someone who thinks that Jesus meant what he said, so when I read "Zechariah son of Berekiah," I believe that's who he meant—the prophet from the book of Zechariah who spoke from around 520 BC to 480 BC. At the same time, I don't think that Jesus was always required to use biblical texts when speaking of biblical history. Some things we can corroborate from texts, some things we must assume were oral history that was left unrecorded in written form.

From that perspective, I lean toward a line of thinking similar to scholar, Gleason Archer Jr., who notes that during the time of that Zechariah's ministry, "The Old Testament contains no record of events during the first few decades of the fifth century BC until about 457, the date of Ezra's return to Jerusalem. But it may very well have been that ... Zechariah the prophet was martyred by a mob in much the same way Zechariah son of Jehoiada was some three centuries earlier."

To me, that seems the most plausible understanding. However, as always, you'll have to make your own decisions about that.

Sources: HWG 55-56; MAT 397; EBD 337-338

Jesus Grieves Over Jerusalem
Matthew 23:37–39

Um, did Jesus really call himself a chicken?

Well, yes, but the image of a hen protecting her chicks wouldn't have seemed as corny back then as it might seem today. Among Jesus' original hearers this simile would've called to mind majestic avian imagery from Old Testament Scriptures about God's faithful protection. As one Bible scholar reports, "Jewish tradition claimed that Jewish people were under God's wings and ... The Old Testament also portrays God as an eagle hovering over its offspring." For example, Psalm 91:4 promises, "He will cover you with his feathers. He will shelter you with his wings. His faithful promises are your armor and protection." Deuteronomy 32:11 reads, "Like an eagle that rouses her chicks and hovers over her young, so he spread his wings to take them up and carried them safely on his pinions." This is the context in which Jesus' lament would've been taken.

It's also important to notice the gender dynamics that Jesus displays in the imagery of Matthew 23:37. Beyond the simple fact that he represents himself as a hen (female), his public lament is itself feminine by nature. In that ancient Hebrew society, professional mourners were employed to come alongside and help the grieving (see, for example, Mark 5:37–40; the historical assumption here is that in order for a crowd of that many mourners to gather so quickly at the home of Jairus, they would've been professional mourners). The ministry of public mourning was traditionally considered woman's work, yet Jesus took on that role for himself anyway. In doing that, he mirrored the biblical symbolism of Rachel weeping over the loss of her children (Jeremiah 31:15; Matthew 2:18).

With that in mind, theologian Anna Case-Winters comments poignantly on this passage: "The feminine image conveys God's compassion; God's care for God's children is like this. Jesus laments the unresponsiveness of God's children.... The image is one of loss and profound sorrow."

Sources: IBB 111; BTC 269

Jesus Speaks about the Future
Matthew 24:1–51

Why did Matthew interrupt his story to point out that Jesus spoke this end-times prophecy on the Mount of Olives?

Jesus' long prophecy about future troubles, recorded in Matthew 24:1–51, is known as "The Olivet Discourse" (variations of which are also recorded in Mark 13 and Luke 21) because it took place on the Mount of Olives. And yes, Matthew seems to have included that information in his text on behalf of his Jewish readers, because that location is significant when taken in context of Scripture and the predicted end times.

The Mount of Olives sits just to the east of Jerusalem, a two-mile ridge that rises about 300 feet higher than the city. If you stand on that mountain range today, you'll have a panoramic view of what's called the "Old City" of Jerusalem, including the impressive Islamic mosque, Dome of the Rock, which dominates the area. In Jesus' day, that same view would've shown you the equally impressive Jewish temple from which Jesus had just come (Matthew 24:1).

On the eastern slope was (and still is) the town of Bethany where Jesus' friends, Mary, Martha, and Lazarus lived. The temple would've been to the west, and in between the two was the Garden of Gethsemane where Jesus prayed just before his arrest (Matthew 26:36–44).

Zechariah 14:4 declares that the Mount of Olives will play host to the conquering return of the Messiah, heralded by an apparent earthquake that splits the mountain in two. Additionally, only a few weeks after this discourse, Jesus himself stood again on the Mount of Olives, spoke final words to his disciples, and then ascended into heaven before their very eyes (Acts 1:6–12).

There are other important historical events that occurred on this mountain (see, for example, 2 Samuel 15:30; Ezekiel 11:23; Matthew 26:30, among others), but those two messianic moments from Zechariah and Acts stand out from the rest.

Source: LOB 137–139

Do we know any details about the destruction of the temple that Jesus predicted?

Yes, we actually know quite a bit about that, thanks to an ancient historian named Josephus. Jesus' prophecy in Matthew 24:2 came true in devastating fashion in AD 70, about forty years or so after he spoke it.

By that time, many Jews in Jerusalem had finally gotten what they wanted: an uprising against the powers of Rome. However, there was infighting among the Jews that split them into three militant factions. They were so preoccupied fighting each other that they didn't notice the Roman army marching toward them until it was too late.

According to Josephus, the Roman general Titus had his troops surround Jerusalem and lay siege to it. That brought severe famine inside the city walls, and horrific suffering. So many people died of starvation and sickness that their bodies were simply stacked like rotting pieces of wood all along the city streets. It was even reported that some mothers resorted to cannibalism, eating the flesh of their dead children in order to survive.

Eventually Titus's massive army breached the walls, raining destruction on everyone and everything within the city. It's said that the general ordered his soldiers to spare the Jewish temple, but by then the soldiers' hatred toward the Jews was so strong that they disobeyed and set fire to it. The temple contained large amounts of gold and silver, and the fire caused it all to melt. Those precious metals liquefied and dripped down into the cracks and crevices of the stones used in the Temple construction.

After the blaze had died down and the gold and silver had hardened, the Romans set about retrieving it for themselves as spoils of war. They took long bars and split apart the stones to extract the gold and silver piece by piece. They were so efficient that, when they were finished, literally not one stone of the temple structure was left upon on another.

Although the temple itself was completely destroyed, a small part of a retaining wall just west of the building did survive the calamity. That wall remnant, now called the Western Wall, still stands in Jerusalem today.

Source: WOE 24–25

How does Matthew 24:4–51 fit with John's book of Revelation?

All right, now we have to talk—briefly—about a topic that theologians call "eschatology"—that is, the study of end times as prophesied in the Bible. Eschatology is a mess for everyone, preachers and teachers included, because so much of what we find in the Bible about it is symbolic and not easily understood until after it takes place. So, read on skeptically, and I'll try to summarize some key approaches to interpreting Matthew 24:4–51 in light of Revelation.

Revelation 20 speaks of a thousand-year period (a millennium) in which Satan is bound and Christ reigns as Judge. Then, at the end of the thousand years, Satan is let out "for a little while" before being thrown into the "fiery lake" (verses 3, 10). *When* one believes this millennium will take place colors the way one interprets the events Jesus describes in Matthew 24. Here's how:

> **VIEW #1:** Some people see the millennium in more spiritual or metaphorical, rather than literal, terms. The millennium, then, began with Christ's coming and continues long past a thousand years. This view, called Amillennialism, typically sees the fulfillment of all of Matthew 24:4–51 in the first century, most specifically in the destruction of the Jewish temple in AD 70.

> **VIEW #2:** Others also see the millennium as more figurative than literal, but they believe the millennium is being fulfilled throughout history through the influence of the church, as the reign of Christ becomes more and more evident in this world. In this view, called Postmillennialism, fulfillment of the Mathew 24 prophecies is happening gradually over time, including the time in which we now live.

> **VIEW #3:** Those who see the millennial reign of Christ as a literal thousand years also interpret Matthew 24 more literally. This view is called Premillennialism. There are, however, some disagreements within this approach. Some people see the whole passage as speaking of the future Great Tribulation described in Revelation; others think that Matthew 24:2–14 has been fulfilled already, while Matthew 24:15–30 will take place during the Great Tribulation.

So how does Matthew 24:4–51 fit with John's book of Revelation? Well, there are different opinions and lots of arguments and no universal agreement in theological circles. My personal impression is that Jesus was talking about some of the same events that John later wrote about in his Revelation—and that Christ also was talking about some things that maybe have happened or will happen before that time.

It's also possible that Jesus spoke of things that both have happened and will happen, using the same imagery for them. My pastor calls this the "law of two mountains." That's the idea that one image can sometimes reference two different things in the same way that one mountain peak seen in the distance may actually turn out to be two or three separate ridges when seen close-up. When it comes to end-times prophecy, the law of two mountains makes sense to me.

Sources: EPB 381; CBP 156–159

Was Jesus mistaken when he said, in verse 34, "This generation will not pass from the scene until all these things take place"?

Matthew 24:34 is typically understood in one of three ways, and that understanding depends on how you interpret the Greek phrase *genea hautē*, "this generation."

First is the view that Jesus did indeed make a mistake, or worse, he was lying to his disciples only days before his crucifixion. That thinking sees *genea hautē* as referring specifically to the people alive at that time. It basically says: Jesus promised the end of the world would come before the last person alive at that time had died (roughly by the end of the first century); that entire generation has long died out; therefore Jesus is a liar.

Second is the view that *genea hautē* refers to the generation of people alive at the time when the symbolic fig tree mentioned in verse 32 has bloomed—that is, the people alive during the future Great Tribulation described in detail in the book of Revelation. This view prefers to look at the whole of Matthew 24 as being important to consider when trying to understand verse 34, particularly the verses just before and after it.

Third is the view that *genea hautē* refers to the Jewish people as a whole, or to the nation of Israel, which will continue until the events of the end times have been completed. According to prominent twentieth-century pastor Ray Stedman, the cornerstone of this thinking is that "in the first century, the word *genea* referred to a group of people of common family stock, of shared nativity or descent. In this sense, everyone who was descended from Jacob ... were all of the same 'generation.'"

I think all three of those opinions are plausible. After all, in Greek the word *hautē* ("this") could mean "referring to a person or thing before mentioned," *and* it could also mean "the chief topic of discourse." If Jesus used it in the first sense, it meant that specific, first-century generation; if he used it in the second sense, it meant either the future generation alive at the Great Tribulation, or perhaps the Jewish people as a group throughout history.

Still, I think I prefer a fourth option put forth by New Testament scholar, Mike Wilkins. See if you agree. Dr. Wilkins says:

> It is perhaps easiest to see a two-fold reference in "this generation," as Jesus has done throughout the discourse. The disciples to whom Jesus spoke on the Mount of Olives will be "this generation" that sees the temple destroyed, which shows the applicability of the discourse to AD 70. Further, within the context of Jesus' statements about the coming of the Son of Man at the end of the age, "this generation" must apply to those at the end of the age who will see the events surrounding the abomination of desolation.... Jesus' saying is a word of warning—to his contemporaries and to those in the future who are unrepentant."

Sources: CWSN 91; WOE 141-143; ZB1 152-153; CWDN 1077; HAC 154-155

Does Matthew 24:36–44 teach that Jesus will rapture the church away before the Great Tribulation?

There are those among scholars and pastors who would say yes, this passage teaches of a rapture before the terrible days of Great Tribulation predicted in John's book of Revelation. For instance, Dr. Michael Vanlaningham of Moody Bible Institute comments: "The man and woman who are taken in vv. 40 and 41 are raptured out of the world before the start of the tribulation, just as Noah was taken out of harm's way before the coming flood."

At the same time, there are others who would disagree pretty strongly with Dr. Vanlaningham's interpretation. They'd say that the doctrine of a raptured church is wishful thinking at best, and potentially harmful theology that makes a promise God does not intend to keep.

Personally, I fall more in line with that second group than with the first. I don't see Jesus speaking of a rapture in these verses. To me, it appears that Christ's talking about the events described in Revelation 19:11–21:27, when he returns to defeat armies of evil and establish the New Jerusalem for his saints.

Entire books have been written on this subject, so I won't attempt to offer any definitive theology on that here. I will admit, though, that my interpretation of Matthew 25 is colored by my general disbelief in the theology of a pre-tribulation rapture. This doctrine of a "secret return of Christ" before his actual Second Coming was never taught by the early church nor by Jesus' disciples. Rapture theory was mostly formulated by the British preacher, John Darby, in 1827—some eighteen-hundred years after Jesus' ministry—and it has proliferated from there. I'd love for it to be true, but I simply don't see it demonstrated in Scripture.

In the end, you'll have to make your own decisions about this one, but I tend to agree with theologian Daniel Doriani when he says, "The New Testament teaches that (1) Jesus returns one more time; (2) his return is public and visible to all, and (3) the dead rise at the time. Rapture theory asserts the opposite at each point.

Sources: MBC 1503; REC2 390–391

Parable of the Ten Bridesmaids
Matthew 25:1–13

Did Jesus endorse polygamy in his parable of the ten bridesmaids?

Well, in reality, Jesus' parable in Matthew 25:1–13 has very little to do with monogamy or polygamy—its whole point was a warning to be prepared for his coming return, continuing the theme from the place where Matthew 24 ends. But some do try to use this parable to promote the idea of polygamy, so let's go ahead and talk about it.

Fact is, in Jesus' day, polygamy was an acceptable, though relatively uncommon, practice. Typically, marriage to multiple wives was reserved only for the wealthy or those in royal positions, often as a function of sealing political alliances. Still, Jewish history didn't blush at telling us that the heroes like Abraham, Jacob, David, Solomon and others practiced polygamy. We also can't simply dismiss that other New Testament Scriptures suggest polygamy was a reality, though not one endorsed by the church (1 Timothy 3:2, 12 NKJV).

Those who use Matthew 25:1–13 to justify multiple wives would approach the Scripture this way. First, they discard our modern cultural understanding of the Greek word, *parthénos*, which is translated as "bridesmaid" in some Bible versions, but more literally translated as "virgin" in others. They insist on "virgin" as the literal translation, which would be a description for a bride. Next, they point out that although a bridegroom (who clearly represents Christ) is featured in the parable, no bride is mentioned, thus defaulting to the idea that the virgins (plural) were intended to represent the bride. Finally, they say that the five wise virgins represent the church as the "bride of Christ," those who are taken by the groom to the wedding (2 Corinthians 11:2; Revelation 19:7–9). As theologian Herbert Lockyear, playing devil's advocate, asks (italics his): "The Bible clearly teaches that all born again believers form the Bride, the Church, [so] how can they be the *bridesmaids* and the *bride* at the same time?" Thus, they say, polygamy is good enough for Jesus, it's good enough for us.

Obviously, I disagree with that method of interpretation of this parable. I can't dismiss that some could feel justified by this perspective, but it seems to me to be convoluted thinking, forcing a meaning into the text in order to fit a predetermined goal.

I prefer the more common interpretation that falls within both the biblical and cultural context of Jesus' time. This takes the view that the *parthénos* of the parable, while literally translated as virgins does in its context describe bridesmaids. Additionally, Drs. Lawrence Schiffman and Paul Achtemeier report that in the Jewish culture of that time, "the central ritual of the marriage ceremony itself was the symbolic bringing of the bride into the groom's house, followed by great rejoicing." If this ritual occurred in the evening, as was known to happen, it would've been a torchlight procession full of joy and celebration. Bible scholar, Craig Evans describes it this way:

> After the wedding feast at the house of the bride's parents, which ends well into the night, the bridegroom escorts his bride to his parents' house. A number of maids await the arrival of the bride and groom and will escort them with lamps to the bridal chamber.

This seems the most straightforward view of Jesus' teaching, so I'd say no, I don't believe this parable endorses the practice of polygamy among Christ's followers.

Sources: HBD 302, 608; CWSN 92; CWDN 1119; ATP 239; MFE2 133; MAT 416

I've been told that oil in the Bible always represents the Holy Spirit? Is that true in this parable?

Oil in Scripture does often beautifully represent the Holy Spirit—but not *always*, and not necessarily in this parable.

There are close to two hundred mentions of oil in the Bible. Given such extensive use, it's no surprise that sometimes oil has spiritual significance, and other times it represents … oil.

For instance, when used in anointing, oil symbolizes the presence of the Holy Spirit (Exodus 30:25; Psalm 23:5; Isaiah 61:1–3). When used in connection with baking, it meant, literally, oil (Numbers 11:8). The miracle of the widow's oil describes it as simply kitchen material, which has value for buying and selling (2 Kings 4:1–7).

Regarding the oil in the parable of the ten bridesmaids, some have interpreted it as symbolizing Christ's Holy Spirit, or as a symbol of the Word of God (the Bible), or good works, or faith, or love, or wisdom, and so on. As I read the parable, though, to me it just seems to represent oil in the practical sense—the fuel needed to keep the lamps lit.

Sometimes, I think, there's no need to impose a symbolic meaning on every part of a Bible story.

Sources: DBI 392, 603; BEC 91–92; MFE2 133

Parable of the Three Servants
Matthew 25:14–30

The parable of the three servants symbolizes God as being a "man going on a long trip." Does that mean that God is not watching over us all the time?

Based on this parable, I can see why a person might reach the conclusion that God is an absentee Father. Three parables in a row represent God with a character that's distant from us and not paying attention until he returns (Matthew 24:45–25:30). If this were the only testimony of Scripture in that regard, I'd be inclined to agree with the idea that God created the universe and then stepped away and chose not to interfere in anything afterward. But that's not what I see here or elsewhere in the Bible.

First, the view of God as uninvolved deity doesn't appear to be the intent of this parable of the three servants. The story itself uses a business metaphor to bring home the idea that God has made us his stewards on this earth. In this way, it symbolizes a postponement of accounting and the promise of a final reckoning. The fact that this master is "away" during this parable is just a literary device to communicate that the servants/stewards have a limited window of opportunity to manage their own careers successfully, using the master's extensive resources as their seed money.

Second, Scripture as a whole overwhelmingly refutes that idea that God is not active in human lives. There are many Bible passages to indicate that, but here are just a few to remember:

> "The Lord keeps watch over you as you come and go, both now and forever" (Psalm 121:8).

> "The LORD is watching everywhere, keeping his eye on both the evil and the good" (Proverbs 15:3).

> "But when you pray, go away by yourself, shut the door behind you, and pray to your Father in private. Then your Father, who sees everything, will reward you" (Matthew 6:6).

> "But Jesus replied, "My Father is always working, and so am I" (John 5:17).

My favorite, though, is the promise of the ongoing work of the Holy Spirit that's recorded in John 14:16–17. May this be an encouragement to you as you go through your day today:

> "And I will ask the Father, and he will give you another Advocate, who will never leave you. He is the Holy Spirit, who leads into all truth."

Source: CEM 333

How much money did the master actually give to his servants?

The money given to the servants in this parable is called "bags of silver" in some Bible translations, while other versions say that it's "bags of gold,"— and just to make matters more confusing, older Bible translations identify it as "talents" with no indication of whether that means gold, silver, or copper. The Greek word in Matthew 25:15 is *talanta*, which translates literally as "talents," with no indication of what kind of metal the currency was. Here's what we do know:

> A talent (regardless of type) wasn't a specific amount of money but indicated the *weight* of a precious metal. In that sense, a "talent" today would be the equivalent of about seventy-five pounds.

> A talent of money in Jesus' day could've been gold, silver, or copper. In this parable, it was almost certainly silver. We know this because in Matthew 25:18 the Greek word translated generically as "money" is *argyrion*, which means "silver" or "silver coin."

> Seventy-five pounds of silver in that time was worth about six thousand denarii. Since a single denarius was the equivalent to a day's wage for a laborer, that meant a single talent of silver was equal to about six thousand days of wages.

> In other words, one servant received nearly twenty years of wages from the master; another received close to forty years; and the third was given almost a hundred years' worth of income to manage.

For a little fun today, go online and look up "hourly wage for general laborer." Then do this:

> Multiply that hourly wage by eight (hours in a workday) to get an average daily wage.

> Next multiply that daily wage by six thousand, which was the number of days a talent of silver could cover in wages.

> Finally, multiply that last number by eight (the number of talents the master distributed.)

That'll give you a rough equivalent, in our modern currency, of how much money the master entrusted to his servants. When I did this exercise at the time of this writing, it totaled over six million dollars!

Sources: CWSN 93; CWDN 1365; RDA 24; REC2 399; ZB1 155-156

Why is the master (God!) so harsh in punishing the last servant in this parable? Was that really deserved?

The parable of the three servants makes a lot of people uncomfortable, particularly because God, in the character of the master, is symbolized as being very harsh and demanding. Plus there's the whole "throw this useless servant into outer darkness, where there will be weeping and gnashing of teeth" verse. That's an extreme punishment which, on the surface, doesn't seem to fit the crime. Some feel compelled to jump to God's defense here, as if Jesus perhaps made a mistake in the way he depicted the Father. They try to soften the text to make it more palatable to our modern ears.

I don't feel that compunction, as I think God does just fine defending himself. However, I do want to tell you what I see in here, and you can decide if you see the same thing.

When I look at this parable, the first thing I notice is the nature of the relationship between the master and his servants. For starters, we've gentrified them a bit by calling them "servants" in our most common translations. The Greek word in Matthew 25:14 is *doulos*, which always means "slave" and also denotes a bondslave or "bond-servant," as in "Paul, *a bond-servant of Christ Jesus*, called as an apostle, set apart for the gospel of God" (Romans 1:1 NASB, italics mine). A bondservant was a unique type of slave in Hebrew culture; this person had been offered freedom but, *out of love for, and devotion to, the master*, had voluntarily chosen to remain a slave for life (Deuteronomy 15:16–17). Given the level of responsibility and enormous amounts of money these slaves received, they were almost certainly bondslaves to their master.

Second, the circumstances of the stewardship arrangement described in this parable show the master as entering into a *partnership* with his bondservant. The lines between slave and master have been blurred by the relationship and the significant responsibility—and the inherent honor—bestowed on the slave. This stewardship arrangement carried with it personal, relational elements that included respect, generosity, and, most importantly, complete trust.

Third, the end of the parable reveals that the master's intent was to bless each bondservant with abundance, wealth, and joy. He returned fully ready to celebrate and reward. Punishment does not appear to be the master's first choice.

Finally, the last bondservant did *nothing*. For a *l-o-n-g* time. Yet he expected a reward. Worse, he justified his indolence by mischaracterizing and insulting the master to whom he had pledged love, loyalty, and responsibility. This was not simply a bad business decision, but a betrayal of trust, of the relationship, of the partnership, and of the master's intent to bless.

Imagine if you gave one million dollars to a 401K fund manager to invest for you. Twenty years later you're ready to retire so you ask to see the progress your investor has made with your money. That person tells you, "Oh, I did nothing. Absolutely zero. For twenty full years. In fact, I buried your cash and forgot about it until you came back."

How would you respond?

So to my mind, the problem of this last servant was not so much bad cash flow, but a failure of character. His was a lifestyle of hypocrisy (akin to the Pharisees) that cost that poor man everything. We'd be wise to learn from his tragic example.

Sources: CWSN 93; VCEN 73; BID 1552

Do "outer darkness," and "weeping and gnashing of teeth" always refer to hell, or are there other interpretations too?

Well, let's see…

The Greek phrase translated as "outer darkness" in the NLT is *skotos to exōteron*. That phrase is exclusive to Matthew's gospel and shows up three times: Matthew 8:12; 22:13; and 25:30. In every instance it's a record of Jesus talking, and all three verses are references to hell. Interestingly, every time he says "outer darkness," Jesus also pairs it with "weeping and gnashing of teeth." "Weeping" by itself obviously has multiple uses and applications in the New Testament, but when combined with the Greek *brygmos tōn odontōn*, "gnashing of teeth," that phrase appears seven times in the New Testament, again always spoken by Jesus. Six of those appearances are in Matthew, as in: Matthew 8:12; 13:42, 50; 22:13; 24:51; and 25:30. The final occurrence is found in Luke 13:28. Again, in every usage, "weeping and gnashing of teeth" refers to an eternal hell, often combined with a description of fire in place of "outer darkness."

Seeing the consistency with which this image of "weeping and gnashing of teeth" is used, it does make one think. We typically assume this is an allegorical, sensory/emotional view of hell. But since Christ described hell this way every time, we must wonder if he was perhaps, giving us a literal peek into that awful, painful place? It'll be best, I think, if we never have to find out.

Sources: CWSN 93; CWDN 1298, 1025, 609, 349, 1027

The Final Judgment
Matthew 25:31-46

Can you explain the symbolism behind "sheep" and "goat" in this passage?

This is one of those instances where the metaphor of sheep and goats doesn't seem to be obviously apparent, other than one group is rewarded and the other is punished. As Dr. Michael Wilkins comments, "There does not appear to be any significant reason why the goat was selected to contrast with the sheep, except for the symbolism that will be attached to both in a surprising manner."

In most cases, flocks of goats wouldn't mix with flocks of sheep, so there'd be no need to separate them. However, Bible historian Daniel Doriani does tell us that in areas surrounding the land of ancient Israel, it was possible for these kinds of flocks to mingle together for grazing. In that situation they'd have to be separated at day's end because goats, with less fur, needed warmer protection at night.

Also, we know that sheep in both Old and New Testament literature were frequently used as a metaphor for God's chosen and well-loved people. This was particularly true in reference to Israel but also referred to Christ's own followers (see, for example, Ezekiel 34 and John 21:15–17). So the symbolism of sheep seems well established.

The goat metaphor in Scripture is harder to pin down. Mention of them in the New Testament is rare, and mostly incidental rather than meaningful. However, according to Dr. Wilkins, "In the Old Testament seventy percent of the references [to goats] concern their use as animals for sacrifice, such as the goat offered for sin sacrifice and the scapegoat, where in a symbolic way sin was removed from the community and sent to the region of desert or death."

It may be that Jesus meant the goats in this parable to symbolize the scapegoat's destiny, but that's speculation at best. The most that we can probably take from this, symbolically speaking, is that Christ will judge us all, rewarding those who served him by serving others and punishing those who hypocritically did not.

Sources: ZB1 157; REC2 411

Is it important that Jesus "will place the sheep at his right hand" (verse 33)?

The right hand of royalty, or authority, held considerable meaning in the ancient world of Jesus. This is especially seen in the parable of the sheep and goats because it's one of the rare times that Jesus called himself a "king" (verse 34).

Pictured as a royal throne room (as it is in this parable), placement at the right hand of a king indicated a few very important things:

> *Close Relationship.* Only the king's intimates were allowed to occupy that position so near to the king.

> *Trust.* The one a king trusted most, for instance, an advisor or a queen, sat at his right side in a throne room.

> *Favor.* Royal favor toward a person, above all others, was demonstrated by his or her position at the king's right side.

> *Honor.* The person to the king's right had been exalted to the highest honor in a kingdom.

> *Highest Authority.* The one at the king's right acted as the agent of the king and, therefore, with the king's authority; the king's "right-hand man," so to speak.

> *Power.* The authority of the king's right hand wasn't simply a decree, but a position that could be backed up by force.

Basically, to sit at the king's right side was to be made equal to the king without taking the position of king. This is why Christ's disciples asked to be seated at his side (Matthew 20:20–21), and why Jesus himself is often depicted in Scripture as being seated at the right hand of Father God for all eternity (for example, Acts 7:56; Romans 8:34; Hebrews 1:3 and others). So the fact that Jesus will place his followers at his right hand in the coming glory emphasizes visually the high honor associated with his promise:

"Come, you who are blessed by my Father, inherit the Kingdom prepared for you from the creation of the world" (verse 34).

Source: ASB 1983

What does it mean that hell was prepared for the devil and his demons?

Most agree that Jesus' reference to "the eternal fire" in Matthew 25:41 is speaking of what the apostle John will later describe in Revelation 20:10 as a "lake of fire"—the final destination for Satan and his allies. With that perspective, I think Pastor David Platt says it best (italics his): "Hell is not a place where the Devil torments sinners; hell is a place where he is tormented *alongside* sinners."

A. Lukyn Williams was a New Testament scholar who lived during the 1800s. In a commentary on these verses, he points out that a majestic kingdom inheritance for the righteous (the "sheep" in this parable) was in God's plans for us at the earliest moments of creation (Matthew 25:35). By contrast, "eternal fire," was an afterthought, fashioned after creation specifically for the devil and his demons. "It seems as though," Williams observes, "there were no proper place for man's punishment; there is no book of death corresponding to the book of life."

This feels tragic to me; it indicates that God's first intention was, from the beginning, extravagant blessing and reward. The blight of eternal punishment was something that needn't ever have existed, but for our participation in Satan's sin. Williams finally concludes:

> How to reconcile this destiny, which seems inconceivably terrible, with God's mercy, love, and justice, has always proved a stumbling-block to free thinkers. It is, indeed, a mystery which we cannot understand, and which Christ has purposely left unexplained. We can only bow the head and say, "Shall not the Judge of all the earth do right?" (Gen. xviii. 25)

Sources: CEM 337; PCXV 484

The Plot to Kill Jesus
Matthew 26:1–5

What can you tell me about Caiaphas, the high priest who plotted to kill Jesus?

Caiaphas (pronounced KY-uh-fuss) was a Sadducee high priest during parts of the lives of both John the Baptist and Jesus. By all accounts, he and his father-in-law, Annas, were fairly corrupt, and also fairly powerful people in Jewish society under Roman rule.

For starters, Caiaphas, along with his father-in-law, ran the crooked Annas Bazaar at the temple, which Jesus violently drove out on two occasions (see the commentary on Matthew 16:1–4 and 21:12–17). Additionally, he was part of a scheme of nepotism that kept his family in power under the authority of Rome.

Annas had been appointed as high priest by the Roman governor of Syria around AD 6 or 7 and then deposed in AD 15. The next seven high priests were all from Annas's family—five sons, one grandson, and of course, Caiaphas his son-in-law.

Caiaphas came to power around AD 18 and ruled the Jewish Sanhedrin for nearly twenty years. He earned a reputation for bribery, thuggery, and for abusing his position to pursue criminal behavior. Worst of all, though, was his hatred for Jesus. When Caiaphas found out that Christ had raised Lazarus from the dead, he called a meeting of the Sanhedrin to discuss it (John 11:1–53). He apparently feared that Jesus would start a rebellion that would bring down the wrath of Roman armies on Jerusalem. His solution? Kill Jesus now so the Romans wouldn't have to kill him later (John 11:49–50). As seen in Matthew 26, Caiaphas was intimately involved in plotting Jesus' murder, having him arrested, presiding over Jesus' sham trial before the Sanhedrin, and pronouncing the death sentence for Christ.

Caiaphas also was likely among those who denied Judas when he tried to return the thirty pieces of silver, and who used that blood money to buy a field which was turned into a graveyard. This high priest's last appearance in the New Testament is in the book of Acts, where he's still fighting against Jesus by having the Christ-followers arrested for healing a man who had been unable to walk for forty years.

History reports that Caiaphas appears to have lived to a ripe old age of sixty or so—"old" for back then. Archaeologists have recovered an ornate bone box (ossuary) from first-century Jerusalem that features the inscription, "Joseph son of Caiaphas." The ossuary contained bones of six people, including bones believed to have belonged to the Caiaphas who succeeded in his plot to have Jesus killed.

Sources: WWW 34, 69; WWA 61; JOB 279-280

Jesus Anointed at Bethany
Matthew 26:6-13

Why is Matthew's account of the woman pouring perfume on Jesus different from the other gospel writers?

The record of this event, or one like it, appears in all four of the Gospels. And, as you mentioned, none of them are exactly the same. This is to be expected when four different people each tell a story from a different perspective (for more on this, see the commentary on Matthew 20:29–34). However, there are some discrepancies this time that require us to take a closer look.

The main question is: Do these Scriptures all refer to the same event, or to different-but-similar events?

The accounts in Matthew 26:6–13 and Mark 14:3–9 appear to be talking about the same moment. They agree that it took place in Bethany, in the home of a person named Simon (formerly a leper), in the days leading up to Jesus' arrest and crucifixion. There a woman poured the perfume on Jesus' head, and the disciples objected to the waste.

John 12:1–8 tells close to the same story. In that account, though, the woman is named as Mary, the sister of Lazarus whom Jesus had raised from the dead. Additionally, John is ambiguous about whose house they were in at the time, simply saying, "A dinner was prepared in Jesus' honor," and indicating that Mary's sister, Martha, served the food. John 12 also mentions perfume on Jesus' feet, which foreshadows his beautiful recollection of Jesus washing the disciples' feet, told in John 13.

John's account is fairly easy to reconcile with Matthew and Mark. It would appear that: (1) A dinner was held in Jesus' honor, (2) in Bethany,

(3) at the house of Simon (the leper), where (4) Martha was the ancient world's equivalent of a caterer, and (5) Mary poured perfume on both Jesus' head and feet.

So it would appear that, even though some minor details are different, all three accounts from Matthew, Mark, and John report the same event. Trying to reconcile those details with Luke 7:36–50 is a different story.

In Luke, the perfume-pouring moment takes place in Galilee, much earlier in Jesus' ministry, at the home of a Pharisee named Simon (which was a very common name in that time). The woman is unnamed, but clearly identified as "a sinner," a designation which was never applied to Mary, the sister of Lazarus. Also in Luke, the woman is weeping in sorrow and kissing Jesus' feet. There's no objection to wasted perfume from the disciples in this account, but instead a parable of forgiveness told to the Pharisee who is overly judgmental toward the sinner-woman. Finally, Jesus blesses the woman with these kind words: "Your faith has saved you; go in peace" (Luke 7:50).

Reading these accounts next to each other, it seems *very* unlikely that Luke 7:36–50 is the same event as the one in the other gospels. Most likely is that these are two different, though similar, moments.

I think that probably, early in Jesus' ministry, the unnamed sinner came to Christ with perfume and received the forgiveness she needed. Perhaps Mary, the sister of Lazarus, heard of that other woman and decided to imitate her beautiful act? We don't know for sure, but sometime later, Mary too poured perfume on Jesus as a spontaneous act of devotion. That seems to make the most sense to me.

Source: IBD2 959–960

How was pouring perfume on Jesus' feet preparing him for burial?

In the time of Christ, one of the earliest steps in a typical burial process was to perfume the corpse. This was because Jews didn't embalm the bodies of loved ones who died.

Let's face it, dead bodies decompose and start to smell bad pretty quickly—especially in a hot climate like the desert regions of Israel. So in that time and place, the first thing to be done with a corpse was to wash it and then gently cover it in scented oils. This masked the increasingly foul odor for several days while mourners came to pay their respects.

Because of that custom, when the woman (identified in John 12:3 as Mary, the sister of Lazarus) poured perfume over Jesus just days before his execution, it was both a beautiful expression of her devotion—and a symbolic prophecy of his death that was soon to come. (For more details about burial customs of the ancient Israelites, see the commentary on Matthew 27:57–61.)

Source: JOB 274

Judas Agrees to Betray Jesus
Matthew 26:14-16

What is known about Judas Iscariot?

Judas Iscariot appears to have been a fine, upstanding man of faith in his day. His zeal for God, at least initially, is evident in the fact that he left everything to become one of Jesus' itinerant followers, a disciple and servant traveling for years with the Son of Man who had "no place to lay his head" (Luke 9:58).

Judas's first name was the Greek version of "Judah" (meaning "praise")—an honored name throughout most of Hebrew history. In fact, it was popular enough that two of Jesus' twelve disciples were named Judas (John 14:22), and one of Jesus' own brothers was a Judas too (Mark 6:3). Judas Iscariot's last name means "man of Kerioth," most likely a reference to the town of Kerioth Hezron once located in southern Israel. That means Judas was the only of Christ's disciples not from the region of Galilee.

Among the twelve, Judas appears to have been well respected. He was trusted enough that "he was in charge of the disciples' money" (John 12:6). Scripture also suggests that Judas performed miracles of healing and exorcisms and was one of the twelve who went from village to village, proclaiming the good news of Jesus and healing the sick (Luke 9:1–6).

Details of the Last Supper (Mark 14:20; John 13:26–27) lead Ronald Youngblood and his colleagues to believe that during that meal "Judas probably was reclining beside Jesus, [more] evidence that Judas was an important disciple." Still, perhaps most revealing of Judas's place among the twelve disciples is found in the exact moment of betrayal. When the "praised man of Kerioth" led soldiers to Christ's hiding place and kissed his master to signal whom the soldiers were to arrest, Matthew 26:50 records that Jesus greeted him with the word:

"Friend."

The end of Judas Iscariot was both awful and despondent. Matthew 27:3–5 reports that he hanged himself in suicide before Christ was crucified. Acts 1:18–19, after Jesus' resurrection, reveals that Judas' body fell and split open on the ground.

Sources: WWA 232; WWC 282-283; JOB 135; NIB 642

Why did Judas choose to betray Jesus?

It's hard to say with certainty why Judas turned against Jesus. Betrayal is such an intimate act that, really, only the one doing it knows why. The best we can do is to theorize about Judas's motives, using inferences from the gospel writers.

THEORY #1: Greed

Matthew 26:14 and Mark 14:10 both report that it was right after Mary had poured expensive perfume on Jesus that Judas went out to cut a deal for betrayal. John 12:4–5 also reveals that, among the other disciples, Judas complained about the loss of "a year's wages" from wasted perfume. And John 12:6 accuses Judas of stealing money from the donations people gave to support Jesus' ministry.

So, the first theory goes something like this: Judas had spent three years living hand-to-mouth with Jesus. He'd seen the way the crowd had celebrated Christ's entry into Jerusalem. In his thief's heart, he had hopes that Jesus would be his ticket to riches. Then seeing Christ's reaction to the "waste" of expensive perfume, he was confronted (again) with the truth that Jesus simply wasn't interested in amassing wealth like he was. And that was the final straw. He figured it was time to cash out, get as much as he could before moving on.

THEORY #2: Judas was just a pawn of Satan.

John 13:27 reports that at the Last Supper, "When Judas had eaten the bread, Satan entered into him" (see also Luke 22:3). Immediately after that, he left to enact his betrayal. This theory suggests that Judas's previous, thieving hypocrisy opened him up to Satan's deceitful control—and the enemy of the saints took full advantage of that.

THEORY #3: Judas wanted a different Messiah.

The thinking here is that Judas simply wanted what he'd signed up for: a Messiah who would deliver Israel from Rome and set up a new, glorious earthly kingdom. And let's be honest—that's what pretty much everyone expected when they spoke of the Messiah.

This theory, then, says that Judas had seen enough to know that Jesus was indeed the promised Messiah. He was also getting impatient, because Jesus kept running away from opportunities to be king (John 6:15, for example). So, he decided to manipulate the situation a bit, to put Jesus into a situation where he'd be forced to act against Rome, and thus set himself up as king.

Are any of these theories the real motivation for Judas? I lean toward the first theory, but honestly, there's absolutely no way to tell. What we do know is that Judas fulfilled his desire to betray Jesus—and paid an awful price for his actions.

Sources: RBD 594; MFE2 152

The Last Supper
Matthew 26:17-30

What was the importance of the Passover meal to Jesus and his disciples, and what did they eat?

The Passover meal is still important in Jewish homes, even to this day. It's a feast which symbolizes beautifully, and in detail, the history of God's work in freeing Israelites from slavery in Egypt. Jesus and his disciples obviously wanted to honor that event along with the rest of their countrymen. Here's what was probably on the table at the Last Supper:

> *Roasted Lamb.* This is a reminder of the lamb's blood smeared on doorposts to signal for the Angel of Death to "pass over" God's people in Egypt (Exodus 12:1–30).

> *Bitter Herbs.* This is a reminder of the bitterness of slavery in Egypt.

> *Bread Made without Yeast.* This is what's known as "unleavened bread," and is a reminder that the Israelites had to hurry out of Egypt—no time even to let the bread dough rise.

> *Wine.* This was drunk at four pre-determined moments during the meal, as reminders of four promises from God that are recorded

in Exodus 6:6–7, "I will free you ... rescue you ... redeem you ... claim you as my own."

Here's what's included in the Passover meal today, and may have also been on Jesus' table:

> *Vegetables with saltwater dip.* This represents tears shed as slaves.

> *Fruit and Mixed Nuts.* This represents mortar that Israelites used for building projects while enslaved in Egypt.

> *Boiled Eggs.* This represents mourning, in association with the Jewish temple.

Source: JOB 314

Why did no one respond when Judas was named as the betrayer at the Last Supper (verse 25)?

You'd think that when Jesus identified Judas as the one who would betray him, then the other disciples would've reacted somehow. But neither Matthew nor any of the other gospel writers give an account of anyone protesting about Judas. Why not?

It would appear that the other disciples simply didn't observe the moment when Jesus said to Judas, "You have said it."

This was a communal meal going on, with thirteen people in attendance. It's likely, given the bombshell Jesus had just dropped about his imminent death, pockets of conversation were going on among smaller groups of the disciples. At this moment during the meal, Peter had motioned for John (reclining on the other side of Jesus), to secretly ask who the betrayer would be (John 13:23–25). That could've been a distraction as well.

Meanwhile, at the table, Judas was reclining right next to Jesus—sitting in a place of honor. This also would've been a seat that afforded privacy between the two. In this position, Judas—knowing he was guilty and hoping to remain undiscovered—probably leaned over to Jesus as he asked, "Rabbi, am I the one?"

New Testament scholar R. V. G. Tasker comments, "Even if Judas spoke the words out loud ... the reply of Jesus was almost certainly not overhead by the rest." The specificity of verse 25 saying that Jesus "told him"—meaning he spoke directly to Judas—adds validity to this viewpoint.

And why did Jesus answer, "You have said it," instead of just saying, "Yes"? That phrase was an idiom which indicated that the questioner had just answered his own question.

Sources: ILJ 243-244; MBC 1507; TYM 246-247

Jesus Predicts Peter's Denial
Matthew 26:31-35

So, did Jesus predict the rooster would crow once, or twice?

Jesus' prediction of Peter's denial "before the rooster crows" appears in Matthew 26:34, Mark 14:30, and Luke 22:34. Matthew and Luke record Jesus as simply saying, "before the rooster crows." Meanwhile, Mark specifies that the rooster will crow "twice" (*dis* in the Greek).

There are a few theories as to why this discrepancy is there:

THEORY #1: There's a mistake in the text.

This tends to be the opinion of those who reject the idea that the Bible truly is the inspired Word of God. In this view, a gospel writer, most likely Mark or a later copyist, made a mistake because some early manuscripts do not include the word "twice."

THEORY #2: There's a mistake in our understanding of the word "twice."

Although the Greek word *dis* in Mark 14:30 is almost always understood as "twice," it can be used figuratively to mean something like "completely" or "utterly," as in Jude 1:12. Applied to this situation, Mark 14:30 would mean something along the lines of "before the rooster finishes crowing completely."

THEORY #3: The rooster crowed twice, which was an important detail for Mark, but not for Matthew and Luke.

This theory allows for the idea that the Gospel writers were free to tell complementary accounts of the same event, rather than identical or competitive ones.

I tend to agree with opinion #3. The first two options strike me as intellectual stretches, and to me it seems clear that the word "twice" in

Mark 14:30 is incidental to the rooster crowing. I suspect that Mark, who wrote down what Peter said, recorded "twice" because it was an important detail to Peter. Matthew and Luke recorded simply that the rooster would crow. They didn't specify one crow, or two, or any particular number, because the number of crows was irrelevant to the thrust of the event, which was Peter's denial of Jesus.

As biblical apologist Gleason Archer Jr. says, "We may be very sure that if the rooster crows twice, he has at least crowed once.... The important part of the prediction, however, lay not in the number of times the rooster would sound out but in the number of times Peter would basely deny."

Sources: ZNS 1450; CWDN 472; DCC 29–30; EBD 339

Jesus Prays in Gethsemane
Matthew 26:36-46

Why did God the Father refuse Jesus' prayer in Gethsemane?

This question, more than any other, addresses the intellectual conflict between God's being all-powerful and God's actions in response to sin. At its core, it simply says:

Why did Jesus have to die?

The skeptic might phrase it this way: *If God really is all-powerful, why didn't he simply speak our release from the power of sin instead of insisting that Jesus suffer and die?*

Could God do that? Of course. Did God choose to do that? No. And why not? The question is valid, but also incomplete because it's restricted by what computer coders call binary thinking—meaning there are only two choices at all times, not many options to choose from. It doesn't take into account two important aspects of our sin situation: (1) the multiplicity of God's intellect, and (2) the nature of God's love for people.

1. The multiplicity of God's intellect

We, as limited beings, look at Jesus' birth (his "incarnation" into humanity) and painful death and ask why that degradation and suffering was not avoided? In our binary thinking we see only two legitimate ways to achieve God's goal of human redemption: (1) The hard way—birth, pain, and death, or (2) the easy way—no need for Jesus to be born, no pain, no death.

Conversely God, the only infinite being, looks at humanity's sin situation and sees—literally—billions and billions of ways to accomplish the goal of human redemption (Isaiah 55:8–9; 1 Corinthians 2:11). God's limitless being provides him with limitless choice.

The fact that Father God chose the hard way and none of the easy ways to achieve our rescue from sin doesn't mean he was unaware of easier ways. Likewise, it doesn't mean that the hard way was the only way to accomplish his purpose, or that he was somehow constrained by our sin and forced to act in this way. Here's what it does mean:

God, in the multiplicity of his fathomless intellect, considered every one of the billions of ways to redeem humankind and, of his own will and volition, chose incarnation (birth into humanity) and suffering as the sole method he would use.

His work, his choice.

Or as Justo González phrased it in a discussion of the theology of William of Ockham, "We are saved by Christ's merits, and this is so, not because it had to be so … but simply because God decided that it would be so."

2. The nature of the love of God

Though God's reasons for choosing the hard way are his alone, I suspect that a motivation for this choice is found in his unfailing love for us (Psalm 6:4; 51:1; Lamentations 3:32). Love—true *agapaó* love—is selfless and determined; it seeks at all times only the best for the object of love, even if that pursuit must sometimes inflict the worst upon the one loving (1 Corinthians 13:4–7).

So why did God choose incarnation and suffering as his method for redemption? I believe it's because that choice alone provided the best, most complete and highest good for those whom God loves and chooses to rescue. For reasons we don't completely understand, the hard way was the best way, and so *God in his love chose the worst for himself in order to achieve the best for us* (John 3:16; Romans 5:8).

This, I believe, is why Father God refused the Son's prayer in Gethsemane. He wanted the best for us and was willing to make enormous sacrifice to ensure that it would be done.

Sources: SOC 435; TGE 3

If Jesus didn't want to die, why did he stay in Jerusalem?

Could Jesus have run away from Jerusalem, and thus escaped his brutal execution? The short answer is yes. Even as late as the prayer at the garden of Gethsemane, Christ still had an exit open to him.

Gethsemane (which literally means "oil press") was a secluded olive grove on the lower slope of the Mount of Olives—the same mountain where he had delivered his Olivet Discourse (Matthew 24:1–25:46). Early traditions in Christian history indicate that this particular olive grove might've been owned by the family of John Mark, the friend of Peter who later wrote the gospel of Mark. From there, the city of Jerusalem was easily seen to the west, with the outline of the temple prominently in view. To the east, though, was nothing but wilderness.

Bible historian Dr. John Beck reports, "Just over the ridge of the Mount of Olives, a forty-five-minute walk into the empty isolation of the Judean Wilderness offered a way of escape." In fact, that wilderness had once hidden King David himself (1 Samuel 23:14; Psalm 63:1).

With that path open to him, why did Jesus stay instead of run away?

The answer is in Christ's Gethsemane prayer: "My Father! If this cup cannot be taken away unless I drink it, your will be done" (Matthew 26:42) As Dr. Beck reminds us, "Of his own accord, the Good Shepherd chose the path of laying down his life for his sheep" (John 10:14–15; 18:11).

Sources: VGG 154-155; SMA 250

Jesus Is Betrayed and Arrested
Matthew 26:47-56

Why did the soldiers need someone to lead them to Jesus?

This is pretty much the same question that Jesus posed on the night of his arrest: "Why didn't you arrest me in the Temple? I was there teaching every day" (verse 55). There were apparently some practical considerations at play.

First, the enemies of Jesus didn't want to arrest him in public because they feared the people would rise to his defense and spark a revolt (see Matthew 26:3–5).

Second, even if the soldiers had known Jesus was in a garden at Gethsemane, they wouldn't have known which one. That area on the Mount of Olives was home to many gated, walled gardens standing side by side. With gates that were pretty much the same in appearance, standing one after another, one needed to know exactly which entrance to go through—and would possibly have even needed keys to enter. Interestingly, there are still gated gardens in this area of the Mount of Olives today.

Third, we must remember it was deep into the nighttime when they came for Christ. In the darkness of that walled garden, it would've been nearly impossible to distinguish one stranger from another. Even though the soldiers might've recognized Jesus in daylight, in the black of night only someone who knew him well would be able to identify him quickly. In the minds of the soldiers, that was how they would prevent Jesus from sneaking away into the night. So Judas was necessary to safely and quickly carry out an arrest.

Sadly, the errant disciple earned his blood money that night.

Sources: SMA 251, 257–258; IBB 177

What was the point of Judas kissing Jesus as part of his betrayal?

Matthew 26:48 reveals that the soldiers sent to arrest Jesus were in need of an unspoken signal to help them identify him. They needed to be sure that, in the darkness and confusion of the night, they got the right man. For reasons known only to Judas and God, the signal he chose was a kiss. It seems, in retrospect, the worst possible choice.

Although a kiss was a common form of greeting among friends, and even among rabbis and their disciples, in this instance, it was a particularly cruel method of betrayal. A kiss was a sign of special affection between friends and family, and when given from a disciple to his master, it was a humble sign of personal honor and admiration.

In this light, theologian Craig Keener comments, "Judas' kiss is thus a special act of hypocrisy…. Matthew's readers encountering this story for the first time would've been horrified…. Judas appears as the most contemptible of traitors."

Source: IBB 122

Why would anybody want to cut off an ear in defense of Jesus?

We know from John 18:10 that it was Peter who drew his sword and defended Jesus from the crowd that came to arrest him. We also know that the person he swung at was Malchus, a servant of the high priest. The general consensus is that good old St. Pete was just a bad aim—that he was trying to kill Malchus, missed, and cut off an ear instead.

Dr. John Beck offers an interesting alternative theory, though. He notes that, as a career fisherman, Peter would've been skilled with a short sword and a knife. Also, he believes it was an intentional choice for the various gospel writers to identify that it was a severed *ear*.

Around 40 BC, or roughly seventy years prior to the Gethsemane arrest, a Jewish leader named Mattathias Antigonus had been arrested for rebellion against Herod the Great. A high priest, according to Mosaic law, could not have any physical deformities. Thus, at the trial, Mattathias Antigonus attempted to discredit the high priest when he surprised everyone by leaning over and biting off the high priest's ear!

Dr. Beck sees a parallel in Peter's actions. Knowing that one disciple could never defeat a full detachment of soldiers, Beck argues, Peter made a symbolic defense instead: "Peter's well-aimed strike on the ear of the representative of the high priest may well have been designed to send his own message about the corruption of the high priest, Caiaphas, who at that time filled the office."

Sources: IBB 177; VGG 156-157

Jesus before the Council
Matthew 26:57-68

I thought the Romans ruled the land of ancient Israel in the days of Jesus. What exactly was the "high council" and why were they allowed to put Jesus on trial?

Yes, the land of ancient Israel was a Roman province in that day. As such, Herod Antipas ruled as Rome's appointed tetrarch—basically, a king over the region of Galilee (Luke 3:1). At the same time, Pontius Pilate (acting under Emperor Tiberius) reigned as Rome's provincial governor over Judea. Those two rulers shared an uneasy alliance that exercised final authority over Jerusalem at that time.

However, under the umbrella of power from those Roman functionaries, the Jewish high council, called the Sanhedrin, was given wide latitude to govern the day-to-day aspects of Jewish society. According to unverifiable tradition, the Sanhedrin had its roots in the days of Moses as the "seventy men who are recognized as elders" (Numbers 11:16), but the institution wasn't formalized until centuries later. The scribe, Ezra, established it under the authority of Persian conquerors who had allowed the Jews to (mostly) govern themselves in local affairs.

In Jesus' time, the Sanhedrin typically consisted of seventy-two members that included: the current high priest; any previous high priests still living; men from aristocratic families (mostly Sadducees); heads of prominent tribes and families (the elders); and the scribes (experts in the religious law). This body was dominated by Sadducees, but also included some well-regarded Pharisees.

As long as they were able to enforce peace, the Sanhedrin exercised full jurisdiction over civil and religious matters, particularly in regard to Moses's law. This group was also allowed to enforce many criminal penalties, and even permitted to maintain its own police force—though it was not allowed to carry out a death penalty. They could *pronounce* a death penalty but, as was seen in the events of Jesus' trial, that had to be approved by the Roman governor before taking effect (John 18:31).

Sources: EOR 61; IBD3 1390–1391; OPB 1408

How did the Jewish leaders manage to convene a high council in the middle of the night? That seems shady.

This midnight-trial of Jesus by the Sanhedrin was filled with, well, let's call them "irregularities." The first, as you've noticed, was that it was held in the dark of night.

Proper procedure would've dictated that Jesus, upon arrest, would be held in a prison cell at the temple until the full Sanhedrin could convene to hear his case, typically on the second or fifth day of the week. In fact, that's what happened when other of Jesus' disciples were later arrested, after Christ's resurrection (Acts 4:3; 5:18). But that's not what happened for Jesus.

It seems apparent that key members of the high council had colluded to create a means for rushing to judgment before there could be any significant objection. In fact, when the soldiers returned with Jesus, a quorum of the Sanhedrin was already in session—despite the lateness of the hour. Most likely, they'd convened before sending out the soldiers and were simply waiting for the arresting guards to bring Jesus to them.

To achieve a voting quorum, the Sanhedrin would've needed a minimum of twenty-three of the seventy-two total members, including the high priest Caiaphas. Dr. Jean-Pierre Isbouts, along with the National Geographic Society and others, indicates that Caiaphas had likely included his cronies in that twenty-three and excluded Sanhedrin members who might've come to Jesus' defense. For instance, Nicodemus and Joseph of Arimathea were both sympathizers of Jesus, but there's no evidence they were at his trial (Mark 15:43; John 3:1)

Additionally, the Sanhedrin had had time enough to recruit a number of people to testify against Jesus—and had them ready to bear witness in the middle of the night. That would've taken some significant prep work and perhaps some incentives offered to the witnesses. Bible scholar R. V. G. Tasker reports that the verb tense that's translated as "were trying to find" (witnesses) in Matthew 26:59 is best understood as having already been in progress. In other words, the Sanhedrin was already at work trying to dig up evidence against Jesus.

What's more, the Jewish legal system prohibited nighttime trials, as well as trials on festival days such as the Passover, which was then just beginning. But this Sanhedrin passed judgment on Jesus at that time anyway. Another irregularity included holding Jesus' trial at the personal home of the high priest. Those proceedings were supposed to take place in the Chamber of Hewn Stones (*Lishkat La-Gazit*) inside the temple. Also, in capital offense cases, testimony on behalf of the accused was supposed to come before testimony against—but that part was skipped in Jesus' trial. It was omitted in favor of a string of false witnesses who couldn't even agree on which crime Jesus was guilty of committing.

Overall, Christ's midnight trial before the Sanhedrin was not an attempt at justice, but a well-orchestrated, late-night sham, convened simply to get rid of one of the high priest's enemies.

Sources: WWC 262-263; TYM 253; IBD3 1390-1391

Peter Denies Jesus
Matthew 26:69-75

Why was Peter so afraid of a little servant girl?

Well, the situation encompassed more than just an idle accusation by a "little" servant girl. We must remember that, at this moment, Peter was standing among enemies in the courtyard of the high priest. This was in March or early April, so it was a cold night. Rather than shiver alone, he had to seek warmth around a fire where armed guards were also standing (John 18:18).

Moments before this, Peter had attacked the high priest's servant and cut off that man's ear (John 18:10). If these guards identified him as that attacker, how would they respond? They would most certainly arrest him. Would they also exact "an ear for an ear" justice? There's no telling, but those guards certainly wouldn't have treated him kindly.

Meanwhile, Jesus' trial was going badly. If these enemies surrounding him knew Peter was a follower of Christ, would they make him suffer the same fate as his master? Add to that the emotional upheaval of the betrayal by his close friend, Judas, and the surprise militia that tore them all from the garden at Gethsemane, and you can see why Peter might have been frayed enough to say, "A curse on me if I'm lying—I don't know the man!" (Matthew 26:74).

And, just for the record, Peter wasn't the only one to turn away from Jesus that terrible night. Matthew 26:56 reports that at the moment of his arrest, "all the disciples deserted him and fled"—including even the gospel writer himself.

Personally, although it breaks my heart to hear Peter's denial and to witness his sorrow afterward, I agree with the late, great theologian Paul Tillich who said that "If the disciples had suppressed the truth about their own profound weakness, our gospels would not be what they are." The church at times, Tillich continues, "has tried to conceal what the disciples openly admitted—that we all forsook him and fled. But this is the truth about all men, including followers of Jesus today."

Sources: WWC 263; TEN 102-103

Judas Hangs Himself
Matthew 27:1–10

Why was Peter able to be forgiven, but Judas was not?

This is a very hard question, and I don't know that I have a complete answer. Remember that, please, as you read the rest of this commentary segment.

Probably the most common answer given for this question is that Peter *repented* while Judas was *remorseful,* and that slight distinction was enough to deny forgiveness to Judas. Dr. Daniel Doriani sums it up this way (italics his):

> Judas "was seized with remorse." The typical Greek word for repentance is *metanoeō.* It means to change one's *mind* or heart. Matthew uses another word of Judas, *metamelomai.* It means to change one's feelings about something. Matthew's choice of terms makes a crucial point. Judas feels sorry and guilty about what he did, but he does not repent…. He is not willing to see himself as a sinner in need of repentance.

I have much respect for Dr. Doriani as a biblical scholar, but very little confidence in this hairsplitting grammatical argument as justification for the eternal condemnation of Judas. For me it falls short because a change in one's feelings inherently reflects a change of one's mind and—more importantly—Matthew uses the Greek root *metamelomai* to clearly mean "repentance" elsewhere in his gospel (see Matthew 21:29).

I think there may be two other things to consider:

1. Jesus indicated that Judas was condemned before he ever acted out his betrayal.

John 6:70–71 reports that long before anyone knew Christ would be crucified, "Jesus said, 'I chose the twelve of you, but one is a devil.' He was speaking of Judas, son of Simon Iscariot, one of the Twelve, who would later betray him."

Also, John 17:12 records Jesus praying this at the Last Supper: "I guarded them, and not one of them perished except the son of destruction, *so that the Scripture would be fulfilled*" (NASB, italics mine). Judas, the betraying "son of destruction," had been identified and written into Bible prophecy hundreds of years before he was born.

The idea that Judas might've been chosen for condemnation before he betrayed, even before he was born, doesn't sit well with any of us, and there are likely extenuating factors unknown by us that make that fact less clear cut. But feeling uncomfortable doesn't mean I can simply dismiss what Jesus said about Judas. I can only admit I don't know the full story and say with the apostle Paul, "Does not the potter have the right to make out of the same lump of clay some pottery for special purposes and some for common use?" (Romans 9:21 NIV).

2. Only one sin is unforgiveable.

Knowing from Jesus' own words that Judas was unforgiven despite his obvious *metamelomai*, we have to acknowledge that—also according to Christ—only one sin is unforgivable: "Anyone who blasphemes the Holy Spirit will not be forgiven" (Luke 12:10).

I think there must've been some aspect of this kind of blasphemy against the Holy Spirit that was inseparable from Judas's betrayal. He was a man who, after all, had *actually worked miracles by the power of the Holy Spirit*, under the direction of Jesus (Matthew 10:1–8). To have experienced that life-giving Spirit firsthand, and then to betray him for thirty coins, seems to me to be a tragic form of unforgivable blasphemy.

Sources: REC2 474; CWSN 77, 104; TGE 405

Jesus' Trial before Pilate
Matthew 27:11–26

What is the history of Pontius Pilate?

Pontius Pilate appears as a historical figure in the biblical record, in Roman records, and on archaeological artifacts.

He was appointed by Emperor Tiberius as the Roman governor (or prefect) of Judea around AD 26, a province which included much of what's modern-day Israel—and which overlapped Herod Antipas's territory. As governor, he was responsible for collecting taxes for Rome, for keeping unstable Judea under control, and for being the top legal judge in the province, which included authority to execute criminals.

The Gospels present Pilate somewhat sympathetically because of his reluctance to order Jesus' execution (see also Mark 15:1–15; Luke 23:1–25; John 18:28–19:16). Still, in his time, he was known for cruelty and provoking the religious ire of his subjects in Judea. He also stole money from the Jewish temple to build an aqueduct into Jerusalem. When Jews inevitably gathered to protest, he had soldiers infiltrate the crowds in disguise and then attack. Many were killed, beaten, and trampled to death in the panicked multitude.

Roman historian, Philo (a contemporary of Pontius Pilate), described him as a man who was prone to "bribes, acts of pride, acts of violence … constant murders without trial, the ceaseless and most grievous brutality." The only thing that Pilate feared, it seemed, was losing favor with Emperor Tiberius—so that's what leaders of the Jewish Sanhedrin used when they brought Christ into Pilate's court for judgment. Here's how biographer Peter Richardson explains it:

> Pilate's patron in Rome was Sejanus, Tiberius's chief lieutenant, who was opposed to Jews. When Sejanus was executed in 31 CE on a charge of treason, the career of protégés such as Pilate would have altered. In Jesus' trial, according to John 19:12, Pilate was accused of being no friend of Caesar's if he let Jesus go. Pilate's position, following the fall of Sejanus … was threatened by doubts of his allegiance; to take a pretender to kingship lightly might have made Pilate, like Sejanus, guilty in Tiberius's eyes.

Ironically, Pontius Pilate's fears came to pass anyway. His favor with the emperor and his rule over Judea came to an abrupt end after he ordered a particularly brutal attack on an unarmed Samaritan crowd. When Rome found out, he was ordered to report to the emperor for judgment. Tradition tells us he was found guilty, banished to the barbaric south of France, and there committed suicide.

Sources: TRF 38; WWA 312–313; DOB 611–612; HER 312

Jesus' trial before Pilate comes across as almost mob justice. What was going on really?

Yes, mob justice is an accurate description of what happened—or, more precisely, mob injustice.

It appears that the leading priests (Sadducees) and elders wanted to give Pilate a tangible threat of an uprising in order to pressure him to concede to their demands that Jesus be executed. They were successful, as verse 24 reports that Pilate saw "a riot was developing" and then agreed to have Christ crucified—even though he clearly thought Jesus was not guilty of any crime.

This trial took place very early in the morning on Friday (verse 1), most likely at dawn before word of Jesus' arrest could spread very far. It's assumed that the proceedings took place at the Antonia Fortress, a palace built by King Herod the Great and named in honor of his Roman patron, Mark Antony. It was a massive complex with four high towers just to the northwest of the Jerusalem temple. This fortress included barracks for Roman troops, and also featured a very large courtyard in which Jesus was probably tried.

Pilate would've sat on a prominently placed "judgment seat" (*bema* in the Greek text, verse 19), a raised platform from which he would make his ruling. A contingent of armed soldiers would've stood near him, ready to enforce his judgment. Jesus, already beaten and weak at this point, and still bound in restraints, would've been placed before him, within earshot. Also, there would've been the chief priests who played the roles of passionate prosecutors demanding Jesus' death.

In the courtyard, or perhaps just outside the fortress entrance, the Sadducees and elders had also gathered a crowd of their own supporters and also perhaps supporters of the insurrectionist Barabbas. It would appear that a number of Sadducees and elders also spread out within the swarm of people, strategically placed so they could whip to a frenzied pitch the most vocal outbursts against Jesus.

The trial lasted several hours, and only reached its end because Pilate realized he was losing control of the crowd. He decided it was better to give in to the mob than to release an innocent man, thus sealing his reputation as a corrupt governor and one of history's greatest cowards.

Sources: TYM 257; JHT 257; ZB1 174; ANT 114; MAT 454

Pilate's wife had a bad dream—why would he care?

We know little about the wife of Pontius Pilate, or why she thought a bad dream would influence her husband's legal judgment absent of any other evidence. The closest thing we have is the so-called *Gospel of Nicodemus*, an apocryphal (fictional) alternative account of Jesus' trial that briefly includes her in it.

According to that story, Pilate's wife was named Claudia Procula and she was a granddaughter of the venerable Caesar Augustus. Supposedly, she was a gentile convert to Judaism (very unlikely, given that her husband famously detested Jews), and later converted to Christianity. Other folklore says that she was the "Claudia" that Paul mentioned in 2 Timothy 4:21. Although likely just a legendary figure, Pilate's wife is actually considered a saint in some Eastern Church traditions.

Regardless, we know there was a woman who was married to Pontius Pilate, that she had a troubling dream about Jesus, and that she warned her husband to set him free.

Heavenly dreams were obviously important in the Jewish culture because their Hebrew Scriptures (our Old Testament) reported many times that God communicated with his people through dreams. In the Roman world, a similar—though more superstitious—regard for dreams was also evident. For instance, a well-known story was that Julius Caesar's wife, Calpurnia, had suffered a premonitory dream about his imminent murder by stabbing. Could that have been why Pilate's wife thought her husband would listen to her dream-inspired instructions?

In spite of this, Pilate ignored his wife's warning, and the rest, as they say, is history.

Sources: AWB 226–227; MAT 453

Why was Barabbas "notorious"?

Barabbas is absent from history except for his mention in the four Gospels. So, although he was apparently "notorious" (*episémos* in the Greek text) for a time, he would be completely unremembered if not for his infamous association with Christ.

Based on some early manuscripts of Matthew's gospel and a comment from ancient church father, Origen, some believe his name might've actually been "Jesus Barabbas." This was entirely possible, as Jesus was a common enough name in that time and place. If that were the case, Rome's appointed governor, Pontius Pilate, may have chosen to offer him as a thoroughly guilty "Jesus" in contrast to the obviously innocent "Jesus who is called the Messiah" (verse 17). Still, all that can be known for sure is that he was called Barabbas, which is kind of a nonsensical name that simply means, "son of father."

Barabbas was leader of a small insurrection against Rome in Jerusalem, which was apparently quickly put down by Pilate (Luke 23:19). Mark tells us he was "a revolutionary who had committed murder" (Mark 15:7) and John calls him a *léstés*, a Greek word that's translated as both "robber" and as "revolutionary" (John 18:40). Context seems to indicate Barabbas was all of the above: robber, revolutionary, and murderer.

Dr. Michael Wilkins suggests he was a rural bandit who instigated social unrest. These *léstés* were considered Robin-Hood-style heroes among common folk because they stole from the rich and sowed anarchy for the hated Roman authorities.

We have no idea what happened to Barabbas after his miraculous, death-row pardon. One could say that he was, in the strictest substitutionary sense, the very first person for whom Jesus died.

Sources: ZB1 173–174; IBD1 175; CWSN 371; TGE 377

The Soldiers Mock Jesus
Matthew 27:27-31

Why were the Roman soldiers so astonishingly cruel to a helpless, already-condemned man?

Well, there was zero justification for what Jesus endured at the hands of these sadistic soldiers. All I can do is try to offer some background as explanation, insufficient though it is.

For starters, Roman soldiers were not, generally speaking, peaceful, gentle types. These were men whose daily life, for years on end, was spent waging war, practicing war, and subjugating those they'd conquered in war. Legionnaires had been trained to inflict heavy casualties in any conflict. They were well accustomed to the gore of close combat, where the stench of blood is simply perfume for a day's work. You can imagine the kind of person who'd be attracted to that career choice.

The typical Roman legionary would've viewed all conquered peoples as somewhat less than human. As one disgusted foot soldier on campaign for Rome complained, "We are here among savage tribesmen, the enemy visible from our very tents." That would've summed up the general opinion toward a Jewish population they viewed as obstinate and threatening.

Also remember that some (maybe all) of these soldiers had been involved in violent reprisals against Jewish terrorists like Barabbas (Luke 23:19).

They probably would've viewed Jesus, a supposed "King of the Jews," as no different from Barabbas or any other would-be revolutionary. They "had probably seen some of their friends killed," comments Bible scholar N. T. Wright. "They were tired of policing such a place, far away from their homes, having to keep the lid on a volatile and dangerous situation with all kinds of rebel groups ready to riot."

Finally, these soldiers knew they'd never be held accountable for any brutality done to this innocent man. Their horrifying abuse of Christ was perverse entertainment to them—something for which history condemns them, even to this day.

Sources: WIX 102; ARF 71; MFE2 181-182

The Crucifixion
Matthew 27:32-44

What was the purpose of that specific form of death—crucifixion?

The purpose of crucifixion, humanly speaking, appears to have been to use sadistic cruelty and utter humiliation as a form of criminal deterrence.

Crucifixion as execution was most likely invented by the ancient Persians, and then transported by the armies of Alexander the Great into the Middle East. The Romans refined the method to cause a very slow and extremely painful death. It was such an offensive punishment that it wasn't allowed to be used on a Roman citizen. Crucifixion instead was reserved only for insurrectionists, delinquent slaves, or the most violent of offenders.

According to famous Roman orator, Cicero, death on a cross was "the most cruel and hideous of punishments." He said, "The very word *cross* should be forbidden in the presence of a Roman citizen. Romans shouldn't have to think of a cross, see a cross, or hear the miserable word." Seneca, a philosopher and advisor to the vicious Emperor Nero, agreed with Cicero. He called crucifixion "the worst torture of all."

Common practice was first to strip a prisoner completely naked, tie him to a post, and then two soldiers would take turns beating him into agony with a *flagrum*—that is, a whip with sharp bits of bone and lead woven into the thongs. The idea was to cut through flesh and promote bleeding. A person could, and did sometimes, die from only this scourging.

Next, the prisoner would be forced to carry a heavy wooden crossbeam (*patibulum*) to the site of his execution. There, a permanently rooted, wooden post would be waiting. Yes, it likely had dried blood and insects on it from previous executions. The crossbeam would be set into place on the post, and then the prisoner would be brutally attached to the resulting cross. In Jesus' case, this was done by hammering spikes through his flesh and into the wood.

After that, at Jesus' crucifixion, it was the duty of the Roman soldiers to stand guard (in case any disciples made a rescue attempt) and to pass the time waiting for their prisoner to finally die. Because crucifixion was designed to be a slow and painful execution, death could've taken days; the fact that Jesus died after only three hours shows how viciously he'd been beaten and abused in the short time that had passed since his arrest the night before.

Added to the intense physical suffering Christ endured was the abject humiliation associated with crucifixion. We've already seen how the Romans felt about their own torture device. Jews added a religious stigma to it as well. According to Deuteronomy 21:22–23, a criminal "executed and hung on a tree … is cursed in the sight of God." But really, across all cultures both Jew and gentile, crucifixion was an intensely shameful way to die. This is partly why Romans later called Christians "degenerates"—because they insisted on worshiping a crucified criminal. And it's why Paul proudly embraced the shame when he told early gentile believers, "The message of the cross is foolish to those who are headed for destruction! But we who are being saved know it is the very power of God" (1 Corinthians 1:18).

Sources: JHT 256–260; ETC 35, 154; VGG 180; MBC 1511

Who was the Simon that carried Jesus' cross, and where was Cyrene?

There are three definitive mentions of Simon of Cyrene in the New Testament, all within the Gospel accounts (Matthew 27:32; Mark 15:21; Luke 23:26). There are also mentions of a "Simon" or "Simeon" (a variant spelling for Simon) in the book of Acts that might have referred to this man who carried the cross of Christ.

Cyrene was a mostly gentile city located in North Africa. Because its population was primarily African peoples, many believe that Simon of Cyrene was therefore a black man. It's also intriguingly possible that this Simon became more than just a load-carrier for Christ, but also was a Christian follower of Jesus, along with his family.

Mark 15:21 tells us that "Simon was the father of Alexander and Rufus." This name-dropping suggests that Mark himself knew those two sons, possibly knew Simon, and probably indicates they were all recognizable people to Mark's mostly non-Jewish readers. Since Mark is believed to have written his gospel while in Rome, Bible historians like Peter Walker think that Simon's son, Rufus, and Simon's unnamed wife may have been friends of Mark. Walker adds that Paul probably knew them as well because, near the end of his letter to the church in Rome, he said, "Greet Rufus, whom the Lord picked out to be his very own; and also his dear mother, who has been a mother to me" (Romans 16:13). Additionally, when Paul and Barnabas were commissioned as missionaries, we're told that "among the prophets and teachers of the church at Antioch of Syria were Barnabas, *Simeon (called "the black man")*, Lucius (from Cyrene) ..." and so on (Acts 13:1, italics mine).

Archaeologists have also uncovered a small tomb in Israel that has inscriptions in both Aramaic and in Greek that refer to someone named "Alexander of Cyrene" and "Alexander, son of Simon." The consensus (or wishful thinking?) is that this tomb holds the bones of Simon of Cyrene's son, Alexander.

From the admittedly circumstantial evidence of the biblical references and the rediscovered tomb, Walker thinks, "It seems likely that the whole family had become Christian believers—almost certainly influenced by the way Simon's life had intersected with Jesus."

Sources: BPB 118; ISJ 165

Were the two men crucified with Jesus rebels or thieves?

Matthew 27:38 and Mark 15:27, tell us that Jesus was crucified with two *léstés*, a Greek word that's translated as both "robber" and "revolutionary" in our English versions. Luke 23:32 calls them *kakourgos*, which we translate as either "criminal," "robber," or "malefactor." If we can assume that Christ took the cross intended for Barabbas the insurrectionist (Luke 23:19), then that means they would've been scheduled to be crucified alongside Barabbas and could've been his coconspirators.

Given all that information, it's probably safe to assume that these crucified criminals were both robbers and violent, would-be rebels. This seems even more probable because of the one criminal's confession: "We deserve to die for our crimes" (Luke 23:41). Most likely they were part of a rural gang of outlaws who wreaked havoc among the Roman authorities until they were finally arrested when Pilate put down Barabbas's uprising in Jerusalem. (For more, see Barabbas the commentary on Matthew 27:11–26.)

Sources: CWSN 371; TGE 320, 377; ZB1 173-174; IBD1 175

What prophecies were fulfilled when Jesus was crucified?

I've heard that in his life, death, and resurrection, Jesus fulfilled close to three hundred messianic prophecies—though I'll admit I've never counted. According to biblical apologist Josh McDowell, Christ fulfilled twenty-nine specific prophecies on the day of his crucifixion:

1. Betrayed by a friend (Psalm 41:9; Matthew 10:4)

2. Sold out for thirty pieces of silver (Zechariah 11:12; Matthew 26:15)

3. Thirty pieces of silver thrown down in the temple (Zechariah 11:13; Matthew 27:5)

4. Thirty pieces of silver used to buy a potter's field (Zechariah 11:13; Matthew 27:7)

5. Abandoned by his disciples (Zechariah 13:7; Mark 14:50)

6. Falsely accused by many witnesses (Psalm 35:11; Matthew 26:59–60)

7. Silent before his accusers (Isaiah 53:7; Matthew 27:12)

8. Wounded and bruised (Isaiah 53:5; Matthew 27:26)

9. Beaten and spit upon (Isaiah 50:6; Matthew 26:67)

10. Ridiculed (Psalm 22:7–8; Matthew 27:29)

11. Too weak to walk (Psalm 109:24–25; Luke 23:26)

12. Hands and feet pierced (Psalm 22:16; Luke 23:33)

13. Executed alongside criminals (Isaiah 53:12; Matthew 27:38)

14. Prayed for those who killed him (Isaiah 53:12; Luke 23:34)

15. Was rejected by his own people (Isaiah 53:3; Matthew 27:17–23)

16. Was hated without cause (Psalm 69:4; John 15:25)

17. Loved ones stood at a distance from him (Psalm 38:11; Luke 23:49)

18. Mockers shook their heads at him (Psalm 109:25; Matthew 27:39)

19. Stared at by gloating enemies (Psalm 22:17; Luke 23:35)

20. People divided his garments and cast lots for his clothing (Psalm 22:18; John 19:23–24)

21. Suffered from thirst (Psalm 69:21; John 19:28)

22. Offered gall and vinegar for thirst (Psalm 69:21; Matthew 27:34)

23. A cry of being forsaken (Psalm 22:1; Matthew 27:46)

24. Committed himself to God (Psalm 31:5; Luke 23:46)

25. Had no bones broken (Psalm 34:20; John 19:33)

26. His side pierced (Zechariah 12:10; John 19:34)

27. His heart broken (Psalm 22:14; John 19:34)

28. Darkness covered the land (Amos 8:9; Matthew 27:45)

29. Buried in a rich man's tomb (Isaiah 53:9; Matthew 27:57–60)

Source: NET 164, 183-192

The Death of Jesus
Matthew 27:45-56

Who was actually to blame for Jesus' death?

Honestly, there's plenty of guilt to go around, as many people colluded to bring about the crucifixion of Christ. Here are the primary players:

> **Powers and Principalities:** This includes Satan and demons. It appears Jesus' incarnation was an invasion of sorts into territory typically under the Enemy's control (Matthew 4:8–9; 11:12;

1 John 3:8). The devil and demons were naturally terrified by this and so tried to kill Christ, thinking that would end the threat (Mark 5:1–20; Luke 22:3–4; and 1 Corinthians 2:7–8, where "rulers of this world" refers to the spiritual powers of evil). They were sorely mistaken.

> **Kings and Politicians**: This would include people like Herod Antipas (Luke 23:6–12), and Pontius Pilate (Matthew 27:11–26). Their motives were political, although I suspect both fear and hubris were also part of what drove them. And, obviously, the actual Roman legionnaires who tortured, mocked, and nailed Jesus to the cross are guilty of his death as well (Matthew 27:27–38).

> **Religious Leaders**: Among this group the most prominent of Jesus' enemies would've been the party of Sadducees/chief priests, including the high priest Caiaphas (Matthew 27:1–2, 56, 65–66) and the former high priest Annas (John 18:12–13). A good number of Pharisees—though not all of them—would've cheered Jesus' execution, as well as scribes ("teacher of the law") and elders (Matthew 27:12; Luke 11:53). These people would've thought they were doing something holy, ridding the world of a heretic messiah. And, of course, power, wealth, and politics would've played a role in their various motivations too.

> **Close Friends**: Ah, poor Judas Iscariot. This tragic figure in human history was one of Jesus' closest friends—and his betrayer (Matthew 27:14–16, 47–50). The world is still trying to figure out why he turned against the Messiah he once loved.

> **Father God**: It feels somehow wrong to state that Father God was complicit in Christ's suffering and execution—yet the Bible is clear this was true. When forced to choose between my personal preferences and Scriptural truth, I must choose truth. But that doesn't mean I have to like it.

Both Old Testament and New Testament state unequivocally that the Messiah's suffering happened because of God's intentional action and insistence. In this way, God Eternal became an enemy of God Incarnate. The end result was unfathomable victory and redemption for you and me, but the resurrection of Jesus doesn't erase the fact that God was the driving force behind the execution of his sinless Son. (For more on that, see: Isaiah 53:6; Isaiah 53:10; Matthew 26:39; Matthew 27:46; John 3:16; Acts 2:23; Romans 3:25; 2 Corinthians 5:21.)

Sources: See scripture references above.

Did God the Father really abandon Jesus when he was on the cross?

While bleeding and dying, Christ uttered the tortured cry: "*Eli, Eli, lema sabachthani?*" which means "My God, my God, why have you abandoned me?" (Matthew 27:46). Previously, Jesus had said, "The Father and I are one" (John 10:30). So, did the Father actually forsake the Son at that hurtful moment? There are two things to consider with this question.

First, if we read Matthew as an accurate record of Christ's death and words, then ... well ... yes, we have to believe that Jesus was not lying when he spoke this heartbreaking prayer. What we don't have to do is understand exactly how that worked. It's enough for us to know that in that moment "the LORD laid on him the sins of us all" (Isaiah 53:6) and "God presented Jesus as the sacrifice for sin ... shedding his blood" (Romans 3:25). "The whole point of the cross," theologian N. T. Wright says soberly, "is that there the weight of the world's evil really did converge upon Jesus." Somehow, in that awful death, the absolute worst part of the dying was a (temporary) severing of Father and Son—something that thankfully we never have to experience or understand.

Second, it must be noted that Jesus, in this cry, was echoing the messianic prophecy of Psalm 22:1: "My God, my God, why have you abandoned me? Why are you so far away when I groan for help?" Fulfilling this prophecy is one more evidence of who Christ really is, and why he was there at the cross in that moment. Ancient church father Cyril of Jerusalem taught that when Jesus called the Father "my God," he did so as a stand-in for you and me, calling out the prophecy as a sinless man forced to bear the punishment for humanity's sin. I like the way that Bible scholar Stanley Hauerwas sums this up: "Hear these words, 'My God, my God, why have you forsaken me?' and know that the Son of God has taken our place, become for us the abandonment that our sin produces, so that we may live."

Sources: MFE2 190; BTCM 240-241

What did it mean that the curtain in the sanctuary of the temple was torn in two when Jesus died?

The tearing of the temple curtain is one of several supernatural phenomena that Matthew recorded as happening in Jerusalem when Jesus died (verse 51).

> The sun was blocked from noon until 3:00 p.m., and darkness covered the land (verse 45).

> There was an earthquake (verse 51).

> Tombs broke open (verse 52).

> People were raised from the dead (verses 52–53).

Roman soldiers, likely superstitious about disturbances in nature, were terrified at all that had suddenly happened (verse 54).

The tearing of the temple curtain, though, is by far the most important event to coincide with Jesus' death (yes, even more important than dead people coming out of their tombs).

In Moses's law, God had directed that this heavy curtain hang in the temple between the Holy Place and the Holy of Holies room (Exodus 26:31–34). The ark of the covenant was kept within the Holy of Holies room, and no one was allowed to enter; it was reserved for God alone. Only once each year, on the Day of Atonement, the high priest would go in and sprinkle the blood of a sacrifice for the sins of the people (Hebrews 9:7–8).

The curtain that hid the Holy of Holies from the rest of the temple was impressive. During Jesus' time, it was a two-layer, fabric wall of immense size. The layers were hung about eighteen inches apart across the opening. It was sixty feet long (just over half a football field) and thirty feet wide. It was thick and heavy, tightly woven with blue, purple, and scarlet yarn as well as twisted linen. To hack through this dual-layered fabric wall would've taken significant effort by a giant man with a sharp sword. Yet at Jesus' death, the thing spontaneously split, from top to bottom.

It signified an unmistakable, astounding change in the relationship between God and humanity. The writer of Hebrews explained it this way:

And so, dear brothers and sisters, we can boldly enter heaven's Most Holy Place because of the blood of Jesus. *By his death, Jesus opened a new and life-giving way through the curtain into the Most Holy Place.*

And since we have a great High Priest who rules over God's house, let us go right into the presence of God with sincere hearts fully trusting him. For our guilty consciences have been sprinkled with Christ's blood to make us clean, and our bodies have been washed with pure water. (Hebrews 10:19–22, italics mine)

At the moment of Christ's death, God himself tore away the obstacle of sin that had previously required separation between people and God. And he miraculously tore through the impenetrable curtain that symbolically hid his presence, inviting us all to "go right into the presence of God with sincere hearts."

To the Jews in Jesus' time—as scholar David Daube has argued—the curtain tearing in two may have held another interesting symbolism: divine anguish. It was customary for Jews to rend their garments in grief over the loss of a loved one. In the Bible, when Jacob was told that his beloved son Joseph had been killed by a wild animal, he tore his clothes and mourned his son (Genesis 37:34). When Elisha's mentor Elijah was taken to heaven, Elisha "took hold of his garment and tore it in two" (2 Kings 2:12). Perhaps the tearing of the "garment" of the temple at the moment Jesus died signaled to the people God's immense grief over the death of his Son, validating what the Roman centurion at the cross proclaimed: "This man truly was the Son of God!" (Matthew 27:54).

Sources: VGG 182-183; NTRJ 23-24

Who were the three women from Galilee that witnessed Jesus' crucifixion?

Of Jesus' male disciples, only one witnessed his execution: John, called "the disciple he loved" (John 19:26). However, Jesus had a larger group of disciples beyond "the Twelve" who traveled with him, and a good number of them were women. When everyone else ran from Christ, these courageous female disciples remained faithful. Matthew reports that as Jesus died, "many women who had come from Galilee with Jesus to care for him were watching from a distance" (verse 55). He names three of them: "Mary Magdalene, Mary (the mother of James and Joseph), and the mother of James and John, the sons of Zebedee" (verse 56). Those names are included likely because Matthew knew them, and because these women were well known among the Christian community after Jesus' resurrection.

Mary Magdalene had been rescued from seven demons by Jesus (Luke 8:2; Mark 16:9). She was from Magdala, a wealthy port city on the west shore of the Sea of Galilee. The New Testament indicates she was a woman of means, and that she, along with other wealthy women, supported Jesus financially (Luke 8:1-3). In stark contrast to the Twelve and Jesus' other disciples, Mary's complete dedication to Christ is unwavering in all of Scripture—even after she thought he was dead and gone. Jesus chose her to be the first person he met after he returned to life (John 20:11-18).

Mary (the mother of James and Joseph) is a little harder to trace historically. She and her sons are mentioned in the gospels of Matthew, Mark, and Luke, so they all must've been known to some extent by the first Christians. This Mary was a disciple who followed Christ to Jerusalem and watched him die on the cross. She also must've been a friend of Mary Magdalene and was present at Christ's burial (Matthew 27:61). Thinking all had been lost, she still went with Mary Magdalene back to the tomb to do the dirty work of preparing Jesus' corpse for final burial (Mark 16:1-8). It's possible this Mary was also the "wife of Clopas" mentioned in John 19:25. If so, she might've been the sister of Jesus' adoptive father, Joseph.

"The mother of James and John" was Salome, the woman who'd asked Jesus to make her sons "sit in places of honor" next to him in his coming kingdom (Matthew 20:21-22). It's commonly believed, because of an unnamed reference in John 19:25, that she was the sister of Jesus' mother, Mary. That would've made her Jesus' Aunt Salome. It speaks volumes about this woman's integrity and loyalty that, even after she believed Jesus was dead and his kingdom exterminated, she remained faithful to her nephew-Messiah. Commenting on John 19:25-27, Frances Vander Velde also made the interesting observation that, "Salome listened as Jesus commended his mother to John and we think that Salome shared this holy duty and honor with her son." After his execution, Salome joined Mary Magdalene and Mary the mother of James to accomplish the unpleasant task of preparing Jesus' cadaver for proper Jewish burial (Mark 16:1-8).

Gratefully, that was a job none of those women ever had to complete.

Sources: ID3 221, 288-289; HAC 133-134; WOM 203

The Burial of Jesus
Matthew 27:57-61

Do we know where Jesus was buried?

Well, archaeologists seem to have a pretty good idea of where the temporary resting place for Jesus was located—at least they've narrowed it down to two choices. First they reconstructed the biblical evidence to determine that the tomb had to have the following characteristics:

> Cut into a rock (Matthew 27:60)

> In a garden near Golgotha, the site of crucifixion (John 19:17, 41)

> Just outside the city of Jerusalem (John 19:20; Hebrews 13:12)

> Entrance low enough to be sealed with a stone (Mark 15:46)

> Room to sit on the right side, where the body had been placed (Mark 16:15; John 20:11–12)

Next, based on other, known historical tombs, they determined that Jesus' borrowed burial place would've had these characteristics as well:

> A small forecourt

> A low entry passage

> Three "couches" on the three interior walls within the burial chamber, to accommodate three bodies

With these considerations in mind, there are two legitimate possibilities for Jesus' tomb. The first is at the location of the Church of the Holy Sepulchre in Jerusalem, a place identified by Rome's Queen Helena, who was the mother of Emperor Constantine the Great. Around AD 326, Constantine had this church built to mark the site of the tomb for history. The church was destroyed in AD 614, rebuilt twelve years later, damaged and rebuilt again over the centuries. It is somewhat worse for the wear, but it still stands.

The second is a place called (no surprise) the "Garden Tomb." This site is less than three hundred yards north of the Church of the Holy

Sepulchre, just outside Old City Jerusalem. This was the spot theorized by nineteenth-century British military man, Charles Gordon. However, there's no connection to this site from Christian history, so most tend to stick with the Church of the Holy Sepulchre as the likely location of Jesus' tomb.

Source: ASB 1615, 1758

Who was Joseph of Arimathea?

Believe it or not, Joseph of Arimathea was a member of the Jewish ruling group, the Sanhedrin (Mark 15:43). He'd chosen to follow Jesus and is mentioned favorably in all four gospel accounts (Matthew 27:57; Mark 15:43; Luke 23:51; John 19:38).

Remember when the high priest, Caiaphas, held Jesus' midnight trial at his home? Historian Jean-Pierre Isbouts suggests he did that precisely to exclude people like Joseph of Arimathea, who were likely to come to Jesus' defense. This Joseph was also wealthy, enough that he owned a tomb cut into rock (Matthew 27:59–60), in a garden (John 19:41–42), and was able to buy seventy-five pounds of burial ointment made from myrrh and aloes (John 19:39). History remembers him best as the courageous man who generously arranged a proper burial for the executed Christ.

Sources: ID2 980; WWC 262–263

What were the burial traditions of Jesus' time?

Jewish burial custom when Jesus died included the following procedures:

1. Washing the body.

2. Dressing the body (much as we might dress a corpse in a suit for burial), or wrap it in cloth strips, tying the feet at the ankles and the arms at the torso. Given how disfigured Jesus was, wrapping it in cloth was probably the only realistic option.

3. Treating the body with scented perfumes to mask the smell of decay. These were usually spices that were wrapped between the layers of the cloths.

4. Covering the face with a separate cloth, about the size of a napkin.

5. Wrapping the full body in a shroud, a broad, single length of cloth large enough to cover the cadaver front and back.

6. Mourning for about a week, followed by closing of the tomb.

7. Retrieving the bones about a year later (long enough for full decay) and placing them in a bone box for final resting.

Joseph of Arimathea had to rush Jesus' burial a bit because the Sabbath was only hours away. So, he did a quick "OK for now" job of step #5 above and moved Jesus' body to his tomb. Along with the other disciples, Mary Magdalene and Mary (the mother of James and Joseph), he clearly planned to come back and give Jesus a proper burial after the Sabbath had passed.

Source: JOB 274-275

The Guard at the Tomb
Matthew 27:62–66

Were tombs of executed criminals normally guarded in Jesus' day?

Um, no.

In fact, bodies of the crucified were typically left on their crosses to rot for a few days, where scavenging birds would feast on them. After being taken down from a cross, unless a family member claimed the body, a criminal's corpse was either discarded into a common grave or dumped in the stinking, burning, garbage heap at the Valley of Hinnom, located just south of Jerusalem.

The efforts that the chief priests and Pharisees undertook to prevent the theft of Jesus' body were extreme, particularly for a crucified criminal with zero net worth and nothing of value to steal in his tomb. After all, violating a grave or tomb was prohibited by both Roman and Jewish law. Punishment for this crime, by order of Caesar, was death.

However, it's often the case that those with wicked intent project similar wickedness onto others, thinking that everyone is just as evil-minded as they are. Such was the case with the Jewish religious leaders. Because they were deceivers themselves, they accused Jesus and his disciples of the same and demanded security precautions from the Roman governor, Pontius Pilate.

This security included:

> *A heavy stone* to cover the tomb entrance. In this case, it was probably a large, thick, flattened, circular stone rolled in a track in front of the tomb.

> *A Roman seal* on the stone, which would reveal if the stone had been moved. The death penalty was prescribed for anyone breaking the seal to enter the tomb.

> *An unspecified number of soldiers* standing sentry to guard against grave robbers.

It's possible that the guards could've been either temple guards (like the ones who arrested Jesus) or actual Roman soldiers sent from Pilate. Verse 65 records the governor's response to the religious leaders' request was, "You have a guard" (NKJV). This is a little bit ambiguous in the original Greek. It could mean Pilate granted his Roman soldiers (that is, "You have what you've asked for"), or that he insisted the Jews provide their own temple guards. Academics are divided on where the guards came from, but it's my view that Pilate granted Roman legionnaires as guards, for several reasons.

First, the Jewish religious leaders could've placed their own guards in front of the tomb without asking Pilate's permission, but they obviously wanted Roman authority behind their security. Second, the noun translated as *guard* in verse 65 is a Latin word, which would suggest Roman soldiers— Latin being the preferred language of Rome. Third, the Greek word *echete* translated as "you have" in that same verse is used in the imperative sense, likely meaning "you can have a guard" rather than "take your own guard." Finally, after the resurrection, the chief priests promised to protect the soldiers from Pilate—something that would've been unnecessary if they'd been their own temple guards (Matthew 28:13–15).

Needless to say, all these precautions against grave-robbing were overkill—and no match for Jesus anyway.

Sources: MAT 470, 473-475; CFC 208; RBD 423; NNI 1201; NIBC 262

The Resurrection!

The Empty Tomb
Matthew 28:1–10

Is it important that women were the first ones to see Jesus after his resurrection?

Yes, it's extremely important that Jesus chose women to be the first to witness his resurrection—but for a surprising reason.

Dr. William Lane Craig reports that, in that ancient, intensely patriarchal society, "Women's testimony was regarded as so worthless that they weren't even allowed to serve as legal witnesses in a Jewish court of law." Theologian Marlo Schalesky adds, "Jewish historian Josephus (AD 37–100) wrote that due to their giddiness and impetuosity women were not to be trusted or believed as witnesses for any matter."

Women were obviously valued in their own families and repeatedly elevated in Jesus' own ministry, but in Jewish society as a whole, they were regarded as significantly "less than" men. For instance, among the common rabbinical sayings of that time were pejorative teachings like, "Blessed is he whose children are male, but woe to him whose children are female" and "Let the word of the Law be burned rather than delivered to women."

Dr. Craig explains why that negative social bias played out so importantly in the events surrounding Jesus' resurrection (italics his):

> In light of this, it's absolutely remarkable that the chief witnesses to the empty tomb are these women who were friends of Jesus. Any later legendary account would have certainly portrayed male disciples as discovering the tomb—Peter or John, for example. The fact that women are the first witnesses to the empty tomb is most plausibly explained by the reality that—like it or not—they *were* the discoverers of the

empty tomb! This shows that the gospel writers faithfully recorded what happened, even if it was embarrassing.

Sources: CFC 217–218; WBS 229

Why do people disbelieve Jesus was raised from the dead?

Well, the core reason that people disbelieve Jesus was raised from the dead is that they disbelieve (or, more often, dislike) the Christian religion. That's understandable given the hateful reputation that Christians have sometimes earned throughout history (even today), and our human need to attempt to disprove that with which we disagree.

However, it should be noted that virtually no one disputes that Jesus' tomb is empty—the dead body of Christ simply is not there. Even the Jewish religious leaders of that time acknowledged this fact (Matthew 28:12–15). If the body of Jesus had been there, it would've been simple work to discredit Christ's disciples just by going to the tomb and producing the corpse.

Regardless of that, there are a few popular conspiracy theories that attempt to justify disbelief in Jesus' resurrection. They include:

CONSPIRACY #1: Christ's disciples stole his body while the guards slept, then perpetrated a lie of resurrection, and started a new religion based on this lie (the Jewish theory).

To my mind, this is the most plausible of all the conspiracy theories about the resurrection. It's the oldest, dating all the way back to the time of the disciples, and if you're willing to overlook some relevant circumstances, I suppose it could've happened. There are many problems with this theory under scrutiny, though.

First, there was the issue of the armed guard protecting Jesus' tomb. Remember, these guards were placed there with one job only, and a very specific one at that: to prevent Jesus' disciples from stealing the body. And, on the Friday of Jesus' execution, his disciples were scattered and terrified that they'd be next in line for death. That those cowards could come up with a successful plan to quickly confront, outwit, and overcome professional Roman soldiers by Sunday morning strains the imagination.

Additionally, this theory depends not only on the guards being grossly derelict in their duty, but also being able to (1) sleep through the noise of a large stone being rolled away right beside them, and (2) adeptly identify nighttime grave robbers while they sleep. Honestly, given Jesus' reputation as a miracle worker, a miraculous resurrection is more plausible than that.

Second, Jesus' disciples gained nothing of significance from this supposed lie. "It's not as though there were a mansion awaiting them on the Mediterranean," says scholar J. P. Moreland. "They faced a life of hardship. They often went without food, slept exposed to the elements, were ridiculed, beaten, imprisoned. And finally, most of them were executed in torturous ways. For what? For good intentions? No, because they were convinced beyond a shadow of a doubt that they had seen Jesus Christ alive from the dead."

CONSPIRACY #2: Jesus was never crucified, and so was never resurrected (the Muslim theory).

According to this view, Jesus was too holy to endure the indignity of crucifixion. Instead, God miraculously made someone else to look like Jesus who was then crucified in his place. Afterward, Jesus rose to heaven alive, like Elijah. As the Koran reads in surah 4:157, "but they killed Him not, nor crucified him. Only a likeness of that was shown to them ... for a surety they killed him not."

Muslim tradition declares that none of Christ's followers actually saw his death, and so instead offers random conjecture about who actually died on the cross. Some theorize Jesus hid while one of his disciples died in his place. Others say Judas was punished by being made to look like Jesus and then crucified. Some believe that Simon of Cyrene (see Simon of Cyrene commentary segment on Matthew 27:32–44) took Jesus' place for the execution. Some even say Satan was actually crucified as punishment for his opposition to Christ.

To my mind, there are a lot of problems with this theory. The biggest (and most obvious) is that it portrays God as a liar, a deceiver, and callously unconcerned about the fate of anyone else. And it contradicts Christ's own teaching about morality and about his death and resurrection. For me, this falls very short of truth.

CONSPIRACY #3: Jesus was resurrected as pure spirit, not in a physical body (the Jehovah's Witnesses theory).

According to the Jehovah's Witness Watchtower organization, "the King Christ Jesus was put to death in the flesh and was resurrected an invisible spirit creature."

There are many who believe this theory, but for me the only way it can be true is if the Gospels and the book of Acts reported untruth. (For examples, see Luke 24:36–43; John 20:24–29; Acts 3:15; Acts 10:40, among others). I find the New Testament to be a more reliable source on first-century events than the historically recent Watchtower organization.

More random conspiracy theories.

There are other attempts to disprove Christ's resurrection, but they are wholly inventive fictions and surprisingly insubstantial. For instance, some say that Jesus must've had a long-lost twin, separated at birth, who impersonated him after the crucifixion [insert eye roll here]. Others say that Jesus—after being severely disfigured from beatings, tortured on the cross, and having a spear shoved deep into his side—simply fainted … briefly. Then he woke up all better and pretended to be resurrected. Some are at least honest about their skepticism, saying they simply disbelieve—even though they can't think of any plausible explanation for Jesus' empty tomb.

The basic fact is, no conspiracy theory about Christ's resurrection is fully supportable. This is hard for non-believers to accept because, as Lee Strobel points out, "The empty tomb, as an enduring symbol of the Resurrection, is the ultimate representation of Jesus' claim to being God." Dr. Timothy Keller, pastor and author, also likes to say, "The issue on which everything hangs is not whether or not you like [Jesus'] teaching but whether or not he rose from the dead."

The apostle Paul agrees, writing in the first century:

And if Christ has not been raised, then all our preaching is useless, and your faith is useless. And we apostles would all be lying about God—for we have said that God raised Christ from the grave. But that can't be true if there is no resurrection of the dead. And if there is no resurrection of the dead, then Christ has not been raised. And if Christ has not been raised, then your faith is useless and you are still guilty of your sins. In that case, all who have died believing in Christ are lost! (1 Corinthians 15:14–18)

Sources: RES 6-7, 9, 34; CFC 205, 246-247; UI 220; RFG 210

The Report of the Guard
Matthew 28:11-15

How could the soldiers get away with saying they fell asleep while on guard duty?

Here's my thinking:

1. The soldiers would have to be in collusion with both the chief priests and the Roman governor of Judea, Pontius Pilate.

The general population of Jews, given its palpable distaste for Roman governance, probably would've enjoyed the embarrassment of the emperor's vaunted soldiers derelict in their duty. Not so much Pilate. Sleeping while on duty was a grave crime, earning anything from a flogging to execution. The merciless Pilate should've immediately punished those soldiers for gross failure in the line of duty and for embarrassing Rome. But Pilate didn't do that; in fact, he did *nothing*.

Likewise, the chief priests should've been furious, demanding blood from those soldiers. They were supposed to be serving the purposes of the chief priests, *specifically ordered* to prevent Jesus' disciples from stealing the body. To say, "Oops, sorry, we fell asleep," should've been cause for cries of harsh punishment from those religious leaders. That just didn't happen, despite the purported circumstances.

Given the conspicuous absence of *any* punishing response from, or even complaints from, both Pilate and the chief priests, collusion with the soldiers appears fairly evident, just as Matthew reports.

2. There had to be some kind of payoff.

Roman soldiers in that day were hardened men, used to combat, and let's face it, greedy. Simple guard duty in front of a Jewish grave would've been easy work for them. To publicly confess that they'd been outwitted by a ragtag group of Jews *because they were asleep* would've been humiliating both to their own personal reputations and to the reputation of Rome. If it had been true, it never would've been confessed. That would've been too degrading and dangerous. So the fact that they did confess to this kind of dereliction suggests that someone had made that false confession worth it. Matthew reports that's exactly what happened, that the chief priests and the elders gave the guards "a large bribe" (verse 12) to spread the news that they'd fallen asleep on the job and the disciples stole the body.

Sources: ZB1 188; SMB 315

The Great Commission
Matthew 28:16-20

Who is Matthew talking about when he says, "When they saw him, they worshiped him—but some of them doubted"?

The New Testament never identifies exactly who were the "some of them" who doubted Jesus' resurrection—even after seeing him with their own eyes. There are a few reasonable possibilities, though.

In verse 17, the Greek phrase *hoi de edistasan* is translated as "some of them doubted." This is a valid translation, but it could be interpreted to imply the meaning, "some of them doubted *at first*." If that's the case, and if it relates specifically to "the eleven disciples" in verse 16, then it would refer to Thomas—the disciple history has affectionately dubbed, "Doubting Thomas." (You can read his story in John 20:24–29.)

However, it's more likely that this gathering on a Galilean mountain was a crowd of disciples, not just the eleven. This is first indicated in verse 10, where Jesus is recorded as saying, "Go tell my brothers to leave for Galilee, and they will see me there." The implication here is that "brothers" refers to the broader group of Christ's disciples beyond just the eleven.

The second indication is Paul's statement in 1 Corinthians 15:6: "He was seen by over five hundred brethren at once" (NKJV). Paul was probably referring to this gathering. So some of the five hundred on the mountain were probably like Thomas, either dumbfounded or stubborn in disbelief at the idea of a risen Jesus ... at least at first.

Sources: CWSN 111, 399, 472, 1024; TYM 277

What does it mean to "make disciples" as Jesus' commanded?

Entire books have been written on this question! I won't attempt to duplicate those efforts and will, instead, highlight a few things I see in this "great commission" of Jesus. Then I'll trust that you'll continue to explore what this means in your own life.

First, for me, it's important to try to understand how Jesus' followers at that time would've heard the word "disciple." The Greek word in Matthew 28:19 is *mathēteusate*, which at its root means "to learn." The implication here is not that discipleship is a one-time experience, but as it was with Jesus' disciples, it's to be an ongoing, lifestyle of somebody who is constantly learning from a respected master teacher. Second, theologian Larry Richards makes an excellent point when he says, "Jesus does not send His followers out to make converts but to make disciples.... Conversion is the first step in disciple-making, but it can never be the last." With these two things in mind, I believe that if we're to "make disciples" we must be willing to take a long-term view. We must be people who ourselves are constantly learning more of Jesus—and teaching others to do the same. Making disciples requires more than a passing influence in another's life. We must be willing to invest a lifetime into the lives of others—hard days, good days, sorrowful days, joyful days and more.

Next, Jesus gives practical instruction for disciple-making:

"Therefore, go..." I've heard it preached that because of this command to "go," we are all obligated to leave our homes and move to a foreign place as missionaries. Obviously I'm not opposed to people doing that, but I disagree with the idea that a missionary career should be a compulsion for everybody. Instead, I'd ask you to consider: What does it mean to "go" where you are? Where can you go in your neighborhood, your home, your work, your family, your hometown to make disciples? And what kind of impact would it make on our world if each of us who claim Christ were to "go" where we already are, where God has placed us today?

"...and make disciples of all the nations..." There is no race, ethnicity, people group—no one—who is not invited to become Jesus' disciple. It's our responsibility, therefore, to be willing to share Christ-life with anyone, as the apostle Paul would say, "Jew or Gentile, slave or free, male and female..." (Galatians 3:28).

"...baptizing them in the name of the Father and the Son and the Holy Spirit..." Note that baptizing is not what makes a disciple, but it is a

natural expression of disciple-making. In other words, we are not baptized to become disciples; we are baptized because we *are* disciples. In the early church, baptism was representational of two things: (1) Repentance (John's baptism), that is, a change of heart to turn away from sin and toward God, and (2) a symbolic picture of the burial of one's old life followed by the raising of the believer to new life, to be lived in Jesus' power." This is what it means to baptize a disciple in the name of the Father and the Son and the Holy Spirit.

"...teach these new disciples to obey all the commands I have given you." It's C. S. Lewis who reminds me that the first priority in teaching is living. "What we practice," he said, "not (save at rare intervals) what we preach, is usually our great contribution to the conversion of others." And my former pastor Chuck Swindoll eloquently describes the practical messages we are to teach other disciples:

> The first stage in discipleship involves introducing new believers to God the Father, who created all things out of nothing and loves us unconditionally. It involves teaching them about God the Son, the incarnate God-man, who was born of a virgin, who died for our sins and rose again, who ascended into heaven, and who will come again as Judge and King. And it involves informing them of God the Holy Spirit, who gives us new life, indwells us for sanctification, empowers us for service, unites us to Christ, and supplies us with gifts for ministry in His church.... We teach that this is a life filled with good works, done not to earn salvation but rather because we have been saved. And we teach that it involves turning from lives of self-serving wickedness and sin to lives committed to the empowerment of the Spirit, marked by the fruit of the Spirit being increasingly manifested in our lives (Gal. 5:22–23).

This, I think, is a fine starting point for what it means to "make disciples" as Jesus has commanded, but I'd be remiss if I stopped here. God-in-resurrected-bones didn't simply give a command to make disciples and then skip away to leave us on our own. Instead, he made an ironclad promise to his original followers—and you and to me: *"And be sure of this: I am with you always, even to the end of the age"* (Matthew 28:20).

To which I can only say: *Amen, thank you Lord Jesus.*

Sources: EDB 226; ETJ 269-270; CSLB 1211; SMB 322

"Remember that the passion of Christ ends always in the joy of the resurrection of Christ, so when you feel in your own heart the suffering of Christ, remember the resurrection has to come. Never let anything so fill you with sorrow as to make you forget the joy of Christ risen."

Mother Teresa

Source: NGL 137

Acknowledgments

This Q&A-style commentary had its roots in a weekly column I wrote some years ago on Beliefnet.com. It was a fun one that I called, "For Bible Study Nerds," and it forced me to finally put down in writing some results of my curiosity about the gospel of Matthew. Without that column, this book never would've been imagined. So when it comes to acknowledgments, first, I need to thank Sharon Kirk at Beliefnet for saying "yes" when I said, "Hey, how about if …?"

This book also would've been impossible without the generous people who faithfully read chapters from Matthew and then sent me questions that came to mind while they were reading. At one point, after I'd completed about a third of the manuscript, my in-house server crashed and took with it everything I had of *Bible-Smart: Matthew*. I hyperventilated for a while. I whined to my editor (of course). I even considered canceling the project. I figured I could rewrite the commentary segments … but there was no way I could reproduce the many insightful, interesting, meaningful questions that these people had sent me. Finally, I made it a matter of prayer, and waited. A close friend of mine, an engineer who had spent thirty years at Hewlett-Packard, stepped in. It took him several weeks, and a few late nights, but in the end, Dave was able to recover (almost) everything I'd lost of this book—including those precious, priceless questions. So, to those of you who sent me your questions: You inspire me. Thank you. I'm grateful to be in your social orbit.

And while I'm at it, yeah, I need to say this: Hey Dave Hanes! Thank you! You're a genius and a good friend, and I very much appreciate you. (P.S. Your wife, Jennifer Hanes, is pretty cool too, especially since she lets me borrow her theology books whenever I ask.)

During the writing of this book, systematic theologian Dr. Mary Vanden Berg generously read and responded to several key chapters. Her insight and encouragement at critical moments was a priceless gift. Thank you, Mary!

Last but certainly not least, I must thank Lynnette Pennings at Rose Publishing. Your steadfast encouragement and thoughtful partnership in this project have been invaluable to me. Thank you for making me part of the Rose Publishing family (and for bringing in talented people like Jessica Curiel and AJ Hanna to the project!). Remind me someday that I owe you a favor.

Best to all,
Mike Nappa

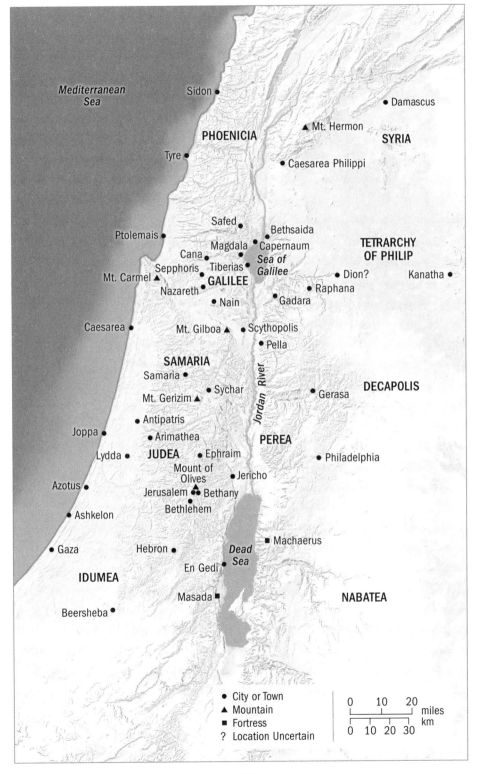

Mediterranean Sea

Sidon •

• Damascus

PHOENICIA

▲ Mt. Hermon

SYRIA

Tyre •

• Caesarea Philippi

Safed •

• Bethsaida

Ptolemais •

Magdala • • Capernaum

TETRARCHY OF PHILIP

Cana •

Sea of Galilee

Sepphoris • Tiberias •

Mt. Carmel ▲

GALILEE

• Dion?

Kanatha •

Nazareth •

• Raphana

• Nain

• Gadara

Caesarea •

Mt. Gilboa ▲ • Scythopolis

SAMARIA

• Pella

Samaria •

Jordan River

Mt. Gerizim ▲ • Sychar

• Gerasa

DECAPOLIS

• Antipatris

• Arimathea

PEREA

Joppa •

Lydda • **JUDEA** • Ephraim

• Philadelphia

Mount of Olives

• Jericho

Azotus •

Jerusalem • ▲ • Bethany

• Ashkelon

Bethlehem •

Dead Sea

■ Machaerus

• Gaza

Hebron •

En Gedi •

IDUMEA

Masada ■

NABATEA

Beersheba •

• City or Town
▲ Mountain
■ Fortress
? Location Uncertain

0	10	20	
			miles
			km
0	10 20	30	

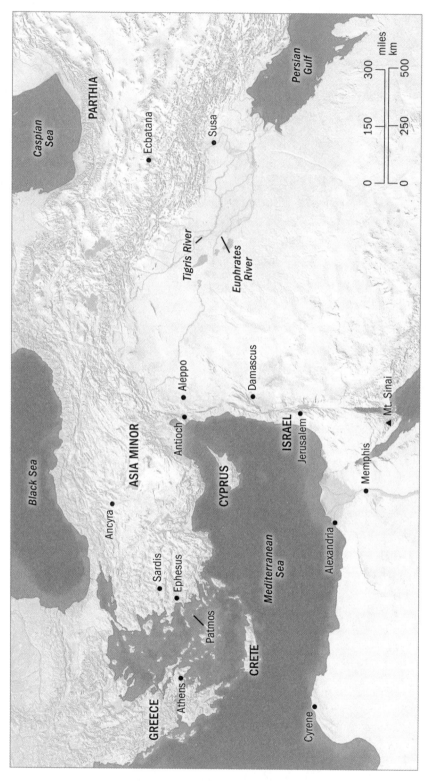

274

Bibliography
Listed Alphabetically by Abbreviation

AAU *Angels Among Us,* by Ron Rhodes (Eugene, OR: Harvest House Publishers, 1994).

ABC *The Abingdon Bible Commentary,* edited by Frederick Carl Eiselen (Nashville, TN: Abingdon-Cokesbury Press, 1929).

ADV *Adventuring Through the Bible: New Testament,* by Ray C. Stedman (Grand Rapids, MI: Discovery House, 1997, 2012).

AMB *All the Men of the Bible,* by Herbert Lockyer (Grand Rapids, MI: Zondervan, 1958).

ANT *Archaeology and the New Testament,* by John McRay (Grand Rapids, MI: Baker Academic, 1991).

APB *All the Prayers of the Bible,* by Herbert Lockyer (Grand Rapids, MI: Zondervan Publishing House, 1959).

ARF *Ancient Rome on Five Denarii a Day,* by Philip Matyszak (London, UK: Thames and Hudson, 2007).

ASB *Archaeological Study Bible, NIV,* edited by Dr. Walter C. Kaiser, Dr. Duane A. Garrett, and Joan Davis Wanner (Grand Rapids, MI: Zondervan, 2005).

AST *The Apologetics Study Bible,* Ted Cabal, general editor (Nashville, TN: Holman Bible Publishers, 2007).

ATP *All the Parables of the Bible,* by Herbert Lockyer (Grand Rapids, MI: Zondervan, 1963).

ATR *Along the Road,* by John A. Beck (Grand Rapids, MI: Discovery House, 2018).

AWB *All the Women of the Bible,* by Herbert Lockyer (Grand Rapids, MI: Zondervan Publishing House, 1988).

BAB *The Bible Answer Book,* by James Stuart Bell and Sam O'Neal (Naperville, IL: Sourcebooks, 2010).

BAH *The Bible Answer Handbook,* by Larry Richards (Grand Rapids, MI: Revell, 1997, 2012).

BAL *The Bible Almanac,* edited by J.I. Packer, Merrill C. Tenney, and William White, Jr. (Nashville, TN: Thomas Nelson Publishers, 1980).

BBH *Bagster's Bible Handbook,* introduction by Dr. Walter Elwell (Old Tappan, NJ: Fleming H. Revell Company, 1983).

BCB *Baker Commentary on the Bible,* edited by Walter A. Elwell (Grand Rapids, MI: Baker Books, 1989).

BEC *The Bible Exposition Commentary, New Testament Volume 1,* by Warren W. Wiersbe (Colorado Springs, CO: Victor Books, 2001).

BIB   *The Baker Illustrated Bible Background Commentary,* edited by J. Scott Duvall and J. Daniel Hays (Grand Rapids, MI: Baker Books, 2020).

BID   *The Baker Illustrated Bible Dictionary,* edited Tremper Longman III (Grand Rapids, MI: Baker Books, 2013).

BIE   *Biblical Interpretation in the Early Church,* edited and translated by Karlfried Froehlich (Philadelphia, PA: Fortress Press, 1984).

BIG   *The Baker Illustrated Guide to Everyday Life in Bible Times,* by John A. Beck (Grand Rapids, MI: Baker Books, 2013).

BKB   *The Bible Knowledge Background Commentary: Matthew-Luke,* edited by Craig A. Evans (Colorado Springs, CO: Victor Books, 2003).

BKN   *The Bible Knowledge Commentary: New Testament,* edited by John F. Walvoord and Roy B. Zuck (Wheaton, IL: Victor Books, 1983).

BKO   *The Bible Knowledge Commentary: Old Testament,* edited by John F. Walvoord and Roy B. Zuck (Wheaton, IL: Victor Books, 1985, 1989).

BKW1 *The Bible Knowledge Word Study: Genesis–Deuteronomy,* edited by Eugene H. Merrill (Colorado Springs, CO: Victor Books, 2003).

BKW2 *The Bible Knowledge Word Study: Joshua–2 Chronicles,* edited by Eugene H. Merrill (Colorado Springs, CO: Victor Books, 2004).

BPB   *The Black Presence in the Bible,* by Rev. Walter Arthur McCray (Chicago: Black Light Fellowship, 1990, 1993).

BSB   *The Bible Source Book,* by Dave Branon (Grand Rapids, MI: Discovery House, 2019).

BTC   *Belief: A Theological Commentary on the Bible, Matthew,* by Anna Case-Winters (Louisville, KY: Westminster John Knox Press, 2015).

BTCM *Brazos Theological Commentary on the Bible: Matthew,* by Stanley Hauerwas (Grand Rapids, MI: Brazos Press, 2006).

CBC   *The Classic Bible Commentary,* edited by Owen Collins (Wheaton, IL: Crossway Books, 1999).

CBP   *The Complete Book of Bible Prophecy,* by Mark Hitchcock (Wheaton, IL: Tyndale House Publishers, 1999).

CBS   *Cultural Backgrounds Study Bible, NIV* (Grand Rapids, MI: Zondervan, 2016).

CEM   *Christ-Centered Exposition: Exalting Jesus in Matthew,* by David Platt (Nashville, TN: B&H Academic, 2013).

CFC   *The Case for Christ,* by Lee Strobel (Grand Rapids, MI: Zondervan Publishing House, 1998).

CGB   *The Complete Guide to the Bible,* by Stephen M. Miller (Uhrichsville, OH: Barbour Publishing, 2007).

CHF   *The Christian Faith,* by Michael Horton (Grand Rapids, MI: Zondervan, 2011).

CSB *The Chronological Study Bible* (Nashville, TN: Thomas Nelson, 2014).

CSLB *The C. S. Lewis Bible,* edited by Marlene Baer Hekkert and Michael G. Maudin (San Francisco, CA: HarperOne, 2010).

CWDN *The Complete Word Study Dictionary: New Testament,* edited by Spiro Zodhiates (Chattanooga, TN: AMG Publishers, 1992, 1993).

CWDO *The Complete Word Study Dictionary: Old Testament,* edited by Warren Baker and Eugene Carpenter (Chattanooga, TN: AMG Publishers, 2003).

CWSN *The Complete Word Study New Testament,* edited by Spiro Zodhiates (Chattanooga, TN: AMG Publishers, 1991).

CWSO *The Complete Word Study Old Testament,* edited by Warren Baker (Chattanooga, TN: AMG Publishers, 1994).

DBI *Dictionary of Biblical Imagery,* edited by Leland Ryken, James C. Wilhoit, and Tremper Longman III (Downers Grover, IL: IVP Academic, 1998).

DBT *A Dictionary of Bible Types,* by Walter L. Wilson (Peabody, MA: Hendrickson Publishers Inc., 1999).

DCC *Documents of the Christian Church, Fourth Edition,* edited by Henry Bettenson and Chris Maunder (Oxford: Oxford University Press, 1943, 1963, 1999, 2011).

DHB *Discovery House Bible Atlas,* by Dr. John A. Beck (Grand Rapids, MI: Discovery House, 2015).

DLJ *Daily Life at the Time of Jesus,* by Miriam Feinberg Vamosh (Herzlia, Israel: Palphot Ltd., 2007).

DOB *A Dictionary of the Bible, Fourth Revised Edition,* by John D. Davis. (Grand Rapids, MI: Baker Book House, 1898, 1903, 1911, 1924, 1954, 1958).

DOS *Dictionary of Saints,* by John J. Delaney. (Garden City, New York: Doubleday & Company, 1980).

EBD *Encyclopedia of Bible Difficulties,* by Gleason L. Archer, Jr. (Grand Rapids, MI: Zondervan, 1982).

EDB *The Expository Dictionary of Bible Words,* by Lawrence O. Richards (Grand Rapids, MI: Regency Reference Library, 1985).

EHB *Eerdmans' Handbook to the Bible,* edited by David Alexander and Pat Alexander (Grand Rapids, MI: William B. Eerdmans Publishing Company, 1973).

EOR *The Emperors of Rome,* by David Potter (New York: Metro Books, 2007).

EPB *Every Prophecy of the Bible,* by John F. Walvoord (Colorado Springs, CO: Chariot Victor Publishing, 1990, 1999).

ESB *The ESV Study Bible,* edited by Lane T. Dennis and Wayne Grudem (Wheaton, IL: Crossway Bibles, 2008).

ETC *Eyewitness to Crucifixion,* by Stephen M. Miller (Grand Rapids, MI: Our Daily Bread Publishing, 2020).

ETJ   *Every Teaching of Jesus in the Bible,* by Larry Richards (Nashville, TN: Thomas Nelson Publishers, 2001).

FCC   "Fertility Cults of Canaan," by Ray Vander Laan, *That the World May Know,* accessed August 26, 2021. https://www.thattheworldmayknow.com/fertility-cults-of-canaan.

FOD   *Fodor's Israel,* edited by Linda Cabasin (New York: Fodor's Travel/Random House, 2014).

GNM   *The Good News According to Matthew,* by Eduard Schweizer, translated by David E. Green (Atlanta, GA: John Knox Press, 1975).

HAC   *The Holman Apologetics Commentary on the Bible: The Gospels and Acts,* Jeremy Royal Howard, general editor (Nashville, TN: Holman Reference, 2013).

HBD   *Harper's Bible Dictionary,* edited by Paul J. Achtemeier (San Francisco, CA: Harper & Row Publishers, 1985).

HER   *Herod,* by Peter Richardson (Columbia, SC: University of South Carolina Press, 1996).

HSB   *Holman Student Bible Dictionary,* by Karen Dockrey and Johnnie & Phyllis Godwin (Nashville, TN: Holman Bible Publishers, 1993).

HSJ   *Hard Sayings of Jesus,* by F. F. Bruce (Downers Grove, IL: InterVarsity Press, 1983).

HTR   *How to Read the Bible for All Its Worth, Fourth Edition,* by Gordon D. Fee and Douglas Stuart (Grand Rapids, MI: Zondervan, 1981, 1993, 2003, 2014).

HWG   *How We Got the Bible,* by Timothy Paul Jones (Torrance, CA: Rose Publishing, 2015).

IB7   *The Interpreter's Bible, Volume VII: General Articles on the New Testament; Matthew; Mark,* edited by George Arthur Buttrick, et. al., exposition by Sherman E. Johnson (Nashville, TN: Abingdon, 1951).

IB8   *The Interpreter's Bible, Volume VIII: Luke; John,* edited by George Arthur Buttrick, et. al. (Nashville, TN: Abingdon, 1952).

IBB   *The IVP Bible Background Commentary: New Testament,* by Craig S. Keener (Downers Grove, IL: InterVarsity Press, 1993).

IBC   *The International Bible Commentary,* edited by F. F. Bruce (Grand Rapids, MI: Marshall Pickering/Zondervan, 1979).

IBD1   *The Illustrated Bible Dictionary, Part 1: Aaron–Golan,* edited by J. D. Douglas (Leicester, England: Inter-Varsity Press, 1980).

IBD2   *The Illustrated Bible Dictionary, Part 2: Goliath–Papyri,* edited by J. D. Douglas (Leicester, England: Inter-Varsity Press, 1980).

IBD3   *The Illustrated Bible Dictionary, Part 3: Parable-Zuzim,* edited by J. D. Douglas (Leicester, England: Inter-Varsity Press, 1980).

ICR   *Institutes of the Christian Religion,* by John Calvin, translated Henry Beveridge (Peabody, MA: Hendrickson Publishers, 2008).

ID2   *The Interpreter's Dictionary of the Bible, Volume 2 E-J,* edited by George Arthur Buttrick (New York: Abingdon, 1962).

ID3   *The Interpreter's Dictionary of the Bible, Volume 3 K-Q,* edited by George Arthur Buttrick (New York: Abingdon, 1962).

ILJ   *The Illustrated Life of Jesus,* by Herschel Hobbs (Nashville, TN: Holman Reference, 2000).

IMK   *Interpretation: A Bible Commentary for Teaching and Preaching, Mark,* by Lamar Williamson, Jr. (Louisville, KY: John Knox Press, 1983).

IMT   *Interpretation: A Bible Commentary for Teaching and Preaching, Matthew,* by Douglas R. A. Hare (Louisville, KY: John Knox Press, 1993).

ISJ   *In the Steps of Jesus,* by Peter Walker (Grand Rapids, MI: Zondervan, 2006).

IWB   *101 Important Words of the Bible,* by Len Woods (Grand Rapids, MI: Our Daily Bread Publishing, 2020).

JAN   *The Jewish Annotated New Testament, Second Edition, New Revised Standard Version,* edited by Amy-Jill Levine and Marc Zvi Brettler (New York: Oxford University Press, USA, 2011, 2017).

JCL   *Jesus Christ Our Lord,* by John F. Walvoord (Chicago: Moody Press, 1969).

JHE   *Jesus & His Enemies,* by Paul Yeulett (Phillipsburg, NJ: P&R Publishing, 2013).

JHT   *Jesus and His Times,* edited by Kaari Ward (Pleasantville, NY: The Reader's Digest Association Inc., 1987).

JOB   *The Jesus of the Bible,* by Stephen M. Miller (Uhrichsville, OH: Barbour Publishing, 2009).

KC   *King's Cross,* by Timothy Keller (New York, Dutton, 2011).

KS   *Kingdom Suffering,* by John Wimber (Ann Arbor, MI: Vine Books, 1988).

LEA   *Leadership: Theory and Practice, Fourth Edition,* by Peter G. Northouse (Thousand Oaks, CA: Sage Publications, 2007).

LEB   *The Lion Encyclopedia of the Bible,* edited by Pat Alexander (Herts, England: Lion Publishing and Reader's Digest Association Inc., 1978, 1986).

LOB   *The Lands of the Bible Today,* by Dave Branon (Grand Rapids, MI: Our Daily Bread Publishing, 2020).

LST   *Lectures in Systematic Theology,* by Henry Clarence Thiessen (Grand Rapids, MI: Wm. B. Eerdmans Publishing Company, 1956).

MAC   *The MacArthur Study Bible,* by John MacArthur (Nashville, TN: Thomas Nelson, 2013).

MAT   *Matthew,* by Craig A. Evans (New York: Cambridge University Press, 2012).

MBC   *The Moody Bible Commentary,* edited by Michael Rydelnik and Michael Vanlaningham (Chicago: Moody Publishers, 2014).

MFE2   *Matthew for Everyone, Part Two,* by Tom Wright (Louisville, KY: Westminster John Knox Press, 2002, 2004).

NAS   *New American Standard Bible: The Open Bible Edition,* (Nashville, TN: Thomas Nelson Publishers, 1975, 1978).

NET   *New Evidence that Demands a Verdict,* by Josh McDowell (Nashville, TN: Thomas Nelson Publishers, 1999).

NGL   *No Greater Love,* by Mother Teresa (New York: Barnes & Noble Books, 1997).

NIB   *Nelson's Illustrated Bible Dictionary,* Ronald F. Youngblood, general editor (Nashville, TN: Thomas Nelson, 1986, 1995, 2014).

NIBC   *New International Biblical Commentary: Matthew,* by Robert H. Mounce (Peabody, MA: Hendrickson Publishers, 1985, 1991).

NMC   *The New Manners and Customs of Bible Times,* by Ralph Gower (Chicago: Moody Press, 1987).

NNI   *Nelson's New Illustrated Bible Commentary,* edited by Earl Radmacher, Ronald B. Allen, and H. Wayne House (Nashville, TN: Thomas Nelson Publishers, 1999).

NSC3   *The New Strong's Exhaustive Concordance of the Bible: Part 3,* "Concise Dictionary of the Words in the Hebrew Bible," compiled by James Strong (Nashville, TN: Thomas Nelson Publishers, 1995, 1996).

NSC4   *The New Strong's Exhaustive Concordance of the Bible: Part 4,* "Concise Dictionary of the Words in the Greek Testament," compiled by James Strong (Nashville, TN: Thomas Nelson Publishers, 1995, 1996).

NTE   *The New Testament Explorer,* by Mark Bailey and Tom Constable (Nashville, TN: Word Publishing, 1999).

NTI   *The New Testament in Its World,* by N. T. Wright and Michael Bird (Grand Rapids, MI: Zondervan Academic, 2019).

NTL   *New Testament Life and Times,* by Lawrence O. Richards (Colorado Springs, CO: Victor, 1994, 2002).

NTRJ   *The New Testament and Rabbinic Judaism,* by David Daube (London: Athlone, 1956).

NTW   *New Testament Words in Today's Language,* by Wayne A. Detzler (Wheaton, IL: Victor Books, 1986).

NUB   *The New Unger's Bible Handbook,* by Merrill F. Unger (Chicago: Moody Press, 1966, 1984).

OCT   *On Christian Teaching,* by Saint Augustine, translated by R. P. H. Green (Oxford: Oxford University Press, 1997, 1999, 2008).

OPB   *The Open Bible, New Living Translation* (Nashville, TN: Thomas Nelson Publishers, 1998).

PCXV   *The Pulpit Commentary Volume XV: Matthew,* edited by H. D. M. Spence and Joseph S. Exell, exposition written by A. Lukyn Williams (Peabody, MA: Hendrickson Publishers, 1892).

PHS   *Precious in His Sight,* by Roy B. Zuck (Grand Rapids, MI: Baker Books, 1996).

PRO   *PROOF,* by Daniel Montgomery and Timothy Paul Jones (Grand Rapids, MI: Zondervan, 2014).

QST   *The Quest Study Bible, New International Version,* edited by Marshall Shelley (Grand Rapids, MI: Zondervan Publishing House, 1994).

RBD   *The Revell Bible Dictionary, Deluxe Color Edition,* edited by Lawrence O. Richards (Old Tappan, NJ: Fleming H. Revell Company, 1990).

RCL   *Reformation Commentary on Scripture, New Testament III: Luke,* edited by Beth Kreitzer (Downers Grove, IL: IVP Academic, 2015).

RDA   *Reader's Digest Atlas of the Bible* (Pleasantville, NY: The Reader's Digest Association, Inc., 1981, 1985).

RDC   *Reader's Digest Complete Guide to the Bible* (Pleasantville, NY: The Reader's Digest Association, Inc.).

REC2 *Reformed Expository Commentary: Matthew, Vol.2,* by Daniel M. Doriani (Phillipsburg, NJ: P&R Publishing, 2008).

RES   *Resurrection,* by Hank Hanegraaff (Nashville, TN: Word Publishing, 2000).

RFG   *The Reason for God,* by Timothy Keller (New York: Riverhead Books, 2008).

RHW   "Ritual Hand Washing Before Meals," by MJL, *My Jewish Learning,* accessed August 15, 2021. https://www.myjewishlearning.com/article/hand-washing/.

SBW   *The Study Bible for Women,* edited by Dr. Dorothy Patterson and Dr. Rhonda Kelley (Nashville, TN: Holman Bible Publishers, 2014).

SGC   *Single, Gay, Christian,* by Gregory Coles (Downers Grove, IL: InterVarsity Press, 2017).

SJP   *Swindoll's New Testament Insights: Insights on James and 1 & 2 Peter,* by Charles R. Swindoll (Grand Rapids, MI: Zondervan, 2010).

SLU   *Swindoll's New Testament Insights: Insights on Luke,* by Charles R. Swindoll (Grand Rapids, MI: Zondervan, 2012).

SMA   *Swindoll's Living Insights: Matthew 1-15,* by Charles R. Swindoll (Carol Stream: IL, Tyndale House Publishers, 2020).

SMB   *Swindoll's Living Insights: Matthew 16-28,* by Charles R. Swindoll (Carol Stream: IL, Tyndale House Publishers, 2020).

SMK   *Swindoll's Living Insights: Mark,* by Charles R. Swindoll (Carol Stream: IL, Tyndale House Publishers, 2016).

SOC   *The Story of Christianity, Volume 1, Revised and Updated,* by Justo L. González (San Francisco, CA: HarperOne, 2010).

SOM   *The Sermon on the Mount,* by R. T. Kendall (Minneapolis, MN: Chosen Books, 2011).

SSB   *The Swindoll Study Bible,* by Charles R. Swindoll (Carol Stream, IL: Tyndale House Publishers, 2017).

ST   *Systematic Theology, Fourth Revised and Enlarged Edition,* by Louis Berkof (Grand Rapids, MI: Wm. B. Eerdmans Publishing Co., 1939, 1941).

TC   *The Teacher's Commentary,* by Lawrence O. Richards (Wheaton, IL: Victor Books, 1987).

TEB   *The Tony Evans Bible Commentary,* by Tony Evans (Nashville, TN: Holman Reference, 2019).

TEF   *That's Easy for You to Say,* by W. Murray Severance (Nashville, TN: Broadman & Holman Reference, 1997).

TEN   *The Eternal Now,* by Paul Tillich (New York, Charles Scribner and Sons, 1956, 1957, 1958, 1959, 1961, 1962, 1963).

TGE   *Thayer's Greek-English Lexicon of the New Testament,* by Joseph H. Thayer (Grand Rapids, MI: Baker Book House, 1977, 1984).

TOR   *The Torah: A Modern Commentary,* edited by W. Gunther Plaut (New York: Union of American Hebrew Congregations, 1981).

TRF   *The Resurrection Factor,* by Josh McDowell (San Bernadino, CA: Here's Life Publishers, 1981).

TTW   *The Theological Wordbook,* by Don Campbell, Wendell Johnston, John Walvoord, and John Witmer (Nashville, TN: Word Publishing, 2000).

TYM   *Tyndale New Testament Commentaries: Matthew,* by R. V. G. Tasker (Leicester, England: Inter-Varsity Press, 1961).

UBP   *Understanding the Bible Commentary Series: Psalms,* by Craig C. Broyles (Grand Rapids, MI: Baker Books, 1999).

UI   *Unveiling Islam,* by Ergun Mehmet Caner and Emir Fethi Caner (Grand Rapids, MI: Kregel Publications, 2002).

VCEN *Vine's Complete Expository Dictionary of Old and New Testament Words: New Testament Section,* by W. E. Vine, Merrill F. Unger, and William White Jr. (Nashville, TN: Thomas Nelson Publishers, 1984, 1996).

VCEO *Vine's Complete Expository Dictionary of Old and New Testament Words: Old Testament Section,* by W. E. Vine, Merrill F. Unger, and William White Jr. (Nashville, TN: Thomas Nelson Publishers, 1984, 1996).

VGG   *A Visual Guide to Gospel Events,* by James C. Martin, John A. Beck, and David G. Hansen (Grand Rapids, MI: Baker Books, 2014).

WBH   *Willmington's Bible Handbook,* by Harold L. Willmington (Wheaton, IL: Tyndale House Publishers, 1997).

WBS   *Women of the Bible Speak Out,* by Marlo Schalesky (Grand Rapids, MI: Our Daily Bread Publishing, 2020).

WEC   *Women's Evangelical Commentary: New Testament,* edited by Dorothy Kelley Patterson and Rhonda Harrington Kelley (Nashville, TN: Holman Reference, 2006).

WET "Wheat's Evil Twin Has Been Intoxicating Humans for Centuries," by Sarah Laskow, *Atlas Obscura*, March 22, 2016, accessed August 9, 2021. https://www.atlasobscura.com/articles/wheats-evil-twin-has-been-intoxicating-humans-for-centuries.

WIW *What I Wish My Christian Friends Knew about Judaism,* by Robert Schoen (Chicago: Loyola Press, 2004).

WOB *The World of the Bible,* by John Drane (Oxford: Lion Hudson, 2009).

WOE *What on Earth is Happening?* by Ray C. Stedman (Grand Rapids, MI: Discovery House Publishers, 2003).

WOM *Women of the Bible,* by Frances Vander Velde (Grand Rapids, MI: Kregel Publications, 1957).

WWA *Who's Who and Where's Where in the Bible,* by Stephen M. Miller (Urichsville, OH: Barbour Publishing, 2004).

WWB *Who's Who in the Bible,* by Joan Comay and Ronald Brownrigg (New York: Bonanza Books, 1980).

WWC *Who's Who in the Bible,* by Jean-Pierre Isbouts (Washington, DC: National Geographic, 2013).

WIX *Working IX to V,* by Vicki Leon (New York: Walker and Company, 2007).

WWW *Who Was Who in the Bible* (Nashville, TN: Thomas Nelson Publishers, 1999).

ZB1 *Zondervan Illustrated Bible Backgrounds Commentary, Volume 1: Matthew, Mark, Luke,* edited by Clinton E. Arnold, Matthew commentary by Michael Wilkins (Grand Rapids, MI: Zondervan, 2002).

ZB2 *Zondervan Illustrated Bible Backgrounds Commentary, Volume 2: John, Acts,* edited by Clinton E. Arnold (Grand Rapids, MI: Zondervan, 2002).

ZNS *Zondervan NASB Study Bible,* Kenneth Barker, general editor (Grand Rapids, MI: Zondervan, 1999).

ZP1 *The Zondervan Pictorial Encyclopedia of the Bible, Volume 1: A-C,* edited by Merrill C. Tenney (Grand Rapids, MI: Zondervan, 1975, 1976).

ZP2 *The Zondervan Pictorial Encyclopedia of the Bible, Volume 2: D-G,* edited by Merrill C. Tenney (Grand Rapids, MI: Zondervan, 1975, 1976).

ZP3 *The Zondervan Pictorial Encyclopedia of the Bible, Volume 3: H-L,* edited by Merrill C. Tenney (Grand Rapids, MI: Zondervan, 1975, 1976).

ZP4 *The Zondervan Pictorial Encyclopedia of the Bible, Volume 4: M-P,* edited by Merrill C. Tenney (Grand Rapids, MI: Zondervan, 1975, 1976).

ZP5 *The Zondervan Pictorial Encyclopedia of the Bible, Volume 5: Q-Z,* edited by Merrill C. Tenney (Grand Rapids, MI: Zondervan, 1975, 1976).

Subject Index

Scripture Index

About the Author

Bestselling and award-winning author, Mike Nappa, is a practical theologian known for writing "coffee-shop theology" and thoughtful Christian living books. He's proud to be a person of color (Arab-American) who is active in Christian publishing.

Mikey (as his friends call him) has written Bible commentary and articles for Beliefnet.com, Christianity.com, and Crosswalk.com, as well as church resources for all ages. He's also authored Bible study books, Christian Living books, devotionals, VeggieTales comics, a few suspense novels, kids' picture books, and, well, much more. Books by Mike Nappa have sold more than two million copies worldwide, and have been translated into many languages such as Turkish, Korean, Spanish, German, and others.

Mikey holds a Master's degree in Bible and Theology from Calvin Theological Seminary, a Master's in English from the University of Northern Colorado, a Bachelor's in Christian Education from Biola University, and a Credential of Readiness from Harvard Business School.

Learn more about Mike Nappa by Googling his name or checking him out on Wikipedia. Find more from Bible-Smart online at www.Bible-Smart.com.